P9-DEW-360

A WHOLE YEAR'S WORTH OF DELICIOUS ANSWERS TO THE QUESTION "WHAT'S FOR DINNER?"

Appetizers
Spicy Artichoke Dip
Almond-Mushroom Pâté

Stews
Hearty Basque Stew
Four-Bean Five-Alarm Chili
Lemony Tempeh and New Potato Stew

Pastas
Ziti with Tofu and Red Pepper Sauce
Fusilli with Broccoli, Seitan, and Pine Nuts
Mediterranean Pasta with Feta and Olives

Casseroles
White Bean and Pumpkin Gratin
Oven-Baked Winter Vegetables and Seitan
Broccoli and Tofu Gratin

Stir-Fries
Summer Garden Stir-Fry
Tofu Stir-Fry with Spinach and Red Peppers
Stir-Fry of Tempeh and Peanuts with Lemon Grass

AND MORE!

ROBIN ROBERTSON is a professional chef and cooking instructor in Virginia Beach, Virginia.

366
Healthful Ways to Cook Tofu

and Other Meat Alternatives

ROBIN ROBERTSON

Nutritional Analysis Provided by Ed Blonz, Ph.D.

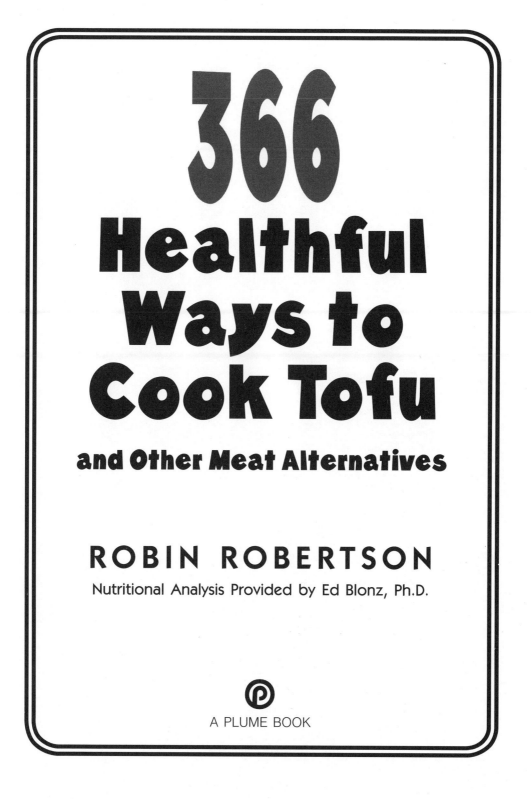

A PLUME BOOK

Nutritional analysis provided by Ed Blonz,
Ph.D. Dr. Blonz is a nationally syndicated
nutrition journalist and author of the "Your
Personal Nutritionist" series (Signet, 1996).
He is president of Nutrition Resource in
Kensington, California. Nutrition analysis was
supplied using the Nutrition IV® software.

Plume
Published by the Penguin Group
Penguin Books USA Inc., 375 Hudson Street,
New York, New York 10014, U.S.A.
Penguin Books Ltd, 27 Wrights Lane,
London W8 5TZ, England
Penguin Books Australia Ltd, Ringwood,
Victoria, Australia
Penguin Books Canada Ltd, 10 Alcorn Avenue,
Toronto, Ontario, Canada M4V 3B2
Penguin Books (N.Z.) Ltd, 182–190 Wairau Road,
Auckland 10, New Zealand

Penguin Books Ltd, Registered Offices:
Harmondsworth, Middlesex, England

First published by Plume, an imprint of Dutton Signet,
a division of Penguin Books USA Inc.

First Printing, April, 1996
10 9 8 7 6 5 4 3 2 1

Copyright © Robin Robertson, 1996
All rights reserved

REGISTERED TRADEMARK—MARCA REGISTRADA

LIBRARY OF CONGRESS CATALOGING-IN-PUBLICATION DATA:

Robertson, Robin (Robin G.)
    366 healthful ways to cook tofu and other meat alternatives / Robin Robertson.
       p.   cm.
    ISBN 0-452-27597-0
    1. Cookery (Tofu)   2. Vegetarian cookery.   I. Title.
TX814.5.T63R63   1996
641.6'5655—dc20   95-41517
                                                             CIP

Printed in the United States of America
Set in Garamond Light
Designed by Leonard Telesca

Without limiting the rights under copyright reserved above, no part of this publication
may be reproduced, stored in or introduced into a retrieval system, or transmitted,
in any form, or by any means (electronic, mechanical, photocopying, recording,
or otherwise), without the prior written permission of both the copyright owner
and the above publisher of this book.

This book is dedicated to the memory of my parents—
to my mother,
who inspired me to cook with love,
and to my father,
who taught me that nothing is impossible.

Contents

Introduction

Not too long ago, people who didn't eat meat were considered "radicals," "hippies," or "health nuts." However, reducing or eliminating meat from our diets has now become a common goal. In the light of recent medical research, alternatives to meat have emerged as an essential preventative measure that can yield impressive rewards in improved health and prolonged life. As scientific reports continue to link a diet high in meats and animal fats to heart disease and cancer, it's easy to understand why more people are choosing to eat less meat. But what are they eating instead?

While the new U.S.D.A. (United States Department of Agriculture) Food Guide Pyramid recommends that we eat more grains and vegetables, it doesn't tell us what to put in that empty space on our dinner plates where the pork chop or beef steak used to be. As a result, many people who try to break free from a meat-based diet find themselves at a loss when it comes time to make dinner.

That's where this book comes in—to introduce you to the variety and versatility of meat alternatives. With *366 Healthful Ways to Cook Tofu and Other Meat Alternatives*, you'll never again have to wonder how to fill that empty space on your dinner plate.

Instead, you will be preparing everything from roasts with all the trimmings to succulent burgers, from rich stews to fabulous stir-fries, and you'll never miss the meat. What's more, these meat alternatives are high in protein, low in fat and cholesterol, inexpensive, and extremely versatile, as the wide array of recipes in this book attests.

Many of these recipes are dishes that are normally prepared with meat but have now been given a healthy new life with meat alternatives. You will find that the recipes do not sacrifice flavor, texture, or appeal. Most are quick and easy to prepare, an essential element to a hectic lifestyle. After all, many of us find ourselves giving in to junk food simply because we don't think we have the time to prepare something "healthy." This book solves that problem.

You'll find a new recipe to try each day of the year to answer the question: "What's for dinner?" The book provides scores of recipes for delicious appetizers, hors d'oeuvres and sandwiches, soups, pasta dishes, and casseroles. There are whole chapters devoted to stir-fries, loaves, and savory pies. You will never again want for meatless casserole ideas and you will be amazed to discover all the non-meat foods that you can sauté, sear, and grill. There are roasts, main dish salads, a chapter on one-dish meals, and much more.

Meat Alternatives

Many of the tempting dishes in this book use basic ingredients such as tofu, tempeh, seitan, beans, and whole grains. The following descriptions will help you become familiar with those that are new to you.

Tofu: Available in soft and firm varieties, tofu can be used in many dishes, from soups and sauces to cutlets and burgers. Tofu is a curd made from soybeans and is high in protein and calcium. Its distinct lack of flavor is what makes tofu a valuable tool to the imaginative cook, since it can be flavored and sauced in a limitless number of ways. In this book you'll find recipes that alter the character and flavor of tofu so drastically that in many cases, you'll have to remind yourself that it's tofu you're eating. Recipes such as Tofu Curry with Plum Chutney (see page 354) and Tofu and Mushroom Salad with Pesto Vinaigrette (see page 314) will dazzle even the staunchest meat eater. Tofu is available in most grocery stores nowadays, although you may find your best price and selection in a natural foods store or Asian grocery store. Use the softer variety for soups and sauces, the firm kind for stir-fries and other recipes requiring that the tofu retain its shape.

Tempeh: Tempeh is made of fermented compressed soybeans formed into firm cakes. It can be found in the refrigerator case in most natural foods stores. Indonesian in origin, tempeh has a distinctive flavor that stands up well to stronger flavors such as curry or hot Thai spices. Given its meaty texture, tempeh can be used to resemble burgers, cutlets, or ground meat. It can also be grated and used to make a fabulous "chickenless" salad. As a general rule, tempeh should be poached before using (see page 12) in order to mellow its flavor and make the tempeh more digestible. High in protein and Vitamin B-12, tempeh is a meat substitute worth keeping on hand.

Seitan: Also known as "wheat meat," because it is literally the meat of the wheat grain, seitan is perhaps the most versatile meat alternative of all. Not only can seitan be used in ground meat recipes, but it also can be sliced thin enough to use as a substitute in elegant sautéed veal and chicken dishes. I have proudly served such delights as Seitan Cutlets with Tarragon-Mustard Sauce (see page 265) to many an unwary dinner guest, who pronounced it the best meal they'd had in ages. Only after dinner did I disclose the secret ingredient. The most exciting aspect of cooking with seitan, however, is that in addition to stir-fries, sandwiches, sautéed dishes, and ground meat dishes, seitan can also be made into wonderful stuffed roasts. There are several recipes in this book for seitan roasts made with a variety of stuffings, all of which are sure to please the most discriminating palate.

Commercially prepared seitan is available in several forms. For example, there is an excellent product available in most natural foods stores called Seitan Quick Mix. Just add water and knead for a few minutes to produce about two pounds of excellent quality seitan, without the bother of making it from scratch. I enjoy the quality of this product so much that I rarely make seitan from scratch any more. Ready-made seitan is available in jars or refrigerated packaging, but is usually marinated and can change the flavors of recipes. The best and most economical seitan, however, is that which you make yourself; see the basic recipe on page 11.

Beans and Whole Grains: Many, many cultures use grain and bean dishes as their daily staple, making beans and whole grains the most widely used "meat alternatives." Rice and bean dishes are common everywhere from Mexico to India to the Middle East to the Far East; they provide an inexpensive and abundant source of protein, as well as being high in fiber and complex carbohydrates. By including several international recipes in your meal planning, you can add variety to your diet while experiencing new and exciting flavors.

When using grains, always use the whole grain variety, such as brown rice instead of bleached white rice, for optimum flavor and nutrition. In so doing, you are giving your body the most direct and complete source of protein available. In this book you will find recipes using a variety of interesting grains, from the well-known brown rice and barley to the lesser-known kamut and quinoa. The featured beans run the gamut from the tiny, nutritious adzuki bean, to the substantial chick-pea, lentil, and fava bean.

These meat alternatives will not only fill the space on your plate, but also provide you with all the protein, vitamins, and minerals you need to be healthy—without the cholesterol and saturated fat that meat contains.

Basic Bean Cooking

Canned beans, rinsed and drained, may be used in any of the recipes calling for cooked beans. However, if you have time to cook dry beans, a bean-cooking chart is included on the following page. Most of the bean recipes in this book call for "cooked beans," in order to give you the option of using canned beans or preparing dried beans in advance.

Soak all dried beans for 4 hours or overnight with the exception of lentils and split peas, which do not require soaking. Sort beans to remove any small stones or sticks, and rinse beans before soaking to remove dust. When cooking beans, you may want to add to the water a 2-inch piece of dried kombu, a sea vegetable widely used in Japanese cooking that helps soften the beans, shortens the cooking time, and adds nutrients. Kombu is available in natural foods stores or Asian grocery stores. For extra flavor, add one or two bay leaves to the bean cooking water. Add salt when beans are almost done, not before, since salt inhibits water absorption in beans.

Bean Cooking Times

(*Note:* All beans except lentils and split peas should be soaked in water overnight prior to cooking.)

Beans (1 cup dry)	Water Amount (in cups)	Cooking Time	Yield (in cups)
Adzuki beans	3	1 hr.	2
Black beans	3	1½ hr.	2¼
Black-eyed peas	3	1 hr.	2
Cannellini beans	3	1½ hr.	2
Chick-peas	4	3 hr.	2½
Great northern beans	3½	2 hr.	2
Kidney beans	3	1½ hr.	2
Lentils	3	45 min.	2½
Pinto beans	3½	2½ hr.	2¼
Split peas	3	45 min.	2½

Basic Grain Cooking

Rinse grains before cooking to remove dust. I find it helpful to cook more grain than I will need in one meal and freeze what is left for use later in the week. If you follow this practice, when you are in a hurry and need two cups of cooked rice to complete a recipe you can place the frozen rice in a colander and run it under warm water. It will thaw in seconds, and be ready to use in your recipe.

Grain Cooking Times

Grains (1 cup dry)	Water Amount (in cups)	Cooking Time	Yield (in cups)
Barley	4	1 hr.	3½
Basmati rice	4	15 min.	3
Brown rice	4	45 min.	3
Bulgur	2	15 min.	3
Couscous	2	5 min.	2
Kamut	4	1½ hr	3½
Millet	3	25 min.	3½
Quinoa	2	20 min.	3½

TVP (texturized vegetable protein): Sold in natural foods stores, TVP is made from soybeans and is available under many brand names. TVP can be used in any recipe calling for ground meat, such as chili, spaghetti sauce, sloppy Joes, or meat loaf. Some brands contain a high amount of sodium, so I usually prefer to use ground seitan or crumbled tofu. However, in a pinch, TVP is a great convenience food to have on hand. It reconstitutes with water or other liquid, and is ready to use immediately. Shop around for a brand you like, and keep some on your pantry shelf.

Nuts: Nuts are a concentrated source of protein, as well as a good source of calcium, iron, and Vitamin B. They have acquired a bad reputation for being high in fat, but don't be afraid to use them in moderation. With nuts, a little goes a long way, and often one or two tablespoons is all you need to add a flavorful crunch to an entire recipe that serves four people. A sprinkling of pine nuts or walnuts on a salad or pasta dish can elevate a meal from ordinary to elegant. Additionally, the use of nut butters and tahini, which is a purée of ground sesame seeds, can add flavor and nutrients to a recipe.

Other Meat Alternatives

There are many commercially prepared meat alternatives now available for adding variety and interest to your recipes. Some of these are used in recipes found in this book. The most popular are tempeh bacon and meatless sausages made from tofu and other forms of vegetable protein.

The freezer cases at natural foods stores and many supermarkets also offer meatless burgers made from grains and vegetables as well as tofu hot dogs, cold cuts (including ham and roast beef), a ground beef lookalike, and meatless pepperoni and Canadian bacon. Many of these products can be used to enhance bean soups, stews, and other dishes, such as Jambalaya (see page 336).

Because there is now such a wide variety of new products and brands available, it is advisable to experiment with them until you find those that work best for you.

About Dairy Products, Oils, and Sugar

Eggs are no longer considered a "healthy" substitute for meat due to their high cholesterol content. Therefore, in these pages you will notice a conspicuous absence of the fritatta, omelet, and soufflé recipes that are often included in meatless cookbooks.

In recipes where eggs or dairy products are included in the list of ingredients, non-dairy alternatives may be easily substituted. An egg replacer product, available at most natural foods stores, is made with potato starch and can be used successfully to replace eggs in most recipes. Often, however, simply using a little water, soft tofu, or other moist ingredient to replace the egg in a recipe works quite well.

Where recipes call for milk or cream, the type of milk product used depends on the needs and preferences of the cook. For example, if you are currently using dairy products, and cholesterol is not a major concern to you, you may want to use heavy cream instead of milk in some of the recipes for extra-rich flavor. Conversely, a low-fat milk will significantly pare down the cholesterol and calorie content of the recipes. For those who do not use dairy products at all, a low-fat soy milk, rice milk, or almond milk may be substituted in exact measure. The same holds true for cheese. There are many dairy-free cheese alternatives available in natural foods stores for those who don't use dairy products at all. However, if you're just trying to reduce your fat intake, simply cut down on the amount of cheese in recipes. A tablespoon or two of Romano or feta is usually enough to impart their special flavor to a recipe.

Regarding cooking oils: as a general rule of thumb, good quality cold-pressed oils are recommended. When buying olive oil, try to choose only "extra-virgin." For general cooking, I favor a good corn oil for its buttery flavor, but safflower and canola oils contain less saturated fat and may be used if you prefer. I use them interchangeably. Sesame oil is available in two varieties: light, or untoasted, which is mild and used for cooking, and dark, or toasted sesame oil, which is strong-flavored and used mainly as a seasoning.

To further trim your intake of oils, you may choose to cut back on the amount of oil specified in some of the recipes. For example, you may want to brush the oil on a pan instead of pouring it on, or take it a step further by poaching food in vegetable broth rather than sautéing or frying it. This will alter the end result somewhat, but in most cases you will still have a tasty dish, significantly lower in calories.

Since sugar and artificial sweeteners provide no nutritional benefit, many health-conscious people avoid using them. In the interest of allowing you to decide which sweetener suits you best, the recipes in this book call for "sugar or a natural sweetener." I prefer to use brown rice syrup or barley malt, since they are the most natural, least refined sweeteners, and can be metabolized most easily for the best nutritional benefit. Molasses, honey, and other natural fruit sweeteners may be used if you prefer. The amounts given for "sweeteners" in these recipes are for refined white sugar. If you are using one of the natural sweeteners, which are generally not as sweet as sugar, you may need to increase the amount to suit your taste.

A Note on Nutrition

All the recipes have been analyzed for their nutritional content, and the resulting information follows each recipe. The data given is for one serving or unit (such as a bar) unless the yield is expressed in cups; in that case the size of the serving is given. When there is a range of servings, such as 4 to 6 servings, the data is based on the mid-range average, in this case 5.

The Basic Recipes

There are certain recipe ingredients used throughout that you may want to make from scratch. These include a basic vegetable stock, which is used in place of a chicken or beef stock, as well a recipe for making your own seitan. All of the recipes using seitan in this book call for prepared seitan, as described in the basic seitan-making recipe on page 11 (or made with the quick mix—see page 3). The only exceptions are the rolled stuffed seitan roast recipes, which specify "raw" (unpoached) seitan. When a recipe calls for "ground seitan," this refers to poached seitan that has been ground with a meat grinder, a food processor, a grater, or simply by mincing with a knife, according to your own preference.

Most of the recipes using beans or grains will state "cooked" beans or grains, giving you the option of using canned beans or precooked grains that you may have on hand. This will help to cut down on the preparation time for each recipe.

In general, it is best to use organic vegetables whenever possible. When organic produce is not available, however, be sure to use extra care in washing and peeling non-organic vegetables. Always begin a recipe by cleaning your vegetables and rinsing grains and beans.

The following recipes are for components that you will use again and again in more complex recipes. One of the most prominent ingredients in many of them is vegetable stock. A large pot of vegetable stock may be made periodically and portioned into small containers to be kept in the freezer for future use. However, it is also a good idea to keep some vegetable bouillon cubes or a powdered vegetable base on hand for those times when no stock is available. When a recipe calls for one cup of vegetable stock, you may simply reconstitute the appropriate amount of vegetable base in a cup of hot water. There are many vegetable bases available in natural foods stores. Try to find one you like that is flavorful but not overly salty. With these convenient products on hand, you will never be at a loss when a recipe calls for vegetable stock. Just be sure to adjust the seasonings in your recipes to account for the particular saltiness of the stock.

Tamari is another ingredient used frequently in this book. Tamari is a high-quality Japanese soy sauce which is preservative free. The low-sodium tamari used in these recipes has the same full-bodied flavor as regular tamari with a fraction of the sodium.

Basic Vegetable Stock

Feel free to add additional vegetables, such as leeks or mushrooms, but stay away from anything too strongly flavored, such as members of the cabbage family.

1 large onion, quartered (including peel)
2 ribs celery, coarsely chopped (including leaves)
2 carrots, coarsely chopped
2 potatoes, unpeeled, sliced
2 cloves garlic, unpeeled, crushed

½ cup coarsely chopped fresh parsley (including stems)
2 tablespoons low-sodium tamari
2 bay leaves
½ teaspoon black peppercorns
½ teaspoon salt

Place all vegetables in a large stock pot and cover them with twice the amount of water (about 8 cups). Add garlic, parsley, tamari, bay leaves, peppercorns, and salt. Bring to a boil, reduce heat to a low simmer, and simmer for 1 hour or more. Strain through a colander into another pot. Stock is now ready to be used in recipes or to portion and freeze for future use.

MAKES ABOUT 6 CUPS (¾-CUP SERVING)

Calories 47.21 • Protein 1.563 gm • Fat 0.187 gm • Percentage of calories from fat 3% • Cholesterol 0 mg • Dietary fiber 1.712 gm • Sodium 255.1 mg • Calcium 25.68 mg

Basic Seitan

(Wheat Gluten, or "Wheat Meat")

½ cup low-sodium tamari
1 bay leaf
1 onion, peeled and quartered
1 piece kombu
1 clove garlic, crushed
2 or 3 slices fresh ginger
  (optional)

12 cups whole-wheat flour
  (approximately 4 pounds)
1 cup wheat-gluten flour
  (optional)
6 to 8 cups water

Place tamari, bay leaf, onion, kombu, garlic, and ginger in a large stock pot over medium heat, and bring to a simmer. In the meantime, place flour(s) in a large bowl, put bowl in sink, and stir in enough water to make a kneadable dough. (Usually the amount of water used is a little less than half the amount of flour. For example, if using 6 cups of flour, you will need approximately 3 cups of water, etc.). Mix the water with the flour, using your hands to form a kneadable dough ball.

Knead the dough about 5 minutes. Then cover the dough in the bowl with water and let it rest about 15 minutes. After 15 minutes, begin kneading out the starch and the bran: Knead dough, in the bowl of water in the sink, until the water turns milky white—that is the starch coming out. Drain the milky water, cover with fresh water, and knead again until the soaking water becomes milky white.

Repeat process, alternating between warm and cool water, each time using fresh water, until the kneading water is almost clear. You will end up with a ball of glutinous dough. This is raw seitan—ready to be poached.

Bring simmering poaching liquid almost to a boil and add seitan, cut into 4 equal pieces. Simmer the seitan in this pot about 1 hour. Do not boil. The longer and slower it cooks, the denser the texture will be. When cooked, remove seitan from the pot and cool on a baking sheet. It is now ready to use in recipes. Seitan can be stored in the cooking liquid in the refrigerator for 4 to 5 days or frozen along with some cooking liquid.

Calories 1401 • Protein 67.53 gm • Fat 7.481 gm • Percentage of calories from fat 5% • Cholesterol 0 mg • Dietary fiber 50.33 gm • Sodium 1235 mg • Calcium 157.9 mg

Note: The nutritional data for Basic Seitan is given for a 1-pound piece.

Tofu Mayonnaise

1 pound soft tofu
1 tablespoon tahini (sesame paste)
¼ teaspoon celery seed
2 tablespoons cider vinegar

2 tablespoons prepared mustard
⅓ cup corn or safflower oil
½ teaspoon salt
⅛ teaspoon cayenne (scant)

Place all ingredients in food processor or blender. Process until well combined. Adjust seasonings.

MAKES ABOUT 3 CUPS (¼-CUP SERVING)

Calories 87 • Protein 3.21 gm • Fat 8.10 gm • Percentage of calories from fat 81% • Cholesterol 0 mg • Dietary fiber 0.031 gm • Sodium 127.5 gm • Calcium 46.3 mg

Note: Commercial brands of tofu mayonnaise are available at natural foods stores.

Basic Poached Tempeh

Poaching commercially prepared tempeh before using it in a recipe improves its flavor and digestibility.

1 pound tempeh   Water

Slice or cube tempeh, according to individual recipe, or leave in slabs, depending on use. Place tempeh in saucepan, add enough water to cover, and bring to a boil. Reduce heat to medium and simmer 10 minutes. Remove tempeh from water. It is now ready to be used in recipes.

Basic Brown Sauce

A rich brown sauce without the fat and extra calories of meat drippings, and so simple to make.

2 cups Basic Vegetable Stock (see page 10)
1 tablespoon low-sodium tamari
½ teaspoon minced fresh parsley
¼ teaspoon dried thyme
⅛ teaspoon dried sage

⅛ teaspoon freshly ground black pepper
2 tablespoons arrowroot or cornstarch
2 tablespoons water

Bring stock to a boil. Add tamari (more or less to taste, depending on strength of stock), parsley, thyme, sage, and pepper. Reduce heat to a low simmer. Dissolve arrowroot or cornstarch in water. Whisk into sauce to thicken. Simmer 5 minutes. Adjust seasonings.

MAKES ABOUT 2 CUPS (¼-CUP SERVING)

Calories 21.65 • Protein .626 gm • Fat 0.054 gm • Percentage of calories from fat 2% • Cholesterol 0 mg • Dietary fiber .453 gm • Sodium 140 mg • Calcium 8.54 mg

You are now armed with a working knowledge of the ingredients and basic recipes that can make you an expert in preparing wonderful dishes without using meat. Don't forget to experiment, entertain, and enjoy the adventure as you try these recipes and discover a whole new way to make dinner.

1
Appetizers, Hors D'oeuvres, and Sandwiches

A tempting array of meatless appetizers are featured in this chapter, from sublime Almond Mushroom Pâté to elegant Eggplant Caviar. Tasty additions to your hors d'oeuvres repertoire include Dim Sum Dumplings, Mini-Pita Pizzas, and Stuffed Grape Leaves. The dazzling tri-colored Quinoa Timbales with Red Pepper Sauce can be plated individually for an elegant first course.

Most of the sandwich selections perform equally well as lunch or light supper fare. When cut into party-sized shapes, they can also be used to fill an hors d'oeuvres tray.

Almond Mushroom Pâté

An elegant alternative to traditional liver pâtés that everyone will enjoy. Almond butter can be found next to the peanut butter and other nut butters in natural foods stores.

2 tablespoons corn oil
½ cup finely minced onion
8 ounces mushrooms, chopped
1 clove garlic, minced
¼ teaspoon salt
1 teaspoon minced fresh tarragon, or ½ teaspoon dried
⅛ teaspoon freshly ground black pepper

1 cup almond butter
1 tablespoon brandy
¼ cup chopped almonds
½ cup whole almonds, toasted (see page 142)
Parsley sprigs for garnish

Heat oil in a medium skillet over medium-high heat, add the onions, mushrooms, and garlic and sauté for 2 minutes. Add the salt, tarragon, and pepper and cook until the liquid is evaporated. In a food processor, combine the almond butter with the brandy and mushroom mixture, and process until smooth. Add the chopped almonds; process with on/off bursts. Cover and chill. Mound the pâté on a serving plate. Garnish with toasted almonds and parsley.

MAKES ABOUT 2 CUPS (½-CUP SERVING)

Calories 161.9 • Protein 4.5 gm • Fat 15.28 gm • Percentage of calories from fat 80% • Cholesterol 0 mg • Dietary fiber 2.5 gm • Sodium 74.35 mg • Calcium 64.8 mg

Tempeh Chutney Pâté

Toasted French bread rounds and a light, fruity Pinot Blanc are perfect complements to this delicate pâté.

1 pound poached tempeh (see page 12), cut in 2-inch pieces
3 scallions, minced
½ cup minced fresh parsley
½ cup chopped almonds
½ teaspoon salt

⅛ teaspoon freshly ground black pepper
¾ cup chutney
½ cup Tofu Mayonnaise (see page 12)

Place the tempeh in a food processor and pulse until finely crumbled. Add the remaining ingredients to the work bowl, pulsing with each addition to combine. Transfer the pâté mixture to a soufflé dish or crock, smooth the top, and cover with a lid or plastic wrap. Chill the pâté several hours or overnight.

MAKES 4 CUPS (½-CUP SERVING)

Calories 219.6 • Protein 12.49 gm • Fat 10.39 gm • Percentage of calories from fat 41% • Cholesterol 0 mg • Dietary fiber 3.127 gm • Sodium 220.7 mg • Calcium 79.48 mg

Lentil Pâté

3 cups cooked lentils
½ cup chopped almonds
1 clove garlic, sliced
2 tablespoons chopped fresh
   parsley
1 teaspoon dried basil
1 teaspoon dried thyme
1 teaspoon paprika

½ teaspoon salt
⅛ teaspoon cayenne
2 tablespoons low-sodium tamari
2 tablespoons olive oil
1 teaspoon lemon juice
2 tablespoons tahini (sesame
   paste)
2 tablespoons chick-pea flour

Preheat the oven to 375 degrees. In a food processor, combine the lentils with the almonds, garlic, and parsley, in short on/off pulses. Add the remaining ingredients except the chick-pea flour. Process until evenly mixed. Do not overprocess. Transfer the mixture to a bowl and stir in the chick-pea flour. Adjust seasonings. Spoon the mixture into a well-oiled loaf pan and bake 30 minutes. Allow to cool before unmolding onto serving plate.

4 TO 6 SERVINGS

Calories 157.4 • Protein 8.584 gm • Fat 5.905 gm • Percentage of calories from fat 33% • Cholesterol 0 mg • Dietary fiber 4.236 gm • Sodium 459.5 mg • Calcium 37.91 mg

White Bean Pâté with Green Apple Chutney

1 cup chopped mushrooms
1 cup Madeira
¾ teaspoon salt
3 cups cooked cannellini beans
  (white kidney beans)
2 tablespoons milk
1½ teaspoons dry white wine

½ teaspoon dried sage, crumbled
½ teaspoon dried basil, crumbled
¼ teaspoon freshly ground black
  pepper
Green Apple Chutney (recipe
  follows)

Simmer the mushrooms in Madeira in a small saucepan until they start to soften, about 5 minutes. Drain, reserving 5 tablespoons of the Madeira.

Lightly oil a 4-cup mold and sprinkle with ¼ teaspoon of the salt. Place the beans in a food processor and purée. Add the reserved Madeira, milk, wine, sage, basil, remaining salt, and pepper and purée again. Place the mixture in a bowl and adjust seasonings. Fold in the mushrooms. Spoon the mixture into the prepared mold. Cover and refrigerate overnight. Serve with Green Apple Chutney.

MAKES 4 CUPS (½-CUP SERVING)

Calories 112.6 • Protein 5.379 gm • Fat 0.419 gm • Percentage of calories from fat 3% • Cholesterol 0.281 mg • Dietary fiber 5.118 gm • Sodium 536.7 mg • Calcium 37.56 mg

Green Apple Chutney

3 cups peeled and chopped
  Granny Smith apples
1¼ cups raisins
¼ cup cider vinegar
2 tablespoons grated fresh ginger
1½ tablespoons minced scallion

2 tablespoons chopped shallot
2 teaspoons ground allspice
1½ teaspoons salt
¼ teaspoon ground cloves
2 cups sugar or a natural
  sweetener

Heat all the ingredients but the sugar in large saucepan over medium heat until bubbling, stirring frequently. Mix in the sugar. Boil until thick, about 20 minutes, stirring constantly toward the end of cooking time. Skim off any foam. Cool to room temperature.

MAKES 4 CUPS (½-CUP SERVING)

Calories 260.6 • Protein 0.817 gm • Fat 0.279 gm • Percentage of calories from fat 1% • Cholesterol 0 mg • Dietary fiber 1.51 gm • Sodium 359.3 mg • Calcium 19.49 mg

Quinoa Timbales with Red Pepper Sauce

Favored by the ancient Incas, quinoa is a tiny grain noted for its high protein content. If you can't find it, millet makes a good substitute in this recipe.

2¼ cups Basic Vegetable Stock
  (see page 10)
2 tablespoons olive oil
1½ cups quinoa
¼ cup minced scallions
¼ cup minced roasted red bell
  pepper (see page 22)

1 tablespoon minced fresh parsley
2 tablespoons fresh lemon juice
½ teaspoon salt
Freshly ground black pepper
Red Pepper Sauce (recipe follows)
Parsley or watercress for garnish

Bring the vegetable stock and 1 teaspoon of the olive oil to a boil in a saucepan over high heat. Stir in the quinoa and scallions. Reduce the heat and simmer, covered, until the liquid is absorbed, 15 to 20 minutes. Remove from the heat and allow to stand 5 minutes. Fluff with a fork. Stir into the quinoa mixture the red pepper, parsley, lemon juice, remaining olive oil, salt, and pepper to taste. Adjust the seasonings. Pack the mixture into 6 timbale molds or custard cups. Cover and refrigerate at least 1 hour. Unmold before serving. Serve on a pool of Red Pepper Sauce garnished with sprigs of parsley or watercress.

6 SERVINGS

Calories 222.1 • Protein 6.398 gm • Fat 7.067 gm • Percentage of calories from fat 28% • Cholesterol 0 mg • Dietary fiber 3.158 gm • Sodium 283.1 mg • Calcium 42.37 mg

Red Pepper Sauce

2 large red bell peppers
1 tablespoon olive oil
1 teaspoon balsamic vinegar

¼ teaspoon salt
⅛ teaspoon freshly ground black
 pepper

Preheat the oven to 500 degrees. Brush peppers lightly with oil and place on a baking sheet. Roast them for 10 to 15 minutes, or until the skin begins to blister. Transfer them to a bowl and cover, or place in a paper bag and close for 10 minutes to allow steam to build as the peppers cool. Remove the charred skins and stems and seeds and discard.

Place the peppers in food processor; add vinegar, salt, and pepper. Purée until smooth. Adjust the seasonings.

MAKES 1 CUP (1-TABLESPOON SERVING)

Calories 20.57 • Protein 0.168 gm • Fat 1.72 gm • Percentage of calories from fat 72% • Cholesterol 0 mg • Dietary fiber 0.323 gm • Sodium 67.1 mg • Calcium 2.24 mg

Butternut Squash and Adzuki Bean Patties

Serve these flavorful patties with a spicy peanut sauce or your favorite chutney.

1 pound butternut squash, peeled and cubed
½ cup cooked adzuki beans
3 scallions, minced
⅛ teaspoon ground cinnamon
⅛ teaspoon ground nutmeg
2 tablespoons flour
Salt and freshly ground black pepper
2 tablespoons corn oil

Steam the squash until soft, about 45 minutes. Allow to cool. In a large bowl, combine the squash, adzuki beans, scallions, cinnamon, nutmeg, flour, salt, and pepper. Mix thoroughly with a fork. Heat 1 tablespoon of the oil in a large skillet over medium heat. Spoon the batter into the hot pan, about 1 heaping tablespoon per patty. Flatten the patties with the back of a spatula to about ¼ inch thick. Cook the patties on medium heat until browned on each side, about 2 minutes per side. Transfer to a plate and keep warm in a 275-degree oven. Repeat with the remaining batter, adding more oil to the pan as necessary.

MAKES 20 PATTIES

Calories 31.61 • Protein 0.731 gm • Fat 1.403 gm • Percentage of calories from fat 38% • Cholesterol 0 mg • Dietary fiber 0.784 gm • Sodium 1.409 mg • Calcium 11.65 mg

Spicy Artichoke Dip

This crowd pleaser is a delightful addition to any gathering. Using tofu mayonnaise helps reduce cholesterol and add protein.

3 14-ounce cans artichoke hearts, drained and finely chopped
½ cup minced scallions
½ cup chopped roasted red peppers (see page 22)
1 cup Tofu Mayonnaise (see page 12)
1 cup grated Pecorino Romano cheese

2 jalapeño peppers, seeded and minced
1 tablespoon fresh lemon juice
1 teaspoon Worcestershire sauce
½ cup sliced almonds, toasted (see page 142)

In a large bowl combine all the ingredients but the almonds and stir until well combined. Transfer the mixture to an oiled baking dish and sprinkle with the almonds. Bake in a preheated 375-degree oven for 25 to 30 minutes, or until the top is golden and the mixture is hot. Serve with crackers or toasted French bread rounds.

8 SERVINGS

Calories 218.6 • Protein 13.02 gm • Fat 11.96 gm • Percentage of calories from fat 44% • Cholesterol 12.67 mg • Dietary fiber 8.471 gm • Sodium 729 mg • Calcium 260.8 mg

Swedish Wheatballs

No one will guess that these savory morsels are made from wheat instead of meat.

½ cup chopped onions
2 tablespoons corn oil
1½ pounds ground seitan (see page 8)
½ cup dried bread crumbs
1 teaspoon salt
¼ teaspoon ground allspice
½ teaspoon ground nutmeg

¼ teaspoon freshly ground black pepper
1½ cups Basic Brown Sauce (see page 13)
½ cup milk or cream
1 tablespoon cornstarch dissolved in 2 tablespoons sherry

In a small skillet sauté the onions in 1 tablespoon of the oil until translucent. In a large bowl combine the seitan, bread crumbs, salt, allspice, nutmeg, and pepper. Add the onion to the seitan mixture and combine well. Refrigerate 1 hour.

Preheat the oven to 325 degrees. Form the mixture into 1-inch balls. Brown lightly in the remaining 1 tablespoon oil, about 5 minutes, and remove with a slotted spoon. Reserve the oil. Place the wheatballs in a covered casserole and bake for 20 minutes.

Heat the Basic Brown Sauce in a saucepan over medium heat. Add the milk and cornstarch mixture. Cook until thick, stirring constantly, 3 to 5 minutes, to obtain desired consistency. Pour over baked wheatballs.

6 SERVINGS

Calories 460.1 • Protein 18.92 gm • Fat 7.314 gm • Percentage of calories from fat 14% • Cholesterol 1.5 mg • Dietary fiber 13.21 gm • Sodium 895.3 mg • Calcium 88.28 mg

Eggplant Caviar

Sometimes called "Poor Man's Caviar." You can serve this delicious spread on crackers or croustades arranged on your best serving tray, or in a bowl so guests can serve themselves. Garnish with parsley sprigs or thinly sliced radish crescents.

2 large eggplants
½ cup olive oil
¼ cup red wine vinegar
¼ cup minced fresh parsley
1 tablespoon Tofu Mayonnaise
  (see page 12)

1 teaspoon Dijon mustard
2 small cloves garlic, minced
Salt and freshly ground black
  pepper

Preheat the oven to 400 degrees. Using a fork, pierce the eggplants all over. Bake until soft, about 40 minutes. Cool, then peel them. Transfer to a bowl and mash well. Stir in the remaining ingredients, except for the salt and pepper. Season with salt and pepper. Cover mixture and refrigerate until well chilled.

MAKES ABOUT 2 TO 3 CUPS (⅓-CUP SERVING)

Calories 227 • Protein 1.396 gm • Fat 22.27 gm • Percentage of calories from fat 85% • Cholesterol 0 mg • Dietary fiber 0.035 gm • Sodium 35.96 mg • Calcium 16.74 mg

Stuffed Grape Leaves

¾ teaspoon salt
1 cup basmati rice
2 tablespoons olive oil
½ teaspoon ground cinnamon
¼ cup golden raisins
⅓ cup walnuts, toasted (see page 326) and finely ground

1½ tablespoons fresh lemon juice
⅛ teaspoon freshly ground black pepper
18–24 grape leaves packed in brine

Bring 2 cups of water and ½ teaspoon of the salt to a boil in a medium saucepan. Add the rice, 1 tablespoon of the oil, and the cinnamon. Return water to a boil, cover, and cook over low heat until the rice is tender, about 15 minutes. Transfer the rice to a bowl and add the raisins, walnuts, and lemon juice. Season with the remaining ¼ teaspoon salt and the pepper.

Rinse and drain the grape leaves, pat them dry, and cut off the stems; spread out the leaves on a flat surface. Using your hands, press approximately 1 tablespoon of the rice mixture into a small cylinder shape and place in the center of each leaf. Fold in the bottom and sides, and roll up toward the top. Brush the rolls lightly with the remaining 1 tablespoon olive oil, arrange in a steamer, and steam over boiling water, covered, for 5 minutes.

Makes 18 to 24

Calories 57.47 • Protein 0.991 gm • Fat 1.893 gm • Percentage of calories from fat 29% • Cholesterol 0 mg • Dietary fiber 0.185 gm • Sodium 79.26 mg • Calcium 6.145 mg

Dim Sum Dumplings

Serve these savory pouches hot or at room temperature, with tamari or other dipping sauces such as a hot mustard sauce or a sweet and sour sauce.

1 tablespoon light sesame oil
1 cup ground seitan (see page 8)
2 tablespoons grated carrot
1 tablespoon minced scallion
1 teaspoon low-sodium tamari

Salt and freshly ground black
  pepper
16 square wonton wrappers, or 4
  egg roll wrappers, quartered

Bring 2 quarts water to a low boil in a large saucepan. Meanwhile, heat the oil in medium skillet over medium heat. Add seitan, carrot, and scallion, and sauté for 5 minutes. Add the tamari and salt and pepper to taste. Transfer the filling to a medium bowl and set aside.

Fill a small bowl with water and keep it on hand when assembling the dim sum. Place a wonton wrapper on a clean work surface. Dip your fingers into the bowl of water, then moisten the edge of the wrapper with a few drops. Place 1 tablespoon of the filling in the center of the wrapper and bring up the two opposite corners to enclose the filling, forming a triangle. Press the edges to seal securely, eliminating any air pockets. Bring the two corners of this triangle toward the center of the wonton. Press the corners together to seal. Set the filled wonton on a plate and repeat with the remaining filling and wrappers.

When the water comes to a boil, carefully add the wontons. Reduce the heat to keep the water below a rolling boil. Stir occasionally with a wooden spoon to keep from sticking. When cooked, the dim sum will float to the top. Remove the dim sum with a slotted spoon and transfer to a serving plate.

MAKES 16 DUMPLINGS

Calories 31.27 • Protein 0.851 gm • Fat 0.952 gm • Percentage of calories from fat 28% • Cholesterol 1 mg • Dietary fiber 0.034 gm • Sodium 58.96 mg • Calcium 4.545 mg

Marinated Tofu

½ cup corn oil
½ cup dark sesame oil
¼ cup low-sodium tamari
¼ cup cider vinegar
1 clove garlic, minced
1 tablespoon sugar or a natural
  sweetener

¼ teaspoon salt
1 pound firm tofu, cut into
  1- × 3-inch bars, ½-inch thick
2 sheets roasted nori

Combine all the ingredients except the tofu and nori in a small saucepan over high heat and bring to a boil. Cut the tofu slices in half lengthwise, and place in a shallow baking dish. Pour the marinade over top. Bake in 350-degree oven for 10 minutes. Turn the tofu bars over and bake another 10 minutes. While tofu is baking, cut the nori sheets into ½-inch strips with scissors. Remove the tofu from marinade with slotted spatula. Wrap a nori strip around center of each tofu slice. Arrange on a platter to serve.

MAKES 16 BARS

Calories 42.17 • Protein 2.024 gm • Fat 3.21 gm • Percentage of calories from fat 67% • Cholesterol 0 mg • Dietary fiber 0.103 gm • Sodium 72 mg • Calcium 9.127 mg

Hummus Spread

This versatile and nutritious spread is delicious on bread, pita, or toasted bagels. To use as a dip, blend in a few tablespoons of water to achieve a thinner consistency.

2 cups cooked chick-peas
¼ cup tahini (sesame paste)
3 tablespoons fresh lemon juice

1 small clove garlic, chopped
1 tablespoon minced fresh parsley
½ teaspoon salt

Pulse chick-peas in a food processor. Add remaining ingredients and pulse again until well blended. Adjust seasonings, store in airtight container in refrigerator.

MAKES 2½ CUPS (¼-CUP SERVING)

Calories 122 • Protein 4.762 gm • Fat 6.4 gm • Percentage of calories from fat 50% • Cholesterol 0 mg • Dietary fiber 2.368 gm • Sodium 227.9 mg • Calcium 21.17 mg

Mini-Pita Pizzas

1 pound firm tofu, quartered
¼ cup tomato paste
1 tablespoon olive oil
2 scallions, minced
⅓ cup grated Pecorino Romano
  cheese
2 tablespoons minced fresh
  parsley
1 teaspoon dried basil, crumbled

⅛ teaspoon dried oregano,
  crumbled
½ teaspoon salt
⅛ teaspoon freshly ground black
  pepper
12 mini-pita pockets, each split in
  half to form rounds
2 medium tomatoes, thinly sliced
1 cup shredded mozzarella cheese

In a food processor, combine the tofu, tomato paste, olive oil, and scallions. Add the Romano cheese, parsley, basil, oregano, salt, and pepper and blend well. Cover and chill at least 1 hour. To assemble, spread a layer of the mixture on each pita round and arrange on a baking sheet. Top each round with a tomato slice. Sprinkle the tomato slices with mozzarella and place the baking sheet under a preheated broiler until cheese melts and turns golden. Serve immediately.

MAKES 24

Calories 90.17 • Protein 5.959 gm • Fat 3.127 gm • Percentage of calories from fat 31% • Cholesterol 6.42 mg • Dietary fiber 0.332 gm • Sodium 177.4 mg • Calcium 102.2 mg

Seitan Egg Rolls

3 tablespoons corn oil
1 tablespoon light sesame oil
1 medium onion, minced
4 scallions, chopped
1 cup ground seitan (see page 8)

1 cup finely chopped bok choy
1 cup grated carrots
2 tablespoons low-sodium tamari
1 cup cooked brown rice
8 egg roll wrappers

Heat 1 tablespoon of the corn oil and the sesame oil in a large skillet over medium heat. Add the onion, scallions, seitan, bok choy, and carrots and sauté until vegetables are soft, adding tamari as desired for flavor. In a large bowl combine sautéed seitan and vegetables with the rice. Adjust seasonings. Put about ⅓ cup of the mixture on each egg roll wrapper and roll up, folding over ends and sealing flap with a little water. Fry egg rolls in the remaining 2 tablespoons of corn oil in large skillet over moderately high heat until golden brown on both sides, about 5 minutes, or bake on oiled baking sheet at 350 degrees for about 15 minutes, or until golden brown, turning once.

8 SERVINGS

Calories 123.7 • Protein 2.315 gm • Fat 7.183 gm • Percentage of calories from fat 52% • Cholesterol 1 mg • Dietary fiber 0.863 gm • Sodium 201.1 mg • Calcium 20.77 mg

Three-Bean Cakes with Salsa

Use your favorite store-bought salsa with these zesty cakes or make your own when fresh tomatoes are available (see following recipe).

3 tablespoons corn oil
1 medium onion, chopped
1 medium green bell pepper, chopped
1 fresh jalapeño pepper, seeded and chopped
1 large clove garlic, chopped
1 cup cooked pinto beans
½ cup cooked black beans
½ cup cooked kidney beans

½ cup Basic Vegetable Stock (see page 10)
¼ cup ketchup
1 teaspoon chili powder
¼ teaspoon ground coriander
Salt and freshly ground black pepper
1 cup cooked brown rice
All-purpose flour
1 cup salsa (recipe follows)

Heat 2 tablespoons of the oil in a large skillet over medium-low heat. Add the onion, bell pepper, jalapeño, and garlic and cook until the onion is translucent, stirring occasionally, about 10 minutes. Add the pinto, black, and kidney beans, stock, ketchup, chili powder, coriander, salt, and pepper and simmer until the liquid evaporates, stirring frequently, about 20 minutes. Transfer the bean mixture to a food processor. Add the rice and process mixture to combine well. Transfer to a bowl. Cover and refrigerate until chilled. Shape the bean mixture into patties, using ¼ cup for each. Dust lightly with the flour. Heat the remaining 1 tablespoon oil in large skillet over medium-high heat. Add the bean cakes to skillet in batches (do not crowd) and fry until crisp, about 2 minutes. Serve with the salsa.

6 SERVINGS

Calories 286.7 • Protein 11.43 gm • Fat 7.971 gm • Percentage of calories from fat 24% • Cholesterol 0 mg • Dietary fiber 2.78 gm • Sodium 216.9 mg • Calcium 71.09 mg

Salsa

To make a milder salsa, omit the jalapeño and reduce the amount of cayenne by half.

1 pound ripe tomatoes, seeded
  and chopped
¼ cup chopped onion
2 scallions, chopped
1 jalapeño pepper, seeded and
  minced

¼ teaspoon salt
1 teaspoon cider vinegar
1 teaspoon lemon juice
¼ teaspoon cayenne

Combine all the ingredients in a bowl. Chill until ready to serve. It is best to make this salsa several hours in advance to allow flavors to bloom.

MAKES 2 CUPS (⅓-CUP SERVING)

Calories 23.36 • Protein 0.927 gm • Fat 0.34 gm • Percentage of calories from fat 11% • Cholesterol 0 mg • Dietary fiber 1.416 gm • Sodium 124.7 mg • Calcium 8.671 mg

Eggless Salad Filling

The only thing better than how this filling tastes is the fact that it contains zero cholesterol. Use it in sandwiches, as a filling for mini-pitas, or for tea sandwiches on a buffet table.

1 pound firm tofu, quartered
¼ cup Tofu Mayonnaise (see
  page 12)
2 tablespoons Dijon mustard
1 large sweet pickle, chopped

¼ cup minced celery
2 scallions, minced
Dash turmeric for color
Salt and freshly ground black
  pepper

Place tofu in a small saucepan, cover with water, and simmer over medium-high heat for 2 to 3 minutes. Drain, press out water, and allow it to cool. Crumble into bowl. Combine tofu with remaining ingredients until well blended. Refrigerate at least 1 hour before using.

4 SERVINGS

Calories 102.9 • Protein 10.5 gm • Fat 4.946 gm • Percentage of calories from fat 43% • Cholesterol 0 mg • Dietary fiber 0.441 gm • Sodium 531.5 mg • Calcium 63.67 mg

Tempeh Reuben

2 tablespoons corn or safflower oil
6 ounces poached tempeh (see
  page 12), cut in ⅛-inch-thick
  slices
1 tablespoon margarine

4 slices rye bread
2 teaspoons Dijon mustard
4 tablespoons sauerkraut
4 ounces Swiss cheese, thinly
  sliced

Heat oil in a large skillet over medium heat, add tempeh, and cook until lightly browned on both sides. Remove from pan. Spread margarine on one side of each slice of bread, and spread mustard on the other side of each slice of bread. Place bread, margarine side down, in a skillet. Layer both slices of bread with tempeh, sauerkraut, and cheese. Top with remaining 2 slices of prepared bread, margarine side up. Fry sandwiches until golden. Turn carefully to brown other side. Serve immediately.

MAKES 2 SANDWICHES

Calories 697.1 • Protein 35.63 gm • Fat 43.81 gm • Percentage of calories from fat 56% • Cholesterol 51.91 mg • Dietary fiber 3.27 gm • Sodium 972.5 mg • Calcium 659.7 mg

Pita Pockets with Marinated Tofu

½ cup olive oil
3 tablespoons balsamic vinegar
½ teaspoon salt
⅛ teaspoon freshly ground black pepper
4 ounces firm tofu, cut into ½-inch dice

1 green bell pepper, chopped
1 carrot, finely shredded
4 radishes, chopped
1 tomato, seeded and chopped
2 whole-wheat pita pockets
4 Boston lettuce leaves

In a large bowl, whisk together olive oil, vinegar, salt, and pepper. Add tofu, bell pepper, carrot, radishes, and tomato. Toss to coat with dressing. Allow to marinate for 1 hour. To assemble, cut pitas in half, place lettuce leaf in each pita half, spoon in vegetable mixture. Repeat for additional sandwiches, or refrigerate extra filling.

MAKES 2 SANDWICHES

Calories 748.7 • Protein 12.21 gm • Fat 57.27 gm • Percentage of calories from fat 67% • Cholesterol 0 mg • Dietary fiber 2.424 gm • Sodium 933.9 mg • Calcium 51.51 mg

Tempeh "Chickenless" Salad

2 tablespoons corn oil
1 pound poached tempeh (see page 12), crumbled
½ cup Tofu Mayonnaise (see page 12)
1 tablespoon prepared mustard
1 teaspoon lemon juice

1 tablespoon minced fresh parsley
¼ cup finely chopped celery
1 large dill pickle, chopped
¼ cup finely chopped scallions
½ teaspoon salt
⅛ teaspoon freshly ground black pepper

Heat oil in medium skillet over moderate heat, add tempeh, and sauté until lightly browned, about 5 to 8 minutes. Allow to cool. Combine Tofu Mayonnaise with mustard and lemon juice and set aside. In a bowl, combine tempeh with the parsley, celery, pickle, and scallions. Add reserved mayonnaise and season to taste with salt and pepper.

4 SERVINGS

Calories 293.5 • Protein 20.03 gm • Fat 19.53 gm • Percentage of calories from fat 60% • Cholesterol 0 mg • Dietary fiber 3.604 gm • Sodium 602.5 mg • Calcium 115.6 mg

B.L.T.'s

1 tablespoon corn oil
8 slices tempeh bacon or other meatless bacon
2 tablespoons Tofu Mayonnaise (see page 12)

4 slices whole-grain bread, toasted
2 Boston lettuce leaves
4 slices ripe tomato
Salt and pepper

Heat oil in a large skillet over medium heat and fry tempeh bacon until browned, turning once, about 3 minutes each side. Remove from pan, drain on paper toweling. Spread Tofu Mayonnaise on toast, place 2 slices of the toast on flat surface, layer each with tempeh bacon, lettuce, and tomato.

Sprinkle with salt and pepper. Top each with remaining slices of toast. Cut in half and serve.

MAKES 2 SANDWICHES

Calories 436.1 • Protein 13.78 gm • Fat 32.4 gm • Percentage of calories from fat 63% • Cholesterol 0 mg • Dietary fiber 6.218 gm • Sodium 1408 mg • Calcium 70.4 mg

Sloppy Joes

Children of all ages will love these served on whole-grain rolls which have been toasted lightly under the broiler.

2 tablespoons corn oil
1 pound firm tofu, crumbled
2 tablespoons low-sodium tamari
1 medium onion, chopped
1 green bell pepper, chopped
1 tablespoon chili powder
½ teaspoon salt

⅛ teaspoon freshly ground black pepper
2 cups tomato sauce
1 tablespoon sugar or a natural sweetener
1 tablespoon Dijon mustard

Heat 1 tablespoon of the corn oil in a large skillet over medium-high heat. Add tofu and tamari; cook until browned. Transfer to a bowl and set aside. Heat skillet over medium-high heat with remaining 1 tablespoon oil, add onion and bell pepper. Cook until onion is translucent, about 5 minutes. Add chili powder, salt, and pepper. Cook 2 minutes. Add tomato sauce, sugar, and mustard. Simmer for 5 minutes. Add tofu. Simmer 10 minutes to blend flavors. Adjust seasonings.

6 SERVINGS

Calories 139.8 • Protein 8.002 gm • Fat 6.524 gm • Percentage of calories from fat 42% • Cholesterol 0 mg • Dietary fiber 0.954 gm • Sodium 655.5 mg • Calcium 52.67 mg

2
Stews and Hearty Soups

What's more soothing than a steaming bowl of soup on a cold winter day? And what's more comforting than a generous serving of rich stew accompanied by a crusty loaf of bread at the first chill of autumn?

With over fifty recipes in this chapter, you could try a new soup or stew every week of the year. The varied selections encompass the globe with Moroccan-Style Seitan with Chick-peas, Hearty Basque Stew, Spicy Tofu Chili, and a delightful Minestrone Soup.

Each soup and stew recipe is chock full of tempting garden vegetables and includes one or more protein-rich ingredients.

Winter Vegetable Soup

2 tablespoons olive oil
1 large onion, chopped
1 large clove garlic, minced
1 rib celery, cut into ½-inch dice
4 new red potatoes, unpeeled, cut into ½-inch dice
2 carrots, halved lengthwise, cut into ¼-inch slices
6 cups Basic Vegetable Stock (see page 10)

4 ounces fresh spinach, washed and chopped
½ teaspoon salt
⅛ teaspoon freshly ground black pepper
2 cups cooked cannellini beans
2 tablespoons chopped fresh parsley

Heat oil in a large saucepan over medium heat. Add onion and garlic; sauté until softened, 3 to 5 minutes. Add celery, potatoes, and carrots; cook, stirring frequently, about 5 minutes. Add stock, increase heat to medium-high, and heat to boiling. Return heat to low. Simmer soup, covered, 10 to 15 minutes. Add spinach, salt, and pepper. Simmer, covered, about 10 minutes. Add beans to soup, adjust seasonings, and simmer another 5 minutes, or until vegetables are tender. Ladle soup into individual bowls; sprinkle with parsley.

4 TO 6 SERVINGS

Calories 297.7 • Protein 11.99 gm • Fat 6.326 gm • Percentage of calories from fat 18% • Cholesterol 0 mg • Dietary fiber 10.62 gm • Sodium 570.4 mg • Calcium 109 mg

Lentil Soup

This is lentil soup the way my mother used to make it. Simple to prepare and simply delicious.

2 tablespoons corn or safflower oil
1 medium onion, diced
1 carrot, diced
1 rib celery, diced
1 pound lentils, rinsed

2 cups tomato juice
2 bay leaves
1 teaspoon salt
⅛ teaspoon freshly ground black
  pepper

Heat oil in a stock pot over medium heat, add onion, carrot, and celery, and cook for 5 minutes. Add lentils, tomato juice, bay leaves, salt, pepper, and 6 cups water; bring to a boil. Reduce heat to medium low and simmer about 45 minutes. If soup becomes too thick, add more water to achieve desired consistency. Adjust seasonings.

6 SERVINGS

Calories 326.8 • Protein 22.32 gm • Fat 5.391 gm • Percentage of calories from fat 14% • Cholesterol 0 mg • Dietary fiber 1.44 gm • Sodium 658.6 mg • Calcium 61.72 mg

Lentil Soup with Red Wine

2 tablespoons olive oil
1 cup minced onion
1 cup grated carrot
½ cup diced celery
2 cloves garlic, minced
6 cups Basic Vegetable Stock
  (see page 10)
1 pound lentils, rinsed
2 cups tomato juice

1 cup dry red wine
½ minced fresh parsley
½ teaspoon minced fresh thyme or
  ¼ teaspoon dried
2 bay leaves
1 teaspoon salt
⅛ teaspoon freshly ground black
  pepper

Heat oil in a large stock pot over medium heat. Add onion, carrot, celery, and garlic and cook about 10 minutes. Add stock, lentils, tomato juice, wine, parsley, thyme, bay leaves, salt, and pepper. Bring to boil. Reduce heat, cover, and simmer until lentils are tender, stirring occasionally, about 45 minutes. Adjust seasonings.

8 SERVINGS

Calories 312.3 • Protein 18.39 gm • Fat 4.265 gm • Percentage of calories from fat 12% • Cholesterol 0 mg • Dietary fiber 2.586 gm • Sodium 515.7 mg • Calcium 75.79 mg

Black Bean Soup

½ pound dried black beans
¾ cup minced onion
⅓ cup minced celery
½ cup minced carrot
½ cup finely chopped green bell
  pepper
3 cups Basic Vegetable Stock (see
  page 10)
1 teaspoon salt
¾ teaspoon dried thyme

1 teaspoon dry mustard
2 cloves garlic, minced
Pinch cayenne
⅛ teaspoon freshly ground black
  pepper
2 tablespoons soy bacon bits or
  minced fresh parsley
Dry sherry, warmed, or lemon
  slices

Soak beans in water overnight. In a large stock pot combine drained beans with onion, celery, carrot, green pepper, and 3 cups of water. Heat over medium heat to boiling, then skim off foam that rises to surface. Reduce heat to low; add the stock, salt, thyme, mustard, garlic, cayenne, and black pepper. Simmer, covered, until beans are tender and soup has thickened, about 2½ hours. Serve soup in individual bowls garnished with soy bacon bits or parsley and sherry or lemon slices.

6 TO 8 SERVINGS

Calories 149.5 • Protein 8.315 gm • Fat 0.708 gm • Percentage of calories from fat 4% • Cholesterol 0 mg • Dietary fiber 1.763 gm • Sodium 428.7 mg • Calcium 70.5 mg

White Bean and Wild Rice Soup

In this unusual soup, the navy beans serve as a delicious meat alternative. I created the recipe during my restaurant years in Charleston, South Carolina. One day I had prepped more wild rice than was necessary for another purpose, yet I still needed to prepare a soup du jour. Sometimes necessity really is the mother of invention.

2 tablespoons corn oil
2 ribs celery, diced
2 carrots, diced
3 shallots, diced
¼ cup minced scallions
½ cup slivered almonds
1 tablespoon chopped pimiento
1 tablespoon chopped fresh dill
½ teaspoon freshly ground black
  pepper

2 bay leaves
¼ teaspoon ground turmeric
3 quarts Basic Vegetable Stock
  (see page 10)
1 cup wild rice
1 teaspoon salt
½ cup basmati rice
3 cups cooked navy beans
2 cups sliced mushrooms

Heat oil in large skillet over medium-low heat. Add celery, carrots, shallots, scallions, almonds, and pimiento and cook, stirring occasionally, for 5 minutes. Add dill, pepper, bay leaves, and turmeric. Turn off heat. Bring 3 quarts stock, wild rice, and salt to boil in a large pot. Reduce heat, add celery mixture, and simmer 45 minutes, adding more stock if soup is too thick. Add Basmati rice, beans, and mushrooms. Simmer 15 minutes longer, or until rice is soft. Discard bay leaves before serving.

6 TO 8 SERVINGS

Calories 466.5 • Protein 17.86 gm • Fat 9.636 gm • Percentage of calories from fat 18% • Cholesterol 0 mg • Dietary fiber 8.675 gm • Sodium 785.4 mg • Calcium 128 mg

Split Pea Soup

Soy bacon bits are available in most supermarkets and add a smoky flavor to this wholesome soup.

2 tablespoons corn or safflower oil
1 onion, cut into ¼-inch dice
1 carrot, cut into ¼-inch dice
1 rib celery, cut into ¼-inch dice
1 potato, cut into ¼-inch dice
1 pound dried split peas, rinsed

1 bay leaf
1 teaspoon salt
⅛ teaspoon freshly ground black pepper
1 tablespoon soy bacon bits

Heat oil in a stock pot over medium heat, add onion, carrot, and celery, and cook for 3 to 5 minutes. Add 6 cups of water, the potato, split peas, bay leaf, salt, and pepper and bring to a boil. Reduce heat to medium low and simmer 45 minutes. If consistency becomes too thick, add more water. Adjust seasonings. Place soup in bowls and sprinkle with soy bacon bits.

6 SERVINGS

Calories 338.9 • Protein 19.86 gm • Fat 5.972 gm • Percentage of calories from fat 15% • Cholesterol 0 mg • Dietary fiber 4.455 gm • Sodium 400.7 mg • Calcium 59.81 mg

Minestrone Soup

Chick-peas may be substituted for the cannellini beans. Either one makes a fine meat alternative in this classic soup. Pastina is a tiny macaroni product the size of a grain of rice. If unavailable, orzo may be substituted.

2 tablespoons olive oil
3 cloves garlic, minced
1 large onion, minced
2 carrots, cut into ¼-inch slices
½ small cabbage, shredded
2 potatoes, diced
1 pound fresh or canned
  tomatoes, peeled and chopped
1 6-ounce can tomato paste
7 cups Basic Vegetable Stock
  (see page 10) or water
1 bay leaf
½ teaspoon fresh oregano or
  ¼ teaspoon dried
½ teaspoon fresh thyme or
  ¼ teaspoon dried

1 tablespoon fresh basil or 1
  teaspoon dried
1 teaspoon salt
⅛ teaspoon freshly ground black
  pepper
¼ cup plus 3 tablespoons minced
  fresh parsley
2 cups cooked cannellini beans
1 zucchini, thinly sliced
1 cup fresh green beans, trimmed
  and cut in half
4 ounces pastina or other very
  small pasta
Freshly grated Parmesan cheese
  (optional)

Heat oil in a large stock pot and add garlic, onion, carrots, and cabbage. Sauté, stirring, over medium heat about 10 minutes. Add potatoes, tomatoes, tomato paste, stock or water, bay leaf, oregano, thyme, and basil. Bring to a boil, reduce heat, cover, and simmer 1 hour. Remove bay leaf. Add salt and pepper to taste, ¼ cup parsley, cannellini beans, zucchini, green beans, and pastina and cook another 15 minutes. Adjust seasonings. Stir in 3 tablespoons parsley. Ladle into bowls and top with freshly grated Parmesan, if desired.

6 TO 8 SERVINGS

Calories 319.6 • Protein 13.13 gm • Fat 5.371 gm • Percentage of calories from fat 14% • Cholesterol 0 mg • Dietary fiber 11.02 gm • Sodium 612.4 mg • Calcium 156 mg

Pasta e Fagioli

My mother made this meatless delight once a week when I was growing up. My first introduction to meat alternatives, it's still one of my favorite dishes.

2 tablespoons olive oil
1 clove garlic, minced
4 tablespoons tomato paste
1 teaspoon salt
½ teaspoon dried basil, crumbled
½ teaspoon dried oregano, crumbled
1 bay leaf

2 cups cooked Great Northern beans
⅛ teaspoon freshly ground black pepper
1 pound elbow-shaped pasta, cooked al dente
Freshly grated Parmesan cheese

Heat olive oil in a large saucepan or stock pot over medium heat. Add the garlic, tomato paste, salt, basil, oregano, and bay leaf. Cook for 3 minutes. Stir in 5 cups of water, the cooked beans, and pepper, and simmer for 15 minutes. Add the pasta, and simmer 5 minutes longer. Remove bay leaf. Serve hot. Pass grated cheese separately.

6 SERVINGS

Calories 227.1 • Protein 9.029 gm • Fat 5.397 gm • Percentage of calories from fat 21% • Cholesterol 0 mg • Dietary fiber 5.278 gm • Sodium 370.6 mg • Calcium 62.38 mg

Spicy Tofu Chili

Tofu that has been frozen takes on a firmer, meatier texture, making it ide-
ally suited for this zesty chili recipe. To freeze tofu, cut it into one-inch thick
slabs and wrap in plastic. Freeze at least 48 hours before thawing for use.

2 tablespoons olive oil
1 large onion, chopped
1 clove garlic, finely minced
1 pound frozen firm tofu, thawed,
  squeezed, and crumbled
1 8-ounce can tomato paste
4 cups hot water
2 cups cooked pinto beans
1½ tablespoons chili powder
¾ teaspoon salt

½ teaspoon ground cinnamon
¼ teaspoon freshly ground black
  pepper
1 teaspoon ground allspice
½ teaspoon Worcestershire sauce
¼ teaspoon cayenne
Freshly cooked pasta shells or
  elbows
1 cup grated cheddar cheese
  (optional)

Heat oil in a large saucepan. Add onion and cook, covered, until softened, about 5 minutes. Add garlic and stir for 30 seconds; add tofu and mix well. Add remaining ingredients, except for the cheese. Simmer 1 hour, stirring occasionally. Serve over cooked pasta shells or elbows and top with grated cheese.

6 SERVINGS

Calories 292.2 • Protein 17.48 gm • Fat 13.21 gm • Percentage of calories from fat 39% • Cholesterol 0 mg • Dietary fiber 6.816 gm • Sodium 563.4 mg • Calcium 227.4 mg

Tempeh Chili

Most welcome on a cold winter day, this easy-to-assemble chili can be ready in a snap.

2 tablespoons corn oil
1 medium onion, chopped
1 pound poached tempeh, finely
  chopped
1 tablespoon chili powder
2 tablespoons low-sodium tamari
1 tablespoon sugar or a natural
  sweetener

2 cups peeled and chopped
  tomatoes (fresh or canned)
3 cups cooked kidney beans
1 cup tomato purée

In a large pot or skillet, heat oil over medium heat, add onion, cover, and cook for 5 minutes. Uncover and stir in tempeh, chili powder, tamari, and sugar. Then stir in tomatoes, beans, and tomato purée. Simmer for 30 to 40 minutes, stirring occasionally, and adding more liquid if chili gets too thick. Adjust seasonings.

6 TO 8 SERVINGS.

Calories 278 • Protein 18.06 gm • Fat 9.577 gm • Percentage of calories from fat 30% • Cholesterol 0 mg • Dietary fiber 9.952 gm • Sodium 583.4 mg • Calcium 93.27 mg

Chili with Chocolate

The chocolate adds a special touch to this flavorful chili.

2 tablespoons corn or safflower oil
1 onion, chopped
1 green bell pepper, chopped
1 clove garlic, minced
2 cups TVP granules combined
  with 2 cups water
2 cups cooked red kidney beans
3 tablespoons chili powder
1 28-ounce can tomatoes,
  chopped, with juice
1 cup Basic Vegetable Stock (see
  page 10)

1 bay leaf
½ teaspoon cayenne
½ teaspoon dried oregano
¾ teaspoon salt
¼ teaspoon freshly ground black
  pepper
1 ounce semisweet chocolate,
  grated
Pinch of cinnamon

Heat oil in a large saucepan over medium heat. Cook the onion and green pepper, stirring, for 4 minutes. Add the garlic, TVP, and kidney beans, and cook for 4 minutes. Add the chili powder and cook mixture over moderately low heat, stirring, for 1 minute. Add the tomatoes, stock, bay leaf, cayenne, oregano, salt, and pepper, bring liquid to a boil, stirring, and simmer chili for 1 hour. Remove the pot from the heat and stir in the chocolate, cinnamon, and additional salt and pepper to taste.

4 TO 6 SERVINGS

Calories 377.9 • Protein 39.38 gm • Fat 9.047 gm • Percentage of calories from fat 19% • Cholesterol 0 mg • Dietary fiber 16.26 gm • Sodium 685.9 mg • Calcium 284.3 mg

Tuscan-Style Pasta and Beans

The meatless pepperoni adds a spicy touch to this fortifying dish, which is equally tasty without it.

2 tablespoons olive oil
1 medium onion, minced
2 ounces meatless pepperoni, chopped (optional)
1 large clove garlic, minced
2 cups tomato sauce
2 cups cooked cannellini beans
½ teaspoon salt
⅛ teaspoon freshly ground black pepper

¼ teaspoon dried oregano
1 bay leaf
6 cups Basic Vegetable Stock (see page 10)
1 pound small shell-shaped pasta, cooked al dente
Freshly grated Parmesan cheese (optional)

Heat oil in a large saucepan or stock pot over medium-high heat. Add onion and meatless pepperoni and sauté about 10 minutes. Add garlic and sauté 30 more seconds. Stir in tomato sauce, beans, salt, pepper, oregano, bay leaf, and stock. Simmer over low heat about 30 minutes. Add cooked pasta and stir; simmer gently 5 minutes. Ladle into bowls and sprinkle with grated cheese, if desired.

6 TO 8 SERVINGS

Calories 403.4 • Protein 14.62 gm • Fat 5.435 gm • Percentage of calories from fat 12% • Cholesterol 0 mg • Dietary fiber 8.175 gm • Sodium 1053 mg • Calcium 70.95 mg

Black Jack Chili

2 tablespoons corn or safflower oil
1 pound seitan (see page 11), cut into ½-inch dice
½ cup diced onion
1 jalapeño pepper, seeded and minced
¼ cup diced green bell pepper
1 teaspoon minced garlic
1 28-ounce can diced tomatoes in purée, with liquid
2 cups cooked black beans, rinsed

3 tablespoons tomato paste
1 cup Basic Vegetable Stock (see page 10)
½ teaspoon ground cumin
1 tablespoon chili powder
¾ teaspoon salt
⅛ teaspoon freshly ground black pepper
1 cup grated Monterey Jack cheese

Heat oil in a large saucepan or Dutch oven over medium heat. Add seitan and cook until lightly browned, about 5 minutes. Remove with slotted spoon and transfer to a bowl. Add onion and jalapeño and bell pepper to pot and cook until softened, stirring occasionally, about 10 minutes. Add garlic, and cook another 2 minutes. Add seitan and remaining ingredients except cheese. Simmer 1 hour to blend flavors, stirring occasionally and adding water if mixture is too dry. Ladle chili in bowls and top with Monterey Jack cheese. Serve immediately.

4 TO 6 SERVINGS

Calories 654 • Protein 33.13 gm • Fat 21.78 gm • Percentage of calories from fat 28% • Cholesterol 40.25 mg • Dietary fiber 18.28 gm • Sodium 1587 mg • Calcium 468.1 mg

Sardinian Stew

Look for tofu sausage links in natural foods stores. If unavailable, substitute other meatless sausage links.

3 tablespoons olive oil
1 pound seitan (see page 11) or tofu sausage links, cut into ½-inch cubes
1 large onion, chopped
1 medium fennel bulb, trimmed, cored, and chopped
2 cloves garlic, minced
½ small green cabbage, cored and chopped

1 cup chopped sun-dried tomatoes packed in oil, drained
2 cups cooked fava beans
½ teaspoon hot red pepper flakes
½ teaspoon salt
⅛ teaspoon freshly ground black pepper
½ cup grated Pecorino Romano cheese

Heat oil in a stock pot over medium-high heat. Add seitan or tofu sausage and brown well, stirring occasionally, about 5 minutes. Add onions and cook until translucent, stirring occasionally, about 5 minutes. Stir in fennel and garlic and cook 30 seconds. Add 4 cups of water and bring to a boil. Reduce heat to medium, add cabbage, tomatoes, beans, red pepper flakes, salt, and pepper. Add more water, if needed, to cover. Cover and simmer, stirring occasionally, about 30 minutes. Sprinkle with cheese just before serving.

6 SERVINGS

Calories 468.5 • Protein 21.6 gm • Fat 13.51 gm • Percentage of calories from fat 24% • Cholesterol 6.583 mg • Dietary fiber 13.9 gm • Sodium 608 mg • Calcium 210.5 mg

Hearty Basque Stew

Protein-rich and meaty in their own right, fava beans enhance this satisfying winter stew.

1 medium carrot, cut into ¼-inch slices
1 medium rib celery, cut into ¼-inch slices
1 small onion, chopped
1 medium potato, cut into ¼-inch dice
1 large clove garlic, minced
3 tablespoons minced fresh parsley
1 bay leaf
⅛ teaspoon hot red pepper flakes
½ pound cabbage, shredded
2 cups cooked fava beans
2 cups cooked Great Northern beans
¼ cup dry red wine
½ teaspoon salt
⅛ teaspoon freshly ground black pepper
4 ¾-inch-thick slices French bread
2 tablespoons olive oil

Pour 4 cups of water into a stock pot and add carrot, celery, onion, potato, garlic, 1 tablespoon of the parsley, the bay leaf, and red pepper flakes and bring to boil. Reduce heat, cover, and simmer 30 minutes. Add cabbage and continue cooking until vegetables are tender, about 15 minutes. Add fava beans and Great Northern beans and cook 15 minutes, adding more water if soup is too thick. Add wine and season to taste with salt and pepper. Preheat oven to 350 degrees. Arrange bread slices in single layer on baking sheet. Brush both sides with olive oil and bake 10 minutes. Turn slices over, bake 10 minutes. Place 1 piece of bread in bottom of each soup bowl. Ladle stew over top. Sprinkle with remaining parsley.

4 SERVINGS

Calories 438 • Protein 20.12 gm • Fat 8.648 gm • Percentage of calories from fat 17% • Cholesterol 0 mg • Dietary fiber 14.87 gm • Sodium 473.6 mg • Calcium 169.4 mg

Tempeh Stew with Peppers

4 tablespoons olive oil
2 medium onions, chopped
½ cup dry red wine
3 red, green, and/or yellow bell
  peppers, seeded and cut into
  1-inch squares
2 cups chopped canned tomatoes,
  drained
2 tablespoons minced fresh
  parsley

1 bay leaf
½ teaspoon salt
⅛ teaspoon freshly ground black
  pepper
12 ounces poached tempeh (see
  page 12), cut into ½-inch cubes

In a large skillet, heat 1 tablespoon of the olive oil. Add half the chopped onions and cook over medium heat for 5 minutes. Remove with a slotted spoon and set aside. Add the wine to the hot skillet and bring to a boil, scraping up any browned bits from the bottom of the pan. Mix the sautéed onions into the wine and boil over moderate heat until the wine is reduced to about 2 tablespoons, 4 to 5 minutes. Remove skillet from heat and set aside.

Heat 2 tablespoons olive oil in stock pot. Add bell peppers and the remaining onion and cook about 5 minutes. Add the wine mixture, the tomatoes, parsley, bay leaf, half the salt, and the black pepper. Bring to a boil over medium-high heat, reduce heat to low, cover, and simmer about 30 minutes. Heat remaining 1 tablespoon oil in the cleaned-out skillet over medium-high heat. Add tempeh and cook until browned on all sides, about 5 minutes. Season with remaining salt. Add tempeh to stew and simmer for 10 minutes, stirring occasionally, to blend the flavors. Remove bay leaf.

4 SERVINGS

Calories 348 • Protein 16.11 gm • Fat 20.5 gm • Percentage of calories from fat 52% • Cholesterol 0 mg • Dietary fiber 6.227 gm • Sodium 307.1 mg • Calcium 96.76 mg

Three-Green Ragoût with Cannellini Beans

The delicate whiteness of the cannellini bean and the orange blush of the sweet potato look lovely against the backdrop of rich greens.

¼ cup olive oil
1 medium onion, chopped
3 cloves garlic, finely minced
1 bay leaf
½ teaspoon sweet paprika
½ teaspoon salt
⅛ teaspoon freshly ground black pepper

2 tablespoons white wine vinegar
4 cups chopped escarole
4 cups chopped kale
1 sweet potato, peeled and cut into ¼-inch dice
3 cups cooked cannellini beans
1 pound fresh spinach, stemmed and coarsely chopped

Heat oil in a large pot over medium heat; add onion and garlic and, stirring, cook for 5 minutes. Add the bay leaf, paprika, salt, pepper, vinegar, and 1 cup of water. Add the escarole and kale, cover, and cook over medium heat until the greens wilt, 3 to 4 minutes. Add sweet potato. Cover and cook over moderately high heat, at a slow boil and stirring occasionally, until the vegetables are tender, about 20 to 30 minutes. Remove bay leaf. Add beans and spinach and cook, stirring, until spinach is wilted, about 4 minutes.

4 TO 6 SERVINGS

Calories 340.4 • Protein 16.59 gm • Fat 12.54 gm • Percentage of calories from fat 31% • Cholesterol 0 mg • Dietary fiber 18.42 gm • Sodium 926.1 mg • Calcium 337.9 mg

Chick-pea and Fennel Stew

Seitan or tempeh would also work in this stew, but the chick-peas are essential to this aromatic Mediterranean dish.

¼ cup olive oil
1 red bell pepper, cut into 1-inch dice
1 fennel bulb, cut into 1-inch pieces
1 large parsnip, cut into ½-inch pieces
3 plum tomatoes, chopped
1 medium zucchini, cut into ½-inch pieces
1 carrot, cut into ½-inch pieces
4 scallions, minced

2 cloves garlic, minced
½ cup chopped fresh parsley
½ cup chopped fresh basil
1 tablespoon white wine vinegar
¼ teaspoon dried thyme
¾ teaspoon salt
½ teaspoon freshly ground black pepper
½ teaspoon hot red pepper flakes
2 bay leaves
3 cups cooked chick-peas

Combine all the ingredients, except the chick-peas and half of the parsley and basil, in a large pot. Stir in 1 cup of water. Cover and cook over medium-high heat, at a slow boil, stirring occasionally, for 45 minutes. Add the chick-peas and another ½ cup of water. Cover and simmer 5 minutes to heat through. Remove the bay leaves and serve sprinkled with reserved parsley and basil.

4 TO 6 SERVINGS

Calories 224.9 • Protein 4.964 gm • Fat 12.1 gm • Percentage of calories from fat 42% • Cholesterol 0 mg • Dietary fiber 7.949 gm • Sodium 555.4 mg • Calcium 85.43 mg

Greek Stew

4 tablespoons olive oil
1 large onion, chopped
2 cloves garlic, minced
1 pound seitan (see page 11), cut
 into 1-inch cubes
½ teaspoon salt
⅛ teaspoon freshly ground black
 pepper
2 bay leaves

½ teaspoon ground cinnamon
½ teaspoon dried rosemary
2 cups chopped, canned tomatoes
 with juice
1 cup dry white wine
1 pound ziti or other small tubular
 pasta
¼ pound feta cheese, crumbled

In a large skillet, heat 2 tablespoons of the oil over low heat. Add onions and garlic and cook 5 minutes, or until onion softens. Add remaining 2 tablespoons of oil to the skillet and increase the heat to medium. Toss the seitan with the salt and pepper and add to the skillet. Cook, stirring frequently, about 3 minutes. Add the bay leaves, cinnamon, rosemary, tomatoes with their juice, and wine. Stir to combine. Bring to a simmer, partially cover, and reduce the heat to low. Cook 30 to 40 minutes, until sauce thickens slightly. Remove bay leaves.

Meanwhile, in a large pot of boiling salted water, cook the pasta until tender but still slightly firm, about 10 minutes. Drain. Transfer the hot pasta to a serving platter. Crumble all but 2 tablespoons of the feta on top. Pour the stew over the pasta, top with remaining cheese, and serve hot.

4 TO 6 SERVINGS

Calories 822.3 • Protein 28.93 gm • Fat 18.77 gm • Percentage of calories from fat 20% • Cholesterol 20.84 mg • Dietary fiber 12.9 gm • Sodium 821.3 mg • Calcium 191.5 mg

Moroccan Tempeh

3 tablespoons corn or safflower oil
1 pound poached tempeh (see
   page 12), cut into 3- × ½-inch bars
1 onion, chopped
½ teaspoon salt
¼ teaspoon freshly ground black
   pepper
⅛ teaspoon ground turmeric
½ teaspoon ground cinnamon
1 cup blanched slivered almonds
1 cup pitted prunes
2 tablespoons sugar or a natural
   sweetener
⅛ teaspoon ground nutmeg

Heat 2 tablespoons of the oil in a large pot over medium heat. Add the tempeh and the onion, season with half the salt and half the pepper, and cook until golden brown, about 10 minutes. Add 3 cups of water, the turmeric, and cinnamon; bring the liquid to a boil and simmer, covered, stirring occasionally, for 15 minutes. Transfer the tempeh to a plate, leaving the onion and broth in the pot.

In a large skillet sauté the almonds in the remaining 1 tablespoon oil over medium-high heat, stirring for 5 minutes, or until golden. Reserve.

Add the prunes to the pot and cook the mixture over moderate heat, stirring occasionally, for 15 to 20 minutes, or until the prunes are just tender. Add the sugar, nutmeg, the remaining ¼ teaspoon of salt and the ⅛ teaspoon of pepper. Cook the mixture, stirring gently, for 5 minutes, or until it has thickened slightly. Add the tempeh to the pot, turning it to coat it with the sauce, and heat the stew, covered, over low heat for 5 minutes. Garnish individual servings with the almonds.

4 SERVINGS

Calories 501.2 • Protein 25.01 gm • Fat 35.83 gm • Percentage of calories from fat 62% • Cholesterol 0 mg • Dietary fiber 6.806 gm • Sodium 279.4 mg • Calcium 178.6 mg

Tempeh and Artichoke Ragoût

4 tablespoons corn oil
1 pound poached tempeh (see
    page 12) cut into 1-inch pieces
½ teaspoon salt
¼ teaspoon freshly ground black
    pepper
1 medium onion, chopped
2 cloves garlic, minced
½ teaspoon minced fresh thyme or
    ¼ teaspoon dried
½ teaspoon minced fresh basil or
    ¼ teaspoon dried

1 bay leaf
2 cups Basic Vegetable Stock (see
    page 10)
½ cup dry white wine
1 red bell pepper, cut into 2-inch
    squares
1 green or yellow bell pepper, cut
    into 2-inch squares
1 10-ounce package frozen
    artichoke hearts, thawed and
    drained

In a large skillet, heat 2 tablespoons of the oil over moderate heat. Add the tempeh, season with the salt and pepper, and cook, turning, until lightly browned, about 5 minutes. When the tempeh browns, transfer to a dish with a slotted spoon and set aside.

Stir into the skillet the onions, garlic, thyme, basil, and bay leaf. Reduce the heat to moderately low, cover, and cook, stirring occasionally, until the onions are tender, about 10 minutes. Add the stock and wine and bring to a boil. Reduce the heat to moderately low, cover, and simmer about 20 minutes.

Meanwhile, in a medium skillet, heat the remaining 2 tablespoons oil over moderately high heat. Add the bell peppers, season with more salt and pepper, and cook, tossing frequently, until lightly browned, about 5 minutes. Add the artichoke hearts and cook for 2 minutes. Combine the tempeh, peppers, and artichokes in a bowl. Strain any cooking liquid and return it to the skillet with stock mixture. Bring to a boil over high heat and boil until the liquid is reduced by one third, about 5 minutes. Season with salt and pepper to taste. Return the tempeh, peppers, and artichokes to the skillet. Simmer gently until heated through, about 5 minutes.

4 SERVINGS

Calories 409.4 • Protein 22.28 gm • Fat 22.66 gm • Percentage of calories from fat 48% • Cholesterol 0 mg • Dietary fiber 9.043 gm • Sodium 473.7 mg • Calcium 150.9 mg

Nature's Bounty Stew

The delicate colors and flavors of this stew make it a perfect choice to welcome Spring.

2 carrots, grated
1 green bell pepper, cut into ¼-inch squares
1 red bell pepper, cut into ¼-inch squares
1 cup small cauliflower florets
¼ pound green beans, cut into 2-inch lengths
2 medium tomatoes, chopped
6 scallions, chopped

2 cups Basic Vegetable Stock (see page 10)
¾ teaspoon salt
⅛ teaspoon freshly ground black pepper
¼ cup chopped fresh dill
1 cup soft tofu
¼ cup fresh lemon juice
4 cups cooked brown rice
½ cup chopped fresh parsley

In a large saucepan, combine the carrots, bell peppers, cauliflower, green beans, tomatoes, and scallions. Add the stock, salt, pepper, and 2 cups of water. Bring to a boil over moderate heat. Reduce heat to low and simmer, partially covered, until the vegetables are tender, about 30 minutes. Add the dill, remove from the heat, and set aside for 5 minutes.

In a small bowl, beat the tofu and lemon juice until blended. Gradually whisk in ¼ cup of the hot stock. Stir the mixture into the hot stew and season with additional salt and pepper to taste. Divide hot rice among 4 bowls, top with stew, sprinkle with the parsley, and serve hot.

4 SERVINGS

Calories 326.6 • Protein 11.72 gm • Fat 3.061 gm • Percentage of calories from fat 8% • Cholesterol 0 mg • Dietary fiber 7.746 gm • Sodium 812.8 mg • Calcium 86.07 mg

Provençal Seitan Stew

A loaf of crusty bread, your favorite wine, and a crisp green salad are all you need to make this an unforgettable meal.

1 cup dry red wine
1 medium onion, thinly sliced
1 teaspoon chopped fresh thyme
  or ½ teaspoon dried, crumbled
1 bay leaf
3 tablespoons olive oil
1 pound seitan (see page 11), cut
  into 1-inch pieces
2 tablespoons minced fresh
  parsley
1 teaspoon grated orange zest

1 teaspoon grated lemon zest
⅛ teaspoon ground allspice
Salt and freshly ground black
  pepper
1 clove garlic, minced
2 cups chopped canned tomatoes,
  with juice
1 pound carrots, cut into ¼-inch
  dice
2 onions, cut into ¼-inch dice

In a large bowl combine wine, sliced onion, thyme, bay leaf, and 1 table-spoon of the oil. Add seitan, stirring to coat it with the marinade, and let it marinate, refrigerated, for at least 1 hour or overnight. Remove seitan and onion slices from the marinade and reserve. Combine the marinade with the parsley, orange zest, lemon zest, and allspice and reserve.

In a large saucepan, heat the remaining 2 tablespoons olive oil over medium-high heat and brown the seitan. Season with salt and pepper and transfer the seitan to a bowl. In the saucepan, cook the reserved onion slices over low heat, stirring, for 5 minutes then add garlic and cook the mixture, stirring, for 1 minute. Add the tomatoes and cook, stirring, for 1 minute. Add the carrots and diced onions and cook the mixture at a simmer, covered, for 30 minutes. Add the seitan, reserved marinade, and ¼ cup of water; bring the liquid to a boil, stirring, and cook, covered, at a simmer, stirring occasionally, for 30 minutes. Season with additional salt and pepper if desired.

4 TO 6 SERVINGS

Calories 464.8 • Protein 15.8 gm • Fat 10.07 gm • Percentage of calories from fat 19% • Cholesterol 0 mg • Dietary fiber 14.27 gm • Sodium 309.6 mg • Calcium 87.51 mg

Seitan Carbonnade

The combination of ginger and beer in this flavorful dish will keep your guests guessing as they ask for seconds. Serve over noodles.

3 tablespoons safflower or corn oil
2 medium onions, cut into ½-inch dice
1 tablespoon sugar or a natural sweetener
2 tablespoons all-purpose flour
1 cup Basic Vegetable Stock (see page 10)
1 cup beer
2 tablespoons minced celery
1 tablespoon minced fresh parsley

½ teaspoon dried thyme, crumbled
1 bay leaf
½ teaspoon minced fresh ginger
1½ pounds seitan (see page 11), cut into 1-inch pieces
½ teaspoon salt
⅛ teaspoon freshly ground black pepper
1 tablespoon red wine vinegar

Heat 2 tablespoons of the oil in a large saucepan over medium-low heat. Add onions, cover and cook until soft, stirring occasionally, about 15 minutes. Stir in sugar. Increase heat to medium and cook uncovered until onions are golden, stirring frequently, about 10 more minutes. Add flour and stir 2 minutes. Add stock, beer, celery, parsley, thyme, and bay leaf. Simmer until liquid thickens, stirring occasionally, about 10 minutes. Set aside. Stir ginger into mixture.

Preheat oven to 350 degrees. Season seitan with salt and pepper. Heat remaining 1 tablespoon oil in a large skillet and add seitan, cooking until browned on all sides, about 5 minutes. Spoon one third of onion mixture into 3-quart baking dish. Add half of the seitan, then continue layering, ending with onion mixture. Cover and bake about 30 to 45 minutes. Stir in vinegar. Remove bay leaf. Adjust seasonings.

4 TO 6 SERVINGS

Calories 556.4 • Protein 21.24 gm • Fat 10.56 gm • Percentage of calories from fat 16% • Cholesterol 0 mg • Dietary fiber 16.37 gm • Sodium 633.2 mg • Calcium 78.33 mg

Seitan Stew with Capers

2 tablespoons olive oil
1 pound seitan (see page 11), cut
 into 1½-inch pieces
1 clove garlic, finely minced
2 cups chopped canned tomatoes,
 with liquid
1 bay leaf

Salt and freshly ground black
 pepper
2 tablespoons tomato paste
 combined with ½ cup water
½ pound mushrooms, sliced
3 tablespoons drained capers

In a large saucepan, heat the oil over medium-low heat, add the seitan, and cook until browned on all sides, about 5 minutes. Add the garlic and cook, stirring, for 30 seconds. Add the tomatoes and tomato liquid, bay leaf, salt, and pepper and bring to a boil, stirring. Add the tomato paste mixture, bring to a boil again, and cook, stirring, for 5 minutes. Add 1 cup of water, bring to a boil again, and simmer the stew, covered, stirring occasionally, for 30 minutes. Add the mushrooms and capers and simmer, uncovered, stirring occasionally, for 15 minutes, or until the sauce thickens slightly. Discard the bay leaf and season the stew with salt and pepper.

4 SERVINGS

Calories 445.7 • Protein 18.87 gm • Fat 9.264 gm • Percentage of calories from fat 18% • Cholesterol 0 mg • Dietary fiber 14.65 gm • Sodium 553.8 mg • Calcium 52.25 mg

Moroccan-Style Seitan with Chick-peas

2 tablespoons olive oil
1 pound seitan (see page 11), cut
  into 1-inch strips
1 onion, chopped
2 cups chopped canned tomatoes,
  with liquid
1 cup dry white wine
1 cup Basic Vegetable Stock (see
  page 10)

¾ teaspoon salt
⅛ teaspoon freshly ground black
  pepper
1 medium zucchini, cut into ½-inch
  dice
2 cups cooked chick-peas
1 tablespoon minced fresh mint or
  1 teaspoon dried

In a large saucepan, heat the oil over medium-high heat and cook the seitan until browned, about 5 minutes; then remove from the saucepan with a slotted spoon and set aside. Add the onion to the saucepan and cook, stirring, until softened, about 5 minutes. Add the tomatoes and the liquid, wine, stock, salt, and pepper and bring it to a boil. Add the zucchini and simmer, covered, for 20 minutes. Stir in the chick-peas, seitan, and mint, and simmer, uncovered, for 15 minutes, or until sauce thickens slightly. Adjust seasonings.

4 SERVINGS

Calories 687.2 • Protein 26.45 gm • Fat 16.48 gm • Percentage of calories from fat 21% • Cholesterol 0 mg • Dietary fiber 20.47 gm • Sodium 1290 mg • Calcium 124.9 mg

Great Northern Bean Stew with Seasonal Vegetables

Studded with many brightly colored vegetables, this delicate stew is a celebration of nature's bounty.

2 tablespoons safflower or corn oil
1 large onion, chopped
¾ pound carrots, cut into ½-inch dice
1 large clove garlic, chopped
1 pound tomatoes, peeled and chopped, or 2 cups chopped canned tomatoes, drained
¼ cup brandy
2 bay leaves
½ teaspoon minced fresh thyme or ¼ teaspoon dried

½ teaspoon salt
⅛ teaspoon freshly ground black pepper
½ pound green beans, trimmed and cut into 1-inch pieces
1½ cups shelled fresh peas, or frozen peas, thawed
2 cups cooked Great Northern beans
1 tablespoon minced fresh parsley
4 cups freshly cooked rice

In a large saucepan heat the oil over medium heat, add the onions and carrots, and cook, stirring, for 5 minutes. Add the garlic and cook, stirring, for 30 seconds. Add the tomatoes and cook, stirring, for 1 minute. Add the brandy and bring to a boil. Add 3 cups of water, the bay leaves, thyme, salt, and pepper; bring to a boil, then simmer, covered, for 20 minutes. Discard the bay leaves. Add the green beans and simmer the stew for 10 minutes. Add the peas and Great Northern beans and simmer 15 minutes if using fresh peas or 5 minutes if using frozen, or until the green beans and peas are tender. Stir the parsley into the freshly cooked rice, which has been seasoned with salt and pepper. Divide the rice among 4 large bowls and top with the stew.

4 SERVINGS

Calories 539.9 • Protein 17.06 gm • Fat 9.879 gm • Percentage of calories from fat 16% • Cholesterol 0 mg • Dietary fiber 12.45 gm • Sodium 353.6 mg • Calcium 138.7 mg

Stewed Tofu and Napa with Noodles

Distinctively Asian, this flavorful stew offers a delightful change of pace. Brown rice vinegar is a mildly flavored vinegar available in natural foods stores. If you can't find it, use a white wine vinegar.

1 pound firm tofu, cut into 1-inch cubes
3 tablespoons sake
1 tablespoon low-sodium tamari
2 teaspoons brown rice vinegar
2 tablespoons corn oil
2 cloves garlic, finely minced
2 tablespoons minced scallions
1 small head napa cabbage, cut into 2-inch pieces (about 6 cups)

½ teaspoon salt
4 cups Basic Vegetable Stock (see page 10)
2 carrots, cut diagonally into ¼-inch slices
8 shiitake mushrooms, stemmed and sliced
8 ounces freshly cooked soba (buckwheat) noodles

Place tofu in a shallow dish. In a small bowl stir together the sake, tamari, and brown rice vinegar; pour over tofu and gently stir to coat with the marinade. Allow to stand, at room temperature, 20 minutes. Drain tofu; reserve marinade. Heat oil in a large saucepan over medium-high heat. Add drained tofu, cook, turning carefully, until golden brown on all sides, about 5 minutes. Remove tofu with slotted spoon to platter. Add garlic and scallions to oil in saucepan, stir-fry about 5 seconds. Add cabbage, stir-fry about 20 seconds, or until coated with oil. Continue to stir-fry, adding salt and 3 tablespoons of the stock, about 3 minutes. Add remaining stock, heat to boiling. Reduce heat to low, add carrots, and simmer, covered, until cabbage is tender, about 15 minutes. Add mushrooms, plus tofu and reserved marinade. Simmer, covered, about 15 minutes. Serve over hot soba noodles.

4 SERVINGS

Calories 459.4 • Protein 24 gm • Fat 9.953 gm • Percentage of calories from fat 18% • Cholesterol 0 mg • Dietary fiber 3.305 gm • Sodium 927.8 mg • Calcium 103.2 mg

Seitan Stifado

This aromatic stew is sure to win accolades from even the staunchest meat eater.

3 tablespoons olive oil
1 ½ pounds seitan (see page 11), cut into 1-inch cubes
1 large onion, chopped
1 clove garlic, minced
2 tablespoons red wine vinegar
⅓ cup dry red wine
1 bay leaf
2 tomatoes, peeled (see page 375), seeded, and chopped

1 tablespoon brown sugar or a natural sweetener
½ teaspoon ground cinnamon
¼ teaspoon ground cloves
½ teaspoon salt
⅛ teaspoon freshly ground black pepper

Heat the oil in a large saucepan, add seitan, and sauté over medium-high heat, until browned, about 6 to 8 minutes. Transfer browned seitan to a plate with a slotted spoon. Add the onion to the saucepan and sauté over medium-high heat until softened, about 10 minutes. Add to the saucepan the garlic, vinegar, wine, bay leaf, tomatoes, sugar, cinnamon, cloves, and 1 cup of water; deglaze the saucepan, scraping up the brown bits on the bottom of the pan. Return the seitan to the pan and season with the salt and pepper. Bring the liquid to a simmer, and simmer, covered, over low heat for 1 hour. Add more water if the liquid evaporates during cooking time to achieve a saucelike consistency.

4 SERVINGS

Calories 664.9 • Protein 25.88 gm • Fat 13.17 gm • Percentage of calories from fat 17% • Cholesterol 0 mg • Dietary fiber 20.16 gm • Sodium 737.5 mg • Calcium 88.28 mg

Seitan Stew with Madeira

4 tablespoons corn or safflower oil
1½ pounds seitan (see page 11),
  cut into ½-inch strips
2 cups Basic Vegetable Stock (see
  page 10)
1 medium carrot, cut into ¼-inch
  dice
1 rib celery, cut into ¼-inch dice

½ cup minced shallots
½ cup dry Madeira
½ teaspoon dry mustard
½ teaspoon minced fresh tarragon
  or ¼ teaspoon dried
¼ teaspoon salt
½ pound green beans, trimmed,
  cut into 2-inch pieces

Heat 2 tablespoons of the oil in a large skillet over medium heat. Add seitan and cook until browned on all sides, about 5 minutes. Remove seitan from skillet and set aside. Add ½ cup of the stock to skillet and cook over medium heat, scraping up browned bits with a spoon. Strain liquid and reserve.

Heat the remaining 2 tablespoons oil in a large saucepan over medium heat. Add carrot, celery, and shallots. Cook, stirring occasionally, about 10 minutes. Stir in the reserved liquid, remaining stock, Madeira, mustard, tarragon, and salt. Heat to boiling; reduce heat. Simmer, covered, stirring occasionally, about 20 minutes. Add green beans and cook another 10 minutes, or until beans are tender. Add reserved seitan and simmer another 5 minutes.

4 SERVINGS

Calories 711.5 • Protein 26.44 gm • Fat 16.57 gm • Percentage of calories from fat 20% • Cholesterol 0 mg • Dietary fiber 19.81 gm • Sodium 742 mg • Calcium 93.32 mg

Fricassee of Autumn Vegetables with Seitan and White Wine Sauce

3 tablespoons corn or safflower oil
1 medium onion, grated
1 tablespoon all-purpose flour
1 cup dry white wine
1 teaspoon salt
½ teaspoon fresh thyme or
  ¼ teaspoon dried
½ teaspoon freshly ground black
  pepper
1 small rutabaga, peeled, cut into
  1-inch cubes

3 carrots, cut into ½-inch slices
1 rib celery, cut into ¼-inch dice
4 small red potatoes, cut into
  1-inch cubes
12 ounces seitan (see page 11), cut
  into ½-inch dice
2 tablespoons capers
1 tablespoon fresh lemon juice
2 tablespoons chopped fresh
  parsley

Heat 1 tablespoon of the oil in a saucepan over medium-high heat. Add the onion and cook about 5 minutes. Add the flour and cook, stirring, for 1 minute. Whisk in the wine, salt, thyme, pepper, and 1 cup water. Bring to a boil, whisking until smooth. Reduce the heat and simmer for 3 minutes. Reserve.

Put the rutabaga pieces, carrots, celery, and potatoes in a large saucepan and add cold water to cover. Bring to a boil and cook for 10 minutes; drain. In a large skillet, heat 1 tablespoon of the oil. Add the seitan and cook over medium heat, until browned, about 5 minutes. Remove seitan from skillet with slotted spoon. Reheat skillet with remaining 1 tablespoon of oil over medium heat and add vegetables. Cook covered about 10 minutes, or until vegetables are browned and tender. Remove lid, add the reserved sauce and seitan to the vegetables in the skillet. Bring to a boil, reduce the heat to a simmer, cover, and cook for 10 minutes to reheat and blend the flavors. Add the capers and lemon juice, simmer for 5 minutes, and serve garnished with the chopped parsley.

6 SERVINGS

Calories 293.6 • Protein 8.442 gm • Fat 7.692 gm • Percentage of calories from fat 23% • Cholesterol 0 mg • Dietary fiber 7.501 gm • Sodium 597.6 mg • Calcium 53.44 mg

Curried Lentil-Vegetable Stew

The symphony of spices in this dish will have your guests requesting an encore. Serve over freshly cooked rice and pass a small dish of chutney.

1 large yellow onion, chopped
1 teaspoon minced fresh ginger
2 cloves garlic, sliced
1 teaspoon hot red pepper flakes
4 tablespoons corn or safflower oil
½ teaspoon ground cardamom
Pinch of ground cloves
4 cups Basic Vegetable Stock (see page 10)
¾ cup coconut milk
1 pound lentils, rinsed

1 pound carrots, cut into ¼-inch dice
2 medium onions, thinly sliced
2 cups cauliflower florets
¼ teaspoon freshly ground black pepper
½ teaspoon dry mustard
⅛ teaspoon ground allspice
⅛ teaspoon ground cinnamon
⅛ teaspoon ground turmeric
Salt

Purée chopped onion, ½ teaspoon of the ginger, garlic, and red pepper flakes in a food processor. Heat 2 tablespoons of the oil in a large saucepan over medium-high heat. Add purée, cover, reduce heat to medium-low, and cook 10 minutes, stirring occasionally. Uncover and cook, stirring constantly, until moisture is evaporated, about 5 minutes (do not allow to burn). Sprinkle with cardamom and cloves and cook 30 seconds. Increase heat to medium, add 3½ cups of the stock, and coconut milk and bring to gentle simmer. Add lentils, cover, and continue cooking 30 minutes.

While lentils are cooking, heat remaining 2 tablespoons oil in a large skillet over low heat. Add carrots, sliced onions, and cauliflower, cover, and cook until vegetables begin to soften, about 10 minutes.

Meanwhile, in a small bowl, combine remaining ½ teaspoon ginger with the black pepper, mustard, allspice, cinnamon, and turmeric. When vegetables begin to brown, sprinkle spice mixture over them and cook 4 to 5 minutes, stirring frequently (do not allow spices to burn). Add remaining ½ cup stock and stir, scraping up any browned bits. Bring mixture to boil, then pour it over lentils when done. Simmer over medium heat, uncovered, until vegetables are tender, about 15 minutes. Add salt to taste. Transfer the stew to a serving dish.

6 TO 8 SERVINGS

Calories 441.6 • Protein 22 gm • Fat 15.14 gm • Percentage of calories from fat 29% • Cholesterol 0 mg • Dietary fiber 4.056 gm • Sodium 186.3 mg • Calcium 93.88 mg

Three-Bean Stew

2 tablespoons olive oil
1 medium onion, chopped
1 carrot, chopped
2 cloves garlic, minced
1 cup chopped celery
1 cup butternut squash, cut into ½-inch pieces
2 cups peeled and chopped tomatoes (see page 375)
1 tablespoon low-sodium tamari
1½ cups cooked fava beans

1½ cups cooked kidney beans
1½ cups cooked black beans
2 cups Basic Vegetable Stock (see page 10)
2 tablespoons chopped fresh parsley
¾ teaspoon salt
⅛ teaspoon freshly ground black pepper
1 bay leaf

In a large pot, heat oil and add onion, carrot, garlic, celery, and squash. Sauté 5 minutes, then add tomatoes and tamari. Stir briefly; add remaining ingredients; stir again. Cover, simmer about 45 minutes, or until vegetables are tender. Remove bay leaf and adjust seasonings. Stew should be thick, not soupy. Serve over cooked grains.

6 TO 8 SERVINGS

Calories 232 • Protein 10.79 gm • Fat 4.708 gm • Percentage of calories from fat 17% • Cholesterol 0 mg • Dietary fiber 6.969 gm • Sodium 856.4 mg • Calcium 77.35 mg

Tofu Stew with Zucchini and Potatoes

4 tablespoons olive oil
1 pound firm tofu, cut into 1-inch
  pieces
Salt and freshly ground black
  pepper
2 onions, finely chopped
2 carrots, cut into ¼-inch dice
2 ribs celery, cut into ¼-inch dice
2 cloves garlic, minced
½ cup dry white wine
1½ cups Basic Vegetable Stock
  (see page 10)

2 pounds new red potatoes,
  quartered
2 pounds tomatoes, peeled (see
  page 375) and chopped, or 2
  cups chopped canned tomatoes
  with liquid
1½ pounds small zucchini,
  scrubbed and cut into ¼-inch
  slices
1 tablespoon minced fresh basil or
  1 teaspoon dried

In a large skillet, heat 2 tablespoons of the oil over medium-high heat; in it brown the tofu, patted dry and seasoned with salt and pepper, for about 5 minutes; then transfer to a bowl. Heat the remaining oil in the skillet over medium-low heat and cook the onions, carrots, and celery, stirring, for 5 minutes. Add the garlic and cook, stirring, for 1 minute. Add the wine, bring to a boil, and cook, uncovered, over moderate heat, stirring, for 5 minutes, or until the liquid is reduced to about ¼ cup. Add the stock and salt and pepper, bring the liquid to a boil, and simmer the mixture, covered, stirring occasionally, for 10 minutes.

Add the potatoes and simmer the mixture, covered, turning the potatoes carefully several times, for 30 minutes. Stir in the tomatoes, zucchini, and dried basil, if using it, and simmer the stew, covered, for 10 minutes. Add the reserved tofu and simmer uncovered for 5 minutes. If a thicker stew is desired, transfer the tofu and vegetables to a bowl and reduce the liquid over moderately high heat, stirring, until it is thickened to the desired consistency. Stir in the fresh basil, if using, and salt and pepper to taste.

4 TO 6 SERVINGS

Calories 410.4 • Protein 16.62 gm • Fat 14.06 gm • Percentage of calories from fat 29% • Cholesterol 0 mg • Dietary fiber 9.48 gm • Sodium 187.5 mg • Calcium 119.5 mg

Fruited Lentil Ragoût

2 cups lentils, rinsed
½ cup raisins
2 tablespoons olive oil
1 onion, finely chopped
2 cloves garlic, minced
1 Granny Smith apple, peeled and chopped

1 ripe plantain, peeled and cut into ¼-inch slices
1 cup cubed fresh pineapple
1 35-ounce can plum tomatoes, drained and chopped
Salt and freshly ground black pepper

Place the lentils and raisins in a large pot. Add enough water to cover the lentils by 1 inch, bring to a boil, and simmer, covered, for 30 minutes, or until the lentils are tender. Turn off the heat.

Heat the oil in a large skillet, sauté the onion and garlic over medium-high heat, stirring occasionally, about 5 minutes, and transfer the mixture with a slotted spoon to the lentils. In the oil remaining in the skillet cook the apple, plantain, and pineapple, stirring occasionally, for 3 minutes, then add the tomatoes and simmer, stirring occasionally, until most of the liquid has evaporated. Add the fruit mixture to the lentils and cook over moderately low heat, stirring occasionally, for 10 minutes; season with salt and pepper.

6 SERVINGS

Calories 406.1 • Protein 20.85 gm • Fat 5.496 gm • Percentage of calories from fat 12% • Cholesterol 0 mg • Dietary fiber 3.929 gm • Sodium 363.7 mg • Calcium 82.79 mg

Creole Seitan Stew

Serve this spicy stew over freshly cooked rice. Meatless sausage links are available in natural foods stores and some supermarkets. Filé powder is a Creole spice mixture, mainly ground sassafras leaves, used in gumbos. It can be found among the spices or in the gourmet food section of most supermarkets.

2 tablespoons corn oil
1 large onion, chopped
1 large green bell pepper, chopped
8 ounces seitan (see page 11), cut into ½-inch cubes
8 ounces meatless sausage links, cut into 1-inch pieces
2 cloves garlic, minced

1 28-ounce can tomatoes, crushed, with liquid
1 bay leaf
1 teaspoon filé powder
1 teaspoon hot pepper sauce
1 teaspoon dried thyme, crumbled
½ teaspoon salt
⅛ teaspoon cayenne

Heat oil in a large saucepan over medium-high heat. Add onion and bell pepper and sauté until tender, about 10 minutes. Add seitan and meatless sausage and cook until brown, about 5 minutes. Stir in garlic and cook 1 minute. Add tomatoes with liquid, ½ cup water, bay leaf, filé powder, hot pepper sauce, thyme, salt, and cayenne. Cover and simmer until heated through, about 30 minutes. Discard bay leaf.

4 SERVINGS

Calories 473.2 • Protein 22.9 gm • Fat 18.18 gm • Percentage of calories from fat 33% • Cholesterol 0 mg • Dietary fiber 10.76 gm • Sodium 1411 mg • Calcium 148.8 mg

Summer Bean Stew

2 tablespoons olive oil
2 medium onions, cut into ¼-inch wedges
2 cloves garlic, minced
3 baking potatoes (about 1 pound), peeled and cut into ¼-inch slices
1 red bell pepper, cut into 1-inch pieces
1 yellow bell pepper, cut into 1-inch pieces

1 green bell pepper, cut into 1-inch pieces
½ teaspoon salt
4 medium tomatoes (about 1 pound), peeled, seeded, and chopped
2 cups cooked cannellini beans
2 cups cooked pinto beans
Freshly ground black pepper

Heat oil in large skillet over medium-low heat. Add onions and garlic and cook until onions are translucent, stirring frequently, about 5 minutes. Reduce heat to low. Add potatoes and bell peppers. Season with salt. Cover and cook 20 minutes, stirring occasionally. Add tomatoes, cannellini beans, pinto beans, and pepper. Cover and cook until potatoes are tender, stirring occasionally, adding water if necessary, about 10 minutes.

4 TO 6 SERVINGS

Calories 336 • Protein 14.15 gm • Fat 6.673 gm • Percentage of calories from fat 17% • Cholesterol 0 mg • Dietary fiber 9.817 gm • Sodium 982.4 mg • Calcium 101.8 mg

Pumpkin and Black Bean Stew

A natural enhancement to a Halloween party, this festive stew is loaded with flavor.

1½ pounds pumpkin or butternut squash, peeled and seeded
2 tablespoons olive oil
1 large onion, chopped
1 clove garlic, minced
½ small chili pepper, seeded and minced
½ green bell pepper, chopped
1 large, ripe tomato, chopped

4 cups Basic Vegetable Stock (see page 10)
¼ teaspoon dried thyme
¼ teaspoon dried marjoram
¾ teaspoon salt
⅛ teaspoon freshly ground black pepper
2 cups cooked black beans

Cut pumpkin or butternut squash into ½-inch chunks and set aside. Heat oil in a large stock pot. Add onion, garlic, chili pepper, and bell pepper. Sauté over medium heat, stirring occasionally, until soft, about 5 minutes. Add tomato, stock, thyme, marjoram, salt, and pepper and stir well. Bring to a boil, lower heat, cover, and simmer until pumpkin is tender, about 1 hour. Add beans to stock pot and add more stock or water if stew is too thick. Cover and continue to simmer about 15 minutes. Adjust seasonings.

4 TO 6 SERVINGS

Calories 252.6 • Protein 9.26 gm • Fat 6.186 gm • Percentage of calories from fat 21% • Cholesterol 0 mg • Dietary fiber 7.64 gm • Sodium 533.5 mg • Calcium 110.3 mg

Country French Seitan Stew

4 tablespoons olive oil
1½ pounds seitan (see page 11),
  cut into 1-inch cubes
Salt and freshly ground black
  pepper
1 large onion, chopped
2 cloves garlic, finely minced
1 teaspoon chopped fresh
  oregano or ¼ teaspoon dried
½ tablespoon chopped fresh
  thyme or ½ teaspoon dried
1 tablespoon chopped fresh basil
  or 1 teaspoon dried

1 bay leaf
¼ cup all-purpose flour
1½ cups Basic Vegetable Stock
  (see page 10)
½ cup dry white wine
¼ cup fresh orange juice
2 tablespoons chopped capers
2 red bell peppers, cut into 1-inch
  pieces
1 tomato, peeled and chopped
½ cup cured black olives, pitted

In a large stock pot, heat 2 tablespoons of the olive oil over medium heat. Cook seitan in batches to avoid overcrowding, until browned, about 5 minutes, adding more oil to the pan as needed. Season with salt and pepper. Remove the seitan with a slotted spoon and reserve.

Add 1 tablespoon of the olive oil to the pot and set over medium heat. Stir in the onion, garlic, oregano, thyme, basil, and bay leaf. Cover and cook, stirring occasionally, until onion is softened, about 5 minutes. Uncover, add the flour, and continue cooking, stirring frequently, about 3 minutes more. Stir in the stock, wine, orange juice, and capers. Bring the stew to a boil, cover, and simmer over low heat for 30 minutes.

In a skillet, heat the remaining 1 tablespoon olive oil over medium-high heat. Add the bell peppers and sauté until browned, about 10 minutes. Add the peppers, tomato, olives, and seitan to the stew. Simmer stew for 20 more minutes to blend flavors. Season to taste with salt and pepper.

6 TO 8 SERVINGS

Calories 438.3 • Protein 15.81 gm • Fat 10.62 gm • Percentage of calories from fat 21% • Cholesterol 0 mg • Dietary fiber 12.44 gm • Sodium 493.4 mg • Calcium 70.78 mg

Ragoût of Seitan and Mushrooms

If porcini mushrooms are unavailable, use all white mushrooms.

¼ cup olive oil
1 pound seitan (see page 11), cut into ½- to 1-inch cubes
2 medium onions, chopped
½ pound white mushrooms, thinly sliced
½ pound porcini mushrooms, thinly sliced
½ teaspoon minced fresh thyme or ¼ teaspoon dried

⅛ teaspoon ground nutmeg
1 cup dry red wine
1½ cups Basic Vegetable Stock (see page 10)
½ cup whipping cream
Salt and freshly ground black pepper

Heat 2 tablespoons of the olive oil in a large skillet over medium-high heat. Add the seitan and brown well on all sides (do not crowd). Transfer to a large saucepan or Dutch oven using a slotted spoon. Repeat with remaining seitan as necessary, adding more oil to skillet if needed. Set aside.

Heat 1 tablespoon of the olive oil in the skillet over medium-high heat. Add onions and sauté until lightly browned, about 5 minutes. Remove with slotted spoon and add to seitan. Heat 1 tablespoon of the olive oil in same skillet. Add mushrooms and cook until limp and lightly browned, about 5 minutes. Transfer them to saucepan with seitan mixture. Stir in thyme and nutmeg. Add wine and stock, and simmer over low heat about 30 minutes. Blend in cream, salt, and pepper and heat through. Transfer ragoût to large casserole dish for serving.

4 TO 6 SERVINGS

Calories 512 • Protein 12.26 gm • Fat 17.95 gm • Percentage of calories from fat 30% • Cholesterol 34.5 mg • Dietary fiber 10.46 gm • Sodium 252 mg • Calcium 67.97 mg

Barbados Seitan Stew

1½ pounds seitan (see page 11), cut into 1-inch pieces
½ teaspoon salt
¼ teaspoon freshly ground black pepper
2 tablespoons corn or safflower oil
2 onions, chopped
2 green bell peppers, chopped
1 clove garlic, finely minced
3 tablespoons tomato paste

2 teaspoons sugar or a natural sweetener
1 bay leaf
2 teaspoons Tabasco sauce
8 pimiento-stuffed green olives, thinly sliced
3 tomatoes, peeled (see page 375) and cut into wedges
2 tablespoons dark rum

Sprinkle seitan with salt and pepper. In a large skillet heat the oil over medium-high heat, and cook the seitan for 5 minutes, or until golden brown, transferring it to a bowl with a slotted spoon. Reduce heat to medium, add the onions and bell peppers, and cook, stirring, for 5 to 6 minutes, or until they are softened. Add the garlic and cook, stirring, for 1 minute. Stir in the tomato paste, sugar, bay leaf, Tabasco, and 1 cup water; bring the liquid to a boil, then let it simmer, covered, stirring occasionally, for 15 minutes. Add the reserved seitan and simmer for 5 to 7 minutes, or until heated through. Add the olives, tomatoes, and rum and heat the stew, stirring, for 1 minute.

4 TO 6 SERVINGS

Calories 546.9 • Protein 22.17 gm • Fat 8.991 gm • Percentage of calories from fat 14% • Cholesterol 0 mg • Dietary fiber 18.33 gm • Sodium 727.1 mg • Calcium 78.43 mg

Cranberry Seitan Stew

The cranberries add a lively touch to this festive stew.

2 tablespoons corn or safflower oil
1½ pounds seitan (see page 11),
  cut into 1-inch cubes
½ teaspoon salt
⅛ teaspoon freshly ground black
  pepper
2 onions, finely chopped
2 cloves garlic, finely minced
¾ cup dry red wine

¾ cup Basic Vegetable Stock (see
  page 10)
2 tablespoons red wine vinegar
1 tablespoon tomato paste
1 cup cranberries
⅔ cup firmly packed brown sugar
  or a natural sweetener
2 tablespoons all-purpose flour

Heat oil in large saucepan or Dutch oven. Add seitan and cook until well browned on all sides, about 5 minutes. Transfer to a plate. Season seitan with ¼ teaspoon of the salt and the pepper.

Reheat saucepan, add onions, and cook over medium heat for 5 minutes, stirring. Add garlic, cook 2 minutes more. Add wine, stock, vinegar, tomato paste, and the remaining ¼ teaspoon salt. Bring mixture to boil. Reduce heat, cover pan, and simmer, stirring occasionally, about 20 minutes. Add seitan and cook another 15 minutes. In a food processor, coarsely chop cranberries with sugar and flour, using on/off pulses. Mix into stew. Cook 10 more minutes.

4 TO 6 SERVINGS

Calories 714.6 • Protein 21.37 gm • Fat 7.861 gm • Percentage of calories from fat 9% • Cholesterol 0 mg • Dietary fiber 17.69 gm • Sodium 656.5 mg • Calcium 113.4 mg

Five-Spice Seitan

This is delicious served over freshly cooked rice with steamed green beans. If five-spice powder is unavailable, combine ½ teaspoon ground ginger with ⅛ teaspoon each of cinnamon, ground aniseed, ground allspice, and ground cloves.

2 tablespoons corn or safflower oil
1½ pounds seitan (see page 11),
  cut into 2- × ½-inch strips
3 tablespoons low-sodium tamari
2 tablespoons dry sherry
1 tablespoon sugar or a natural
  sweetener

1 teaspoon minced fresh ginger
1 clove garlic, minced
1 teaspoon Chinese five-spice
  powder
1 tablespoon cornstarch mixed
  with ½ tablespoon cold water

Heat oil in large skillet or saucepan over medium-high heat. Add seitan and brown all sides well, adding more oil if necessary. Stir in 1 cup water and the tamari, sherry, sugar, ginger, garlic, and five-spice powder. Bring mixture to a boil. Reduce heat, cover, and simmer about 30 minutes, stirring occasionally. Remove seitan from skillet using slotted spoon. Thicken sauce with cornstarch mixture. Return seitan to skillet and spoon sauce over the pieces.

6 SERVINGS

Calories 406.6 • Protein 17.29 gm • Fat 6.367 gm • Percentage of calories from fat 14% • Cholesterol 0 mg • Dietary fiber 12.23 gm • Sodium 632.8 mg • Calcium 43.53 mg

Tempeh Goulash

Serve this robust stew over noodles with a crisp, chilled Gewürztraminer.

1 pound fresh or canned
   sauerkraut
3 tablespoons corn oil
1½ pounds poached tempeh (see
   page 12), cut into 1-inch cubes
½ cup chopped onions
2 tablespoons sweet Hungarian
   paprika
2 cloves garlic, minced
½ cup dry white wine
1 teaspoon caraway seed

¼ cup tomato purée
1½ cups (or more) Basic Vegetable
   Stock (see page 10)
¼ cup whipping cream
¼ cup sour cream
1 tablespoon all-purpose flour
Salt and freshly ground black
   pepper
2 tablespoons minced fresh
   parsley

Rinse sauerkraut under cold running water and drain well. Transfer to a large bowl. Heat oil in a large saucepan or Dutch oven over medium heat. Add tempeh and brown on all sides, about 5 to 8 minutes; then remove it with a slotted spoon and reserve. Add onions and paprika to pot and cook, stirring occasionally, until onions are soft, about 10 minutes. Add garlic and cook 1 to 2 more minutes. Stir in half the wine and bring mixture to boil. Reduce heat to medium, add tempeh. Place sauerkraut over tempeh. Sprinkle caraway seed over top. Combine tomato purée and remaining ¼ cup wine in small bowl and whisk until blended. Stir tomato mixture and stock into pot. Bring mixture to boil. Reduce heat, cover, and simmer, stirring occasionally, about 30 minutes. (If stew seems dry, add more stock.)

Remove tempeh and sauerkraut from pot and keep warm. Combine cream, sour cream, and flour in small bowl, blending well. Whisk cream mixture into sauce and cook over low heat, stirring constantly, 10 minutes. Return tempeh and sauerkraut to pot and spoon sauce over all. Season with salt and pepper to taste. Sprinkle with parsley and serve.

8 SERVINGS

Calories 259.7 • Protein 15.46 gm • Fat 15.23 gm • Percentage of calories from fat 51% • Cholesterol 11.11 mg • Dietary fiber 4.641 gm • Sodium 438.1 mg • Calcium 105.6 mg

Seitan and Fennel Stew

The splash of Pernod enhances the licorice flavor of the fennel. Ground turmeric makes an affordable substitute for the saffron in this dish.

2 tablespoons olive oil
1½ pounds seitan (see page 11),
  cut into ½-inch dice
½ cup minced fennel bulb
2 carrots, minced
2 ribs celery, minced
1 leek, carefully washed and
  minced
2 cloves garlic, minced
5 tomatoes, peeled (see page
  375), seeded, and diced

⅛ teaspoon ground saffron or
  turmeric
2 cups Basic Vegetable Stock (see
  page 10)
½ cup chopped fresh basil
1 tablespoon Pernod
Salt and freshly ground black
  pepper

Heat oil in a large skillet over medium-high heat. Add seitan and sauté until lightly browned, about 5 minutes. Remove seitan with slotted spoon to a platter and reserve. Reduce heat to medium. Add fennel, carrots, celery, leek, and garlic. Cover and cook about 10 minutes. Increase heat to medium-high. Add tomatoes and cook, stirring constantly, until most of tomato liquid has evaporated. Dissolve saffron or turmeric in about ¼ cup stock. Stir into vegetables, blending thoroughly. Add remaining stock and bring to a boil. Stir in seitan, chopped basil, and Pernod. Season with salt and pepper to taste. Cover and cook 10 minutes. Serve immediately.

6 SERVINGS

Calories 336 • Protein 14.02 gm • Fat 5.168 gm • Percentage of calories from fat 13% • Cholesterol 0 mg • Dietary fiber 11.59 gm • Sodium 317.5 mg • Calcium 65.81 mg

White Bean and Butternut Squash Stew

This stew is also wonderful without the sausage, in which case you may want to increase the amount of beans.

1 butternut squash, peeled and seeded
2 tablespoons olive oil
1 large onion, chopped
2 cloves garlic, minced
½ teaspoon salt
⅛ teaspoon freshly ground black pepper
2 tablespoons all-purpose flour
4 cups Basic Vegetable Stock (see page 10)

2 tomatoes, peeled (see page 375), seeded, and chopped
1 tablespoon low-sodium tamari
Juice of 1 lemon
½ teaspoon dried thyme, crumbled
1 bay leaf
2 cups cooked navy beans
8 ounces meatless sausage links (optional)
¼ cup minced fresh parsley

Cut squash into ½-inch cubes. Heat oil in large saucepan over medium heat. Add squash, onion, and garlic and cook for 5 minutes. Season with salt and pepper. Reduce heat to low, add flour, and cook until vegetables are browned, stirring constantly. Stir in stock, tomatoes, tamari, lemon juice, thyme, and bay leaf. Add beans and bring to a boil. Reduce heat, cover, and simmer until squash is tender, about 1 hour. Discard bay leaf. Adjust seasonings. For a thicker stew, purée some of the beans and reblend into stew. If using meatless sausage, cut sausage into ½-inch pieces. Heat a little olive oil in a skillet over medium-high heat. Add sausage pieces, and brown on all sides. Add to stew. Sprinkle with parsley and serve.

6 SERVINGS

Calories 222.7 • Protein 8.374 gm • Fat 5.272 gm • Percentage of calories from fat 20% • Cholesterol 0 mg • Dietary fiber 6.842 gm • Sodium 458.9 mg • Calcium 106.2 mg

Spicy Tempeh and Seitan Stew

1 tablespoon cider vinegar
1 tablespoon fresh lime juice
1 teaspoon chili powder
12 ounces poached tempeh (see page 12), cut into 1-inch cubes
4 tablespoons corn or safflower oil
12 ounces seitan (see page 11), cut into ¼-inch strips
2 cups thinly sliced onion
1 clove garlic, minced

2 jalapeño peppers, seeded and chopped
1 tablespoon minced fresh ginger
1 28-ounce can whole tomatoes, drained (reserve liquid) and chopped
¼ teaspoon ground turmeric
Salt and freshly ground black pepper
6 cups freshly cooked rice

Combine vinegar, lime juice, and chili powder in medium bowl and stir well. Add tempeh and marinate, stirring frequently to coat, about 15 minutes.

Heat 2 tablespoons of the oil in large pot or Dutch oven over medium-high heat. Add seitan in batches, browning well on all sides. Remove from pot. Brown tempeh on all sides, then add the marinade. Bring to a boil, reduce heat, add seitan, cover, and simmer about 5 minutes. Transfer tempeh and seitan to a platter with any marinade. Wipe pot, heat remaining 2 tablespoons oil over medium heat. Add onion and cook until softened, about 10 minutes. Add garlic, jalapeños, and ginger and cook another 3 minutes. Add tomatoes and liquid, ¾ cup water, turmeric, salt, and pepper to taste. Simmer covered for 15 minutes. Uncover and simmer 10 minutes more. Add reserved tempeh and seitan and simmer until heated through. Adjust seasonings. Serve over rice.

6 SERVINGS

Calories 554.9 • Protein 22.11 gm • Fat 14.99 gm • Percentage of calories from fat 23% • Cholesterol 0 mg • Dietary fiber 10.8 gm • Sodium 446.3 mg • Calcium 108.2 mg

Tuscan-Style Seitan Stew

1½ pounds seitan (see page 11),
  cut into 1-inch cubes
½ teaspoon salt
⅛ teaspoon freshly ground black
  pepper
2 tablespoons olive oil
1 onion, minced
2 cloves garlic, minced
2 teaspoons minced fresh
  rosemary or 1 teaspoon dried

2 pounds tomatoes, peeled (see
  page 375) and chopped, or a
  2-pound can whole tomatoes,
  drained and chopped
3 cups shelled fresh peas (about 3
  pounds unshelled), or frozen
  peas, thawed

Pat the seitan dry and season with salt and pepper. Heat the oil in a large, heavy saucepan or Dutch oven over medium-high heat, and brown the seitan on all sides, about 5 minutes. Transfer to a bowl with a slotted spoon. In the oil remaining in the pot, cook the onion until soft, 5 to 8 minutes. Add the garlic and rosemary over moderately low heat and stir for 1 minute; then stir in tomatoes, the reserved seitan, and ½ cup water. Bring liquid to a boil, stirring, then simmer the mixture covered, stirring occasionally, for 20 minutes, and simmer it uncovered, stirring, for 10 minutes, or until the liquid is reduced slightly. Add the peas to the stew and simmer, stirring, for 15 minutes, or until the peas are tender and the liquid is reduced. Season to taste with salt and pepper.

4 SERVINGS

Calories 685.1 • Protein 30.38 gm • Fat 10.63 gm • Percentage of calories from fat 13% • Cholesterol 0 mg • Dietary fiber 21.88 gm • Sodium 730.6 mg • Calcium 141.1 mg

Provençal Stew with Seitan and Fennel

1 pound fennel bulbs
2 tablespoons olive oil
1½ pounds seitan (see page 11), cut into 1-inch cubes
1 medium onion, chopped
1 tablespoon freshly grated orange peel
1 large clove garlic, minced
½ teaspoon chopped fresh basil
½ teaspoon chopped fresh marjoram

½ teaspoon salt
⅛ teaspoon freshly ground black pepper
1 tablespoon all-purpose flour
½ cup dry vermouth
2 cups Basic Vegetable Stock (see page 10)
¼ cup cured black olives, pitted
1 tablespoon capers, rinsed and drained

Trim off tops of fennel bulbs, reserving about 2 tablespoons of the tops. Cut fennel into ½-inch slices. Reserve. Heat olive oil in a large skillet over medium-high heat. Add seitan in batches and brown on all sides, adding more oil if necessary. Transfer seitan with a slotted spoon to a large saucepan. In oil remaining in skillet, cook onion over medium heat until softened, about 5 minutes, stirring frequently. Add orange peel, garlic, basil, marjoram, salt, and pepper and stir about 30 seconds. Sprinkle with flour and stir 30 more seconds, watching carefully so flour does not brown. Stir in vermouth, scraping up any browned bits, and bring to boil. Continue boiling until mixture is reduced by about half. Pour in stock and return to boil. Pour mixture over seitan in saucepan. Place over medium-high heat and bring to simmer. Reduce heat to low, add fennel slices, cover, and cook about 1 hour. Stir olives and capers into stew. Taste and adjust seasonings. Garnish with reserved fennel tops.

4 SERVINGS

Calories 699.5 • Protein 27.77 gm • Fat 11.92 gm • Percentage of calories from fat 14% • Cholesterol 0 mg • Dietary fiber 20.27 gm • Sodium 1042 mg • Calcium 153.8 mg

Lemony Tempeh and New Potato Stew

The delicate whisper of lemon and fresh cilantro in this stew provides a refreshing balance to the tempeh and potatoes. Cilantro, or Chinese parsley, is also sometimes referred to as coriander, since it is the leaves of the coriander plant.

¼ cup plus 1 tablespoon fresh lemon juice
3 tablespoons olive oil
1 large clove garlic, minced
¼ teaspoon coriander seed, ground
⅛ teaspoon freshly ground black pepper
1 pound poached tempeh (see page 12), cut into 1-inch cubes

1 large onion, chopped
⅛ teaspoon ground cumin
⅛ teaspoon ground allspice
2 cups Basic Vegetable Stock (see page 10)
3 tablespoons tomato paste
Salt
1 pound new potatoes, boiled until tender, thinly sliced
1 tablespoon chopped cilantro

Combine ¼ cup lemon juice, 1 tablespoon oil, garlic, coriander seed, and pepper in a large shallow bowl. Add tempeh and stir to coat. Cover and refrigerate 1 hour or overnight, stirring mixture occasionally. Remove tempeh from marinade with slotted spoon; reserve marinade. Heat remaining 2 tablespoons olive oil in a large saucepan or Dutch oven over medium-high heat. Add tempeh in batches (do not crowd) and brown on all sides, about 5 minutes. Remove tempeh with slotted spoon and reserve.

Place saucepan over medium-low heat, add onion, and cook, covered, until soft, stirring frequently, about 5 minutes. Stir in cumin and allspice and cook 30 seconds. Add stock, tomato paste, and reserved marinade and stir, scraping up any browned bits. Bring mixture to boil. Add reserved tempeh, cover, and simmer 30 minutes over medium-low heat. Add salt to taste, potato slices, and 1 tablespoon lemon juice. Simmer, uncovered, 15 minutes. Garnish with chopped cilantro.

6 SERVINGS

Calories 277.4 • Protein 15.29 gm • Fat 12.76 gm • Percentage of calories from fat 40% • Cholesterol 0 mg • Dietary fiber 5.266 gm • Sodium 99.89 mg • Calcium 83.96 mg

Nigerian Groundnut Stew with Tempeh

In Africa, as well as other places, the peanut is known as the groundnut and is a popular ingredient in many appetizing dishes.

2 tablespoons corn oil
1 pound poached tempeh (see page 12), cut into 1-inch dice
1 large onion, chopped
2 green bell peppers, chopped
1 clove garlic, minced
1 cup peanut butter
1 cup Basic Vegetable Stock (see page 10)

1 large tomato, peeled (see page 375) and quartered
½ teaspoon salt
⅛ teaspoon freshly ground black pepper
4 cups freshly cooked rice

Preheat oven to 350 degrees. Heat oil in a large skillet over medium-high heat. Add tempeh and sauté until browned on all sides, about 5 minutes. Remove with slotted spoon and place in casserole dish. In same skillet, cook onion, bell peppers, and garlic, until onion is transparent, about 5 minutes. Add to casserole. Place peanut butter in a saucepan and add stock slowly, stirring, to make a thick creamy sauce over medium heat. Add tomato, salt, and pepper and simmer gently for 2 minutes; pour over tempeh mixture in casserole. Cover and bake for 30 minutes. If sauce is too thin, add more peanut butter; if it is too thick, add more stock. Serve over rice.

4 SERVINGS

Calories 874.8 • Protein 39.79 gm • Fat 48.09 gm • Percentage of calories from fat 48% • Cholesterol 0 mg • Dietary fiber 9.868 gm • Sodium 651.2 mg • Calcium 145.1 mg

Cajun Stew

3 tablespoons corn oil
½ pound seitan sausage (see page 6), cut into ½-inch pieces
½ pound tempeh bacon, chopped
½ cup chopped celery
1 large onion, chopped
1 green bell pepper, chopped
2 large cloves garlic, minced
1 28-ounce can crushed tomatoes, drained (reserve liquid)
2 cups Basic Vegetable Stock (see page 10)
2 tablespoons tomato paste
½ teaspoon salt
½ teaspoon freshly ground black pepper
½ teaspoon paprika
¼ teaspoon cayenne
⅛ teaspoon ground allspice
2 cups cooked fava beans
2 tablespoons chopped fresh parsley
1 tablespoon low-sodium tamari

In a large saucepan or Dutch oven, heat 2 tablespoons of the oil over moderately high heat. Add seitan sausage and tempeh bacon and sauté, tossing, until just browned, about 4 minutes. With a slotted spoon, remove seitan and tempeh bacon to a plate and set aside. Add to the saucepan the celery, onion, green pepper, and garlic. Reduce the heat to medium and cook, stirring occasionally, until the onions are translucent, about 5 minutes. Add the crushed tomatoes and the vegetable stock and bring to a simmer. Stir in the tomato paste, salt, black pepper, paprika, cayenne, and allspice. Reduce the heat to low and return the sausage and bacon to the pan. Add the fava beans, parsley, and tamari, and simmer for 20 minutes before serving.

4 TO 6 SERVINGS

Calories 545 • Protein 21.29 gm • Fat 23.16 gm • Percentage of calories from fat 36% • Cholesterol 0 mg • Dietary fiber 12.28 gm • Sodium 1609 mg • Calcium 132.5 mg

Persian Seitan Stew

Who needs dessert when you have this exotic stew brimming with plump fruit and aromatic spices?

2 tablespoons canola or safflower
  oil
1 pound seitan (see page 11), cut
  into 1-inch cubes
1 large onion, chopped
1 teaspoon ground cinnamon

¾ teaspoon salt
6 dried apricots, halved
6 pitted prunes
2 tablespoons fresh lemon juice
1 tablespoon sugar or a natural
  sweetener

Heat the oil in a large saucepan or Dutch oven, add the seitan, and cook over moderate heat for 5 minutes, turning occasionally, until browned on all sides. Using a slotted spoon, remove the seitan and set aside. Add the onion to the saucepan and cook over low heat for 5 minutes, until soft. Return the seitan to the saucepan, pour in 2 cups water, and add the remaining ingredients. Cover and simmer over low heat for 40 minutes. Serve over couscous.

6 SERVINGS

Calories 330 • Protein 11.88 gm • Fat 5.945 gm • Percentage of calories from fat 15% • Cholesterol 0 mg • Dietary fiber 10.09 gm • Sodium 559.4 mg • Calcium 51.89 mg

3
Pasta Dishes

In recent years, pasta dishes have become increasingly popular in restaurants as well as at home. Once we knew little more about pasta than the basic spaghetti with tomato sauce, but we can now choose from pastas in every color of the rainbow, in a fascinating array of shapes and sizes and with a full complement of sauces. Whether you start with Ziti with Tofu and Red Pepper Sauce, or Penne with Cannellini Beans and Sage, these pasta recipes will give you many nutritious ways to serve a simple and delicious meal.

Radiatore with Sage-Walnut Sauce

4 tablespoons olive oil
2 cloves garlic, crushed and peeled
4 ounces tempeh bacon, chopped
½ cup chopped walnuts
1 pound radiatore or other similar
  pasta

2 tablespoons chopped fresh sage
  or ½ teaspoon dried sage
⅓ cup grated Romano cheese
¼ teaspoon salt
⅛ teaspoon freshly ground black
  pepper

Heat 2 tablespoons of the olive oil in a large skillet. Add the garlic and cook over low heat until golden, 4 to 6 minutes. Remove garlic and discard it. Add tempeh bacon and walnuts to oil remaining in the skillet and cook, stirring occasionally, until the walnuts are lightly toasted and the tempeh bacon is browned, about 5 minutes. If using dried sage, add to walnut mixture now. Remove from the heat and set aside.

Bring a large pot of salted water to a boil. Add the pasta and stir until the water returns to a boil. Cook until just tender, about 12 to 15 minutes. Drain and toss pasta with the walnut mixture. Add the remaining 2 tablespoons of oil, the fresh sage leaves, if using, Romano cheese, salt and pepper, and toss to combine. Serve immediately.

4 TO 6 SERVINGS

Calories 610.1 • Protein 18.54 gm • Fat 28.34 gm • Percentage of calories from fat 41% • Cholesterol 5.214 mg • Dietary fiber 2.666 gm • Sodium 569.6 mg • Calcium 127.9 mg

Angel Hair Pasta with Tofu-Basil Sauce

5 tablespoons olive oil
2 medium cloves garlic, minced
¼ cup pine nuts
½ teaspoon salt
¼ teaspoon freshly ground black pepper
1 pound angel hair pasta

1 pound firm tofu, cut into ½-inch cubes
½ cup packed fresh basil leaves, chopped
Freshly grated Romano cheese (optional)

In a large saucepan, heat 3 tablespoons of the oil over medium-low heat. Add the garlic and cook until softened but not browned, about 2 minutes. Add the pine nuts, increase the heat to medium, and cook, stirring frequently, until the nuts are lightly browned, about 2 minutes. Remove the garlic and pine nut mixture from the heat and season with salt and pepper.

Bring a large pot of salted water to a boil. Add the pasta and cook until just tender, 2 to 4 minutes. Meanwhile, add tofu to garlic and pine nut mixture. Cook over medium-high heat, tossing frequently, 2 to 3 minutes. Remove from the heat and season with additional salt and pepper, if desired. Drain the pasta, add to the tofu, and toss. Add remaining 2 tablespoons of oil, basil, and Romano cheese, if desired, and toss again. Serve immediately.

6 SERVINGS

Calories 460.7 • Protein 17.48 gm • Fat 17.47 gm • Percentage of calories from fat 34% • Cholesterol 0 mg • Dietary fiber 1.906 gm • Sodium 231.3 mg • Calcium 52.18 mg

Cavatelli with Arugula and Pine Nuts

Pine nuts and Romano cheese team up to provide the protein in this tasty meatless dish. Cavatelli is a small, bullet-shaped pasta that can be found in Italian food shops. I prefer the frozen variety for its chewy texture.

1 pound frozen or dried cavatelli
6 tablespoons olive oil
¼ cup pine nuts
½ pound arugula, chopped
½ teaspoon salt

¼ teaspoon freshly ground black pepper
½ cup grated Pecorino Romano cheese

Bring a large pot of salted water to a boil. Stir in the cavatelli and cook according to package directions: 10 minutes for dried, and 15 to 20 minutes for frozen. Meanwhile, heat the oil in a large skillet over moderate heat. Add the pine nuts, arugula, salt, and pepper. Cook until the arugula is tender, about 2 minutes. Drain the cavatelli and put in a serving bowl. Add arugula sauce, sprinkle with the grated cheese, and toss well. Serve immediately.

4 TO 6 SERVINGS

Calories 358.3 • Protein 11.97 gm • Fat 24.54 gm • Percentage of calories from fat 59% • Cholesterol 10.13 mg • Dietary fiber 1.109 gm • Sodium 417.8 mg • Calcium 220.8 mg

Orecchiette with Broccoli Rabe and Capers

Orecchiette means "little ears" in Italian. If unavailable, substitute radiatore or another small pasta shape.

½ pound broccoli rabe
¾ teaspoon salt
1 pound orecchiette or other small
  pasta
3 tablespoons olive oil
4 ounces meatless sausage links,
  cut into ¼-inch pieces

2 large cloves garlic, minced
3 tablespoons capers, chopped
¼ teaspoon freshly ground black
  pepper
½ cup grated Pecorino Romano
  cheese

Peel the stems of the broccoli rabe and cut stems and leaves into ½-inch pieces. Place in a steamer, sprinkle with ¼ teaspoon of the salt, and steam until just tender, about 3 minutes. Add the pasta to a large pot of boiling water over high heat and cook until just tender, about 10 minutes. Meanwhile, heat the oil in a skillet over medium-high heat, add sausage, and cook until browned, about 5 minutes. Add garlic and capers and cook for 2 minutes over moderately low heat. Add broccoli rabe and the remaining ½ teaspoon salt and the pepper. Toss with hot drained pasta and the grated cheese. Serve immediately.

4 TO 6 SERVINGS

Calories 518.2 • Protein 20.38 gm • Fat 16.51 gm • Percentage of calories from fat 28% • Cholesterol 10.13 mg • Dietary fiber 3.31 gm • Sodium 848.1 mg • Calcium 161.7 mg

Spicy Udon with Seitan and Watercress

Cut the cayenne by half for a less incendiary version.

½ cup peanut butter
4 tablespoons toasted sesame oil
   heated with ½ teaspoon cayenne
3 tablespoons minced scallions
3 tablespoons low-sodium tamari
2 tablespoons brown rice vinegar
1 teaspoon finely minced garlic

1 teaspoon sugar or a natural
   sweetener
¼ teaspoon freshly ground black
   pepper
1 bunch watercress, chopped
1 pound udon noodles

Combine all the ingredients except the watercress and noodles in small bowl; add water if thinner consistency is desired. Lightly steam the watercress over boiling water about 2 minutes. Remove from heat and reserve. Cook noodles in boiling water until tender but still firm, checking frequently to avoid overcooking. Drain and transfer to serving bowl. Add watercress and sauce; toss lightly.

6 SERVINGS

Calories 479.9 • Protein 17.36 gm • Fat 21.15 gm • Percentage of calories from fat 39% • Cholesterol 0 mg • Dietary fiber 4.254 gm • Sodium 1109 mg • Calcium 19.98 mg

Ziti with Tofu and Red Pepper Sauce

4 tablespoons olive oil
½ pound firm tofu, cut into ¼-inch dice
2 cloves garlic, minced
1 35-ounce can Italian plum tomatoes, with liquid
¾ teaspoon salt

¾ teaspoon red pepper flakes
1 pound ziti or other tubular pasta
½ cup grated Pecorino Romano cheese
Salt and freshly ground black pepper

Heat 2 tablespoons of the oil in large skillet over medium-low heat. Add tofu and garlic and cook, stirring frequently, about 10 minutes. Remove with slotted spoon and set aside. Add tomatoes with liquid to skillet, along with salt and red pepper flakes, and boil until thick, breaking up tomatoes, about 30 minutes. Cook pasta in a large pot of boiling salted water. Drain and put in a serving bowl. Add tofu to sauce and toss to coat. Add to pasta. Mix in cheese and remaining 2 tablespoons of oil. Season with salt and pepper. Serve immediately.

4 SERVINGS

Calories 684.1 • Protein 25.71 gm • Fat 19.78 gm • Percentage of calories from fat 27% • Cholesterol 10.48 mg • Dietary fiber 5.241 gm • Sodium 1149 mg • Calcium 234.8 mg

Fusilli and Asparagus with Tofu-Dill Sauce

Be sure to try this dish as soon as tender young asparagus becomes available.

1 tablespoon olive oil
2 cloves garlic, finely minced
8 ounces soft tofu, patted dry and
  cut into coarse pieces
¼ cup fresh lemon juice
1 tablespoon Dijon mustard
2 tablespoons chopped fresh dill

¾ teaspoon salt
⅛ teaspoon freshly ground black
  pepper
⅓ cup corn oil
1 pound fusilli or other curly pasta
½ pound fresh asparagus, cut in
  diagonal 1-inch pieces

Heat the oil in a small skillet, add the garlic, and cook over medium-low heat until fragrant, about 3 minutes. In a food processor blend the garlic, tofu, lemon juice, mustard, dill, salt, and pepper until the mixture is smooth. With the processor running add the corn oil in a stream and blend the sauce until emulsified. Meanwhile, cook fusilli in a large pot of boiling salted water until tender, 12 to 15 minutes. During the last 3 to 4 minutes of cooking time, add the asparagus to pasta. Drain, and toss with sauce.

4 TO 6 SERVINGS

Calories 456.3 • Protein 14.43 gm • Fat 21.23 gm • Percentage of calories from fat 41% • Cholesterol 0 mg • Dietary fiber 2.661 gm • Sodium 447.1 mg • Calcium 28.57 mg

Linguine with Pistachio Pesto

Pistachios provide an interesting difference in this pesto recipe. Soft tofu adds creaminess as well as protein.

2 large cloves garlic
½ teaspoon salt
½ cup pistachio nuts, shelled
1 cup packed fresh basil leaves
¾ cup packed fresh parsley leaves

¾ cup olive oil
2 tablespoons fresh lemon juice
4 ounces soft tofu
1 pound linguine

Blend garlic and salt in food processor to a paste, about 30 seconds. Add pistachios, using several on/off pulses until finely ground. Add basil and parsley and process, scraping down sides of bowl as needed. With machine running, slowly add olive oil. Blend in lemon juice and tofu. In the meantime, cook linguine in a large pot of salted water until just tender, about 12 minutes. Toss pasta with sauce and serve immediately.

4 TO 6 SERVINGS

Calories 642.8 • Protein 13.59 gm • Fat 42.35 gm • Percentage of calories from fat 58% • Cholesterol 0 mg • Dietary fiber 3.485 gm • Sodium 254.4 mg • Calcium 46.52 mg

Soba with Tahini Sauce

Gomasio, a mixture of ground sesame seeds and sea salt, is available in most natural foods stores. Sprinkle it on pasta for a tasty calcium-rich alternative to grated cheese.

1 large clove garlic, chopped
¼ cup fresh lemon juice
2 cups cooked chick-peas
½ cup tahini
4 tablespoons low-sodium tamari
⅛ teaspoon cayenne

2 tablespoons chopped fresh
  parsley
1 pound soba (buckwheat)
  noodles
Gomasio (optional)

In a food processor, combine the garlic, lemon juice, chick-peas, tahini, tamari, cayenne, and 1 tablespoon of the parsley and process until smooth. Adjust seasonings. If saltier flavor is desired, add more tamari. Cook soba until tender according to package directions. As pasta is cooking, with food processor running, slowly add warm water to sauce until desired consistency is reached. Toss with cooked soba noodles. Garnish with remaining 1 tablespoon parsley and gomasio, if desired. Serve immediately.

4 SERVINGS

Calories 813.2 • Protein 35.09 gm • Fat 29.06 gm • Percentage of calories from fat 30% • Cholesterol 0 mg • Dietary fiber 7.945 gm • Sodium 1809 mg • Calcium 148.5 mg

Rotini with Yellow Squash, Tofu, and Capers

3 tablespoons olive oil
2 large cloves garlic, crushed and
  peeled
¼ cup minced scallions
4 medium yellow squash, cut into
  ¼-inch dice
½ teaspoon salt
¼ teaspoon hot red pepper flakes

4 ounces firm tofu, cut into ¼-inch
  dice
1 tablespoon capers
1 pound rotini or other curly pasta
½ cup chopped fresh parsley
¼ cup chopped fresh mint
Freshly ground black pepper

In a large saucepan, heat the oil and garlic. Cook over moderate heat until the garlic is browned, 3 to 4 minutes. Then lift it out and discard. Add the scallions to the oil and cook until tender but not browned, about 2 minutes. Add the squash, salt, and red pepper flakes. Cover and cook over moderately low heat, stirring occasionally, until the squash has softened, about 5 minutes. Add tofu and capers, and keep warm on very low heat. Meanwhile, bring a large pot of salted water to a boil. Add the rotini and cook until just tender, about 10 minutes; drain and put in a serving bowl. Add the parsley and mint to the squash and tofu mixture. Season with black pepper to taste. Toss the sauce with the rotini. Serve hot.

4 TO 6 SERVINGS

Calories 454.2 • Protein 14.99 gm • Fat 10.52 gm • Percentage of calories from fat 21% • Cholesterol 0 mg • Dietary fiber 4.261 gm • Sodium 303.6 mg • Calcium 80.58 mg

Ziti with Spicy Bean Sauce

Beans in the creamy sauce provide the flavorful meat alternative in this hearty dish.

3½ tablespoons olive oil
1 carrot, finely chopped
1 onion, minced
1 clove garlic, minced
1 tablespoon chopped fresh
  marjoram or 1 teaspoon dried
2 cups cooked pinto beans
3 cups Basic Vegetable Stock (see
  page 10)

½ teaspoon salt
⅛ teaspoon freshly ground black
  pepper
1 pound ziti
1½ teaspoons hot red pepper
  flakes
½ cup grated Parmesan cheese
2 tablespoons chopped fresh
  parsley

In a large saucepan, heat 1 tablespoon of the oil over low heat. Add the carrot, onion, garlic, and marjoram and sauté until onion is soft, about 4 minutes. Add beans and 2 cups of the stock and simmer about 20 minutes. In a food processor, purée bean mixture until almost smooth. With the machine running, slowly add 2 tablespoons of the oil. Season with salt and pepper.

Cook ziti in a pot of boiling salted water until tender, about 12 minutes. In a large skillet, heat remaining ½ tablespoon of the oil over medium heat. Add the red pepper flakes, stir in the bean purée, and up to 1 cup of the vegetable stock. Add the drained ziti and heat through. Remove pan from heat. Stir in the cheese and parsley. Season to taste with salt and pepper. Serve immediately.

4 SERVINGS

Calories 716.8 • Protein 25.47 gm • Fat 17.55 gm • Percentage of calories from fat 22% • Cholesterol 12.67 mg • Dietary fiber 4.941 gm • Sodium 1063 mg • Calcium 237.3 mg

Sicilian Angel Hair Pasta

Pine nuts and cheese provide the protein, but the meaty eggplant is the real star of this zesty pasta dish.

1 large eggplant, cut into ½-inch dice
1½ teaspoons salt
2 red bell peppers, halved and seeded
4 tablespoons olive oil
2 large cloves garlic, smashed and peeled
4 large tomatoes, peeled (see page 375) and chopped, or 1 35-ounce can peeled tomatoes, drained and chopped

2 tablespoons capers, drained
12 oil-cured black olives, pitted and chopped
¼ cup chopped fresh basil or 2 teaspoons dried
¼ teaspoon freshly ground black pepper
1 pound angel hair pasta
¼ cup pine nuts
¼ pound grated Pecorino Romano cheese

Place the eggplant in a colander and toss with 1 teaspoon of the salt. Put a plate on top and weight it with a heavy can. Let drain for 1 hour. Meanwhile, roast the peppers directly over a gas flame or under the broiler, until skin is charred, about 5 minutes. Place in a paper bag and steam for 10 minutes. Rub off the skins and cut into 1-inch squares. Squeeze the eggplant gently with paper towels to dry.

In a large skillet, heat 3 tablespoons of the olive oil. Add the garlic and cook over low heat until browned, about 5 minutes, then discard it. Increase the heat to medium-high. Add the eggplant to the skillet and sauté, tossing, until lightly browned, about 10 minutes. Pour the remaining 1 tablespoon of oil into the pan. Add the tomatoes and remaining ½ teaspoon salt and bring to a boil. Reduce the heat to medium low, cover, and simmer for 5 minutes. Add the roasted peppers to the sauce; simmer, covered, for 5 minutes. Add the capers, olives, basil, and black pepper. Simmer, covered, for 15 minutes. Cook the pasta in a large pot of boiling salted water until just tender, 2 to 4 minutes. Drain, put in a serving bowl, and toss in the hot sauce. Add the pine nuts and cheese and toss again. Serve immediately.

4 TO 6 SERVINGS

Calories 585.7 • Protein 17.62 gm • Fat 22.49 gm • Percentage of calories from fat 33% • Cholesterol 4.921 mg • Dietary fiber 3.784 gm • Sodium 887.6 mg • Calcium 104.7 mg

Linguine with Vegetables and Peanut Sauce

East meets West in this satisfying pasta dish. Peanut butter fills the role of meat alternative in the spicy sauce.

¾ cup peanut butter
1 clove garlic, minced
1 small onion, chopped
1 teaspoon red pepper flakes
1 tablespoon brown sugar or a natural sweetener
3 tablespoons fresh lemon juice
2 tablespoons low-sodium tamari
1½ cups Basic Vegetable Stock (see page 10) or water
3 tablespoons corn or safflower oil

3 cups broccoli florets, blanched for 1 minute
2 large carrots, cut in ¼-inch thick julienne strips, blanched for 30 seconds
Salt and freshly ground black pepper
1 pound linguine
2 tablespoons chopped fresh cilantro

In a food processor blend together the peanut butter, garlic, onion, red pepper flakes, and brown sugar. Add the lemon juice, tamari, and ¼ cup of the stock, and blend the mixture until smooth. Transfer the mixture to a saucepan and stir in the remaining stock. Heat the sauce over moderately low heat, stirring, until it is hot; keep it warm.

Heat the oil in a large skillet over moderately high heat, add the broccoli and carrots, and sauté until just tender; add salt and pepper to taste. In a large pot of boiling salted water, cook the linguine 10 to 12 minutes, or until tender, drain it, and, in a serving bowl, toss pasta with the vegetables, peanut sauce, and cilantro

4 TO 6 SERVINGS

Calories 628.1 • Protein 22.2 gm • Fat 30.31 gm • Percentage of calories from fat 41% • Cholesterol 0 mg • Dietary fiber 7.456 gm • Sodium 557.8 mg • Calcium 61.27 mg

Linguine with Fava Beans, Olives, and Capers

Fava beans, olives, and capers are among the flavorful tidbits used to create this delightful linguine recipe. If porcini mushrooms are unavailable, substitute regular fresh white mushrooms.

4 tablespoons olive oil
1 medium onion, minced
¼ cup minced carrot
1 tablespoon minced celery
4 ounces fresh porcini mushrooms, chopped
2 tablespoons minced fresh parsley
1 tablespoon minced fresh basil or 1 teaspoon dried
1½ teaspoons minced garlic
½ teaspoon minced fresh oregano or ¼ teaspoon dried
1 cup Basic Vegetable Stock (see page 10)

1 pound fresh or canned tomatoes, peeled (see page 00 for fresh) and chopped
¼ teaspoon freshly ground black pepper
1 pound linguine
2 cups cooked fava beans
12 oil-cured black olives, pitted and chopped
1 tablespoon capers
½ teaspoon salt
½ cup grated Pecorino Romano cheese

Heat 2 tablespoons of the oil in a large skillet over medium heat. Add the onion, carrot, and celery to the skillet and cook, stirring frequently, about 10 minutes. Add mushrooms and stir 1 minute. Add parsley, basil, garlic, and oregano and stir 30 seconds. Stir in stock, scraping up any browned bits, and cook 2 minutes. Boil gently until most of the liquid is evaporated, about 10 minutes. Add tomatoes and pepper. Simmer uncovered 5 minutes.

Cook linguine in a pot of boiling salted water until tender, about 12 minutes. Drain, put in a serving bowl, and toss with remaining 2 tablespoons olive oil. Stir fava beans, olives, and capers into skillet with tomato mixture and heat through. Season with salt. Toss sauce with linguine. Serve immediately, passing cheese separately.

4 SERVINGS

Calories 679.4 • Protein 26.19 gm • Fat 23.46 gm • Percentage of calories from fat 30% • Cholesterol 12.67 mg • Dietary fiber 12 gm • Sodium 662.5 mg • Calcium 192.1 mg

Soba with Cannellini Beans and Kale

1 pound red potatoes, cut into
  ½-inch chunks
1 bunch kale, trimmed and
  chopped (about 3 cups)
6 tablespoons olive oil
2 cloves garlic, minced
1 tablespoon minced fresh sage or
  1 teaspoon dried

2 shallots, minced
2 cups cooked cannellini beans
1 pound soba (buckwheat)
  noodles
Salt and freshly ground black
  pepper
½ cup freshly grated Parmesan
  cheese

Place the potatoes in a medium saucepan of salted water to cover. Bring to a boil over moderate heat. Reduce the heat slightly and cook until the potatoes are tender, about 12 minutes. Drain, rinse under cold water, and drain again. In a medium saucepan of boiling salted water, cook kale until tender, about 5 minutes. Run under cold water and let cool. Drain well and squeeze out as much water as possible. In a large skillet, heat the oil over low heat. Add garlic and cook, stirring occasionally, about 2 minutes. Add the sage and shallots and cook, stirring, about 5 minutes. Add the potatoes, kale, and beans and toss to coat with oil. Cook, covered, until heated through, about 5 minutes. Keep warm. In a large pot of boiling water cook the soba noodles until tender but still firm, about 3 minutes. Drain immediately and transfer to a large bowl. Add the kale-potato mixture and toss gently. Season with salt and pepper to taste. Add Parmesan cheese and toss again.

6 SERVINGS

Calories 560.8 • Protein 22.55 gm • Fat 17.51 gm • Percentage of calories from fat 27% • Cholesterol 6.583 mg • Dietary fiber 8.152 gm • Sodium 773.3 mg • Calcium 240.2 mg

Mediterranean Pasta with Feta and Olives

The creamy sharpness of the feta cheese will make this dish a favorite.

4 tablespoons olive oil
1 large onion, chopped
¾ teaspoon hot red pepper flakes
2 cloves garlic, minced
1 tablespoon chopped fresh basil
1 teaspoon minced fresh oregano
  or ¼ teaspoon dried
1 bay leaf
1 35-ounce can Italian peeled
  tomatoes, chopped, with liquid
¾ teaspoon salt
2 zucchini, cut into ¼-inch slices

¼ teaspoon freshly ground black
  pepper
1 pound penne or other tubular
  pasta
12 oil-cured olives, halved and
  pitted
8 ounces feta cheese, cut into
  ½-inch chunks
¼ cup minced fresh parsley
Freshly grated Pecorino Romano
  cheese (optional)

In a large saucepan or Dutch oven, heat 2 tablespoons of the olive oil. Add the onion and red pepper flakes and cook, over moderate heat, stirring occasionally, until tender and lightly browned, about 10 minutes. Add the garlic, basil, oregano, and bay leaf and cook about 2 minutes. Stir in the tomatoes and liquid. Add ½ teaspoon of the salt and bring to a boil. Reduce heat to medium-low, cover, and simmer, stirring occasionally, until the sauce is thick and chunky, about 30 minutes. In a large skillet, heat the remaining 2 tablespoons oil over medium heat. Add the zucchini, season with remaining ¼ teaspoon salt and black pepper, and cook, turning occasionally until lightly browned, about 10 minutes. Drain on paper towels.

In a large pot of boiling salted water, cook penne until just tender, 8 to 10 minutes. Drain well. Add the pasta to the tomato sauce and cook, stirring, until it absorbs most of the liquid, about 5 minutes. Stir in the olives and cook 1 minute longer. Remove from the heat and stir in half the feta and parsley; cover and let stand 1 minute. Serve topped with the zucchini and remaining feta. Pass the romano cheese separately.

6 SERVINGS

Calories 537.8 • Protein 18.19 gm • Fat 19.74 gm • Percentage of calories from fat

33% • Cholesterol 33.27 mg • Dietary fiber 4.987 gm • Sodium 1090 mg • Calcium 267.6 mg

Fettuccine with Chick-peas and Broccoli Rabe

Also called rapini, broccoli rabe can be found in most supermarkets. If unavailable, peeled and sliced broccoli stalks and chopped broccoli leaves may be substituted.

1 pound broccoli rabe (about 2 bunches)
2 cloves garlic
½ cup olive oil
⅓ cup grated Romano cheese

2 tablespoons capers
2 cups cooked chick-peas
Salt and freshly ground black pepper
1 pound fettuccine

Peel stems of broccoli rabe, and coarsely chop stems and leaves. In a food processor, mince garlic and broccoli rabe. Heat olive oil in a skillet over medium heat and cook broccoli rabe and garlic until vegetable is wilted, about 4 minutes. Add ½ cup water and cook, covered, until broccoli rabe is tender but still green, about 5 minutes more. Purée the mixture in a food processor until smooth. Transfer purée back to skillet. Add the grated cheese, capers, and chick-peas. Season to taste with salt and pepper. Keep warm. Cook the pasta in a large pot of boiling, salted water until tender. Drain, put in a serving bowl, and toss with the chick-peas and sauce. Season to taste with additional salt and pepper, if desired.

4 TO 6 SERVINGS

Calories 719.4 • Protein 20.65 gm • Fat 30.97 gm • Percentage of calories from fat 38% • Cholesterol 10.44 mg • Dietary fiber 9.569 gm • Sodium 467.5 mg • Calcium 227.2 mg

Radiatore with Spring Vegetables

Celebrate spring by preparing this lovely dish that features asparagus and fresh herbs.

1 pound radiatore or other small, shaped pasta
1 tablespoon olive oil
12 asparagus spears, cut diagonally in 1-inch lengths
1 cup Basic Vegetable Stock (see page 10)
1 carrot, cut in ¼-inch thick diagonal slices
½ cup chopped mushrooms
½ cup chopped scallions

½ cup frozen peas, thawed
½ cup heavy cream
1 tablespoon minced fresh tarragon
1 tablespoon minced fresh chives
1 tablespoon minced fresh parsley
1 teaspoon lemon juice
Salt and freshly ground black pepper
Freshly grated Pecorino Romano cheese (optional)

Cook radiatore in a large pot of salted water until tender, 10 to 12 minutes; drain and transfer to large serving bowl. Toss with olive oil and keep warm. In the meantime, steam asparagus over boiling, salted water for 2 minutes. Refresh under cold water and set aside. Bring stock and ½ cup water to a boil in a medium saucepan. Add the carrot slices, cover, and simmer over medium heat until tender, about 10 minutes. Then, with a slotted spoon, remove them to a large bowl. Add mushrooms and scallions to saucepan, cover, and simmer about 5 minutes. Transfer to the bowl. Add the peas to the saucepan, bring to a boil, and cook, uncovered, just until tender, about 1 minute. Transfer peas to the bowl and drain liquid from the bowl into the saucepan. Bring vegetable cooking liquid to a boil and cook until reduced to ¼ cup, about 5 minutes.

Whisk cream into cooking liquid, bring to a boil and cook, whisking often, until sauce is reduced by half, about 4 minutes. Transfer sauce to a large saucepan and bring to a simmer. Add tarragon, chives, parsley, lemon juice, salt and pepper to taste. Add reserved vegetables to sauce and simmer over medium heat, stirring gently, until warmed. Toss gently with warm pasta and serve immediately. Pass grated cheese separately.

6 SERVINGS

Calories 139.5 • Protein 3.281 gm • Fat 9.885 gm • Percentage of calories from fat 61% • Cholesterol 0 mg • Dietary fiber 2.285 gm • Sodium 68.15 mg • Calcium 39.53 mg

Rigatoni with Tofu and Arugula

Watercress may be used if arugula is unavailable. Whichever you use, this dish is sublime.

1 pound firm tofu, cut into ½-inch cubes
½ teaspoon salt
⅛ teaspoon ground black pepper
½ teaspoon ground allspice
5 tablespoons olive oil
2 cloves garlic, peeled and crushed
½ cup dry white wine
1 35-ounce can Italian plum tomatoes, drained
½ cup Basic Vegetable Stock (see page 10)

¼ cup chopped fresh basil or 1 tablespoon dried
2 bunches arugula or 1 bunch watercress
1 pound rigatoni or other tubular pasta, cooked in boiling salted water 10 to 12 minutes and drained
Freshly grated Parmesan cheese (optional)

Sprinkle tofu with salt, pepper, and allspice. Heat 2 tablespoons of the oil in a large saucepan or Dutch oven over medium-high heat. Add tofu and brown lightly on all sides, about 5 minutes. Remove from pan. Add garlic and stir until lightly browned. Remove from pan. Stir in wine, scraping up browned bits, and bring to boil. Add tomatoes, stock, and basil, and bring to boil. Cover and simmer for 10 minutes. Return tofu and garlic to saucepan. Remove from heat.

Add arugula to saucepan. Cover and let stand until arugula is bright green and just wilted, about 3 minutes. Toss drained pasta with remaining 3 tablespoons oil. Divide rigatoni among plates. Spoon tofu and arugula sauce on top of pasta. Pass grated cheese separately.

6 SERVINGS

Calories 502.6 • Protein 18.34 gm • Fat 16.15 gm • Percentage of calories from fat 29% • Cholesterol 0 mg • Dietary fiber 3.431 gm • Sodium 580.1 mg • Calcium 121.2 mg

Fusilli with Portobello Mushrooms

5 tablespoons olive oil
4 ounces minced tempeh bacon
1 medium onion, minced
1 teaspoon minced fresh rosemary or ¼ teaspoon dried
1 teaspoon minced fresh thyme or ¼ teaspoon dried
4 ounces Portobello mushrooms, chopped
8 ounces white mushrooms, sliced
½ cup dry white wine

1 bay leaf
4 cups Basic Vegetable Stock (see page 10), reduced to 1 cup
1 pound fusilli or other spiral pasta
½ cup light cream
½ teaspoon salt
⅛ teaspoon freshly ground black pepper
Freshly grated Pecorino Romano cheese (optional)

Heat 2 tablespoons of the oil in a large skillet over medium heat. Add tempeh bacon and onion with fresh rosemary and thyme, if using. Cook just until onion begins to color, about 5 minutes. Increase heat to medium-high. Add mushrooms and sauté about 5 minutes. Add wine and bay leaf with dried rosemary and thyme, if using, and boil until evaporated, about 5 minutes. Stir in reduced stock and simmer slowly until liquid is reduced to thick glaze, stirring occasionally. Discard bay leaf and remove mixture to a bowl.

Cook pasta in a large pot of boiling salted water until tender, 10 to 12 minutes. Drain well. Heat remaining 3 tablespoons olive oil in the large skillet over medium-high heat. Add mushroom mixture and cook until bubbling. Stir in cream and boil 1 minute. Add drained pasta and toss gently until heated through and pasta is well coated, about 3 minutes. Season with salt and pepper. Serve immediately. Pass cheese separately.

6 SERVINGS

Calories 543.8 • Protein 15.61 gm • Fat 20.91 gm • Percentage of calories from fat 34% • Cholesterol 7.417 mg • Dietary fiber 4.668 gm • Sodium 644 mg • Calcium 73.07 mg

Orecchiette with Hazelnuts and Fresh Herbs

½ cup hazelnuts, hulled
3 tablespoons olive oil
1 cup minced shallots
2 ounces tempeh bacon, chopped
2 tablespoons minced fresh basil
  or 1 ½ teaspoons dried
1 cup heavy cream

Salt and freshly ground black
  pepper
12 ounces orecchiette or other
  small, shaped pasta
3 tablespoons snipped fresh
  chives

Spread the hazelnuts on a baking sheet and toast lightly in a 350 degree oven for 5 minutes, stirring once. Allow to cool, chop, and set aside. Heat 3 tablespoons of the oil in a large skillet over medium-low heat. Add shallots and tempeh bacon and cook until shallots are translucent, stirring frequently, about 5 minutes. Mix in basil and cook about 2 minutes. Pour in cream and simmer until reduced by ¼, 6 to 8 minutes. Season with salt and pepper. Cook pasta in boiling salted water until just tender, about 10 minutes. Meanwhile, bring cream mixture to a simmer. Adjust seasonings. Drain pasta, toss with sauce in skillet. Divide pasta among serving plates, sprinkle with hazelnuts and chives, and serve immediately.

4 SERVINGS

Calories 806 • Protein 16.49 gm • Fat 50.16 gm • Percentage of calories from fat 55% • Cholesterol 69 mg • Dietary fiber 3.561 gm • Sodium 380.3 mg • Calcium 113.5 mg

Fusilli and Cannellini Beans with Garlic-Caper Sauce

1 pound fusilli or other spiral pasta
¼ cup olive oil
1 clove garlic, minced
¼ cup drained capers
  (1 tablespoon liquid reserved)
2 cups cooked cannellini beans

½ cup minced fresh basil
2 tablespoons minced fresh
  parsley
1 teaspoon hot red pepper flakes
¼ cup grated Pecorino Romano
  cheese

Cook pasta in a large pot of boiling, salted water until just tender, stirring occasionally, 12 to 14 minutes. Meanwhile, heat oil in a large skillet over medium-low heat. Add garlic and stir 2 minutes. Add capers, reserved liquid, and beans, and heat through. Drain pasta and add to skillet. Mix in basil, parsley, and red pepper flakes. Sprinkle with cheese and serve.

4 SERVINGS

Calories 666.6 • Protein 23.78 gm • Fat 17.17 gm • Percentage of calories from fat 23% • Cholesterol 5.428 mg • Dietary fiber 7.719 gm • Sodium 393.5 mg • Calcium 150.3 mg

Fettuccine with Seitan and Red Pepper Strips

2 tablespoons corn or safflower oil
1 leek, halved lengthwise, rinsed,
  and chopped
4 ounces seitan (see page 11), cut
  into ¼-inch strips
1 red bell pepper, cut into ¼-inch
  strips

Salt and freshly ground black
  pepper
2 cups heavy cream
12 ounces fettuccine
Grated Pecorino Romano cheese

Heat oil in a large skillet over medium-high heat. Add leek, seitan, and pepper, and sauté until vegetables are softened and seitan is browned. Season with salt and pepper and set aside. In a saucepan, bring cream to a boil. Reduce heat to a simmer and cook about 5 minutes. Add leek, bell pepper, and seitan. Season to taste and simmer for 15 minutes over low heat to reduce cream by half. Meanwhile, cook fettuccine in a large pot of boiling, salted water until tender, 12 to 14 minutes. Drain, toss pasta with sauce, and divide among 4 plates. Pass the grated cheese separately.

4 SERVINGS

Calories 894 • Protein 18 gm • Fat 52.79 gm • Percentage of calories from fat 52% • Cholesterol 163 mg • Dietary fiber 6.018 gm • Sodium 131.9 mg • Calcium 121.8 mg

Penne with Cannellini Beans and Sage

To do this recipe justice, try to make it with fresh sage leaves instead of dried.

4 tablespoons olive oil
1 medium onion, minced
2 ounces tempeh bacon, chopped
1 tomato, seeded and cut into
  ¼-inch dice
¼ cup loosely packed fresh sage
  leaves, minced

2 cups cooked cannellini beans
2 tablespoons balsamic vinegar
½ teaspoon salt
¼ teaspoon freshly ground black
  pepper
1 pound penne or other tubular
  pasta

Heat 2 tablespoons of the oil in a large skillet over medium-high heat. Add the onion and tempeh bacon and cook until the onion is translucent, stirring occasionally, about 5 minutes. Add tomato and sage and cook 2 minutes. Add beans. Reduce heat to low, mix in remaining 2 tablespoons of oil, vinegar, salt, and pepper and cook 2 minutes. Taste and adjust seasonings. In the meantime, cook penne in large pot of boiling, salted water until tender, about 10 minutes. Drain and toss with bean mixture in a serving bowl.

6 SERVINGS

Calories 477.1 • Protein 16.2 gm • Fat 13.51 gm • Percentage of calories from fat 25% • Cholesterol 0 mg • Dietary fiber 5.806 gm • Sodium 325.9 mg • Calcium 86.18 mg

Mostaccioli with Watercress, Tofu, and Pine Nuts

For a simple yet elegant meal, accompany with freshly baked bread and a dry white wine. Mostaccioli is a small tubular pasta similar to ziti or penne.

¼ cup pine nuts
2 tablespoons olive oil
1 clove garlic, minced
8 ounces firm tofu, cut in ½-inch dice
¼ teaspoon hot red pepper flakes
2 cups chopped watercress
1 cup Basic Vegetable Stock (see page 10)

1 pound mostaccioli or other tubular pasta
½ cup grated Pecorino Romano cheese
Salt and freshly ground black pepper

Toast pine nuts in medium skillet over medium-low heat, shaking pan frequently, until lightly browned, about 5 minutes. Remove from heat and reserve. Heat oil in the skillet, add garlic, tofu, and red pepper flakes and sauté 2 minutes, or until tofu is golden brown. Remove with a slotted spoon and reserve. Add watercress to the skillet and cook over medium heat 1 minute. Add stock and simmer 5 minutes. Meanwhile, cook pasta in boiling, salted water for 12 minutes, or until just tender. Drain well. Return pasta to pan. Add watercress mixture, reserved tofu, cheese, and salt and pepper to taste. Toss well. Divide among serving plates and top with toasted pine nuts.

4 TO 6 SERVINGS

Calories 501.7 • Protein 20.95 gm • Fat 14.59 gm • Percentage of calories from fat 25% • Cholesterol 10.13 mg • Dietary fiber 2.771 gm • Sodium 211.2 mg • Calcium 163.3 mg

Linguine with Red Bell Pepper Sauce

This sauce provides a light and refreshing change from tomato sauce.

¼ cup olive oil
1 large onion, thinly sliced
2 pounds red bell peppers, cut into
  ½-inch strips
2 tablespoons chopped fresh basil
  or 1½ teaspoons dried
½ teaspoon salt
¼ teaspoon freshly ground black
  pepper

1½ cup Basic Vegetable Stock (see
  page 10)
1 cup TVP combined with 1 cup
  water
1 pound linguine
¼ cup freshly grated Parmesan
  cheese
2 tablespoons minced fresh
  parsley

Heat the olive oil in a large skillet. Add the onion and peppers and cook over moderately high heat, stirring frequently, until the onion slices begin to brown, about 10 minutes. Reduce the heat to medium and add the basil, salt, and pepper. Cook for 5 minutes, or until the peppers are tender. Add 1 cup of the stock to the skillet and cook for 5 minutes longer. Pour the pepper sauce into a food processor and purée until it is the consistency of a thick tomato sauce. Transfer sauce to a saucepan, add the TVP, and cook over medium heat until heated through, 2 to 3 minutes. If the sauce is too thick, add as much of the remaining stock as necessary to achieve the desired consistency. In the meantime, cook the pasta in a large pot of boiling, salted water until tender but still firm, 10 to 12 minutes. Drain well. Toss the pasta with the hot sauce in a serving bowl. Garnish with grated Parmesan and parsley.

4 TO 6 SERVINGS

Calories 432.9 • Protein 28.6 gm • Fat 5.39 gm • Percentage of calories from fat 11% • Cholesterol 3.95 mg • Dietary fiber 10.48 gm • Sodium 599.8 mg • Calcium 187.8 mg

Seitan Lo Mein

8 ounces soba, udon, or lo mein
  noodles
1 tablespoon sesame oil
2 tablespoons corn or safflower oil
4 ounces seitan (see page 11), cut
  into ¼-inch strips

2 scallions, minced
½ cup sliced mushrooms
½ cup sliced carrots, blanched
1 cup bok choy in ¼-inch strips
1 tablespoon low-sodium tamari

Cook noodles according to package directions. Drain and set aside; toss with the tablespoon of sesame oil. Heat the corn oil in a large skillet or wok over medium-high heat, add seitan, and stir-fry until browned, 3 to 5 minutes. Add scallions, mushrooms, carrots, and bok choy and continue stir-frying about 3 minutes. Add tamari to taste. When the vegetables are soft, combine with pasta and toss. Serve immediately.

4 SERVINGS

Calories 359 • Protein 13.28 gm • Fat 8.381 gm • Percentage of calories from fat 20% • Cholesterol 0 mg • Dietary fiber 5.913 gm • Sodium 762.1 mg • Calcium 20.23 mg

Soba with Lentils and Kale

Soba, or Japanese buckwheat noodles, have a unique hearty flavor.

1 bunch kale, washed and cut away
   from stems
2 medium carrots, cut in diagonal
   ¼-inch slices
1 rib celery, diced
½ cup lentils, rinsed
1 bay leaf
5 tablespoons olive oil
1 clove garlic, minced

2 shallots, minced
4 scallions, finely chopped
Salt and freshly ground black
   pepper
1 cup Basic Vegetable Stock (see
   page 10) or lentil-cooking liquid
8 ounces soba noodles
2 tablespoons chopped fresh
   parsley

Cut kale into ½-inch strips to equal about 3 cups. Reserve. In a pot of boiling salted water, add carrots, celery, lentils, and bay leaf. Cook at a slow boil until tender, about 25 minutes. Drain, reserving up to 2 cups cooking liquid (if using). Toss lentil mixture with 2 tablespoons of the olive oil and set aside.

Slowly warm remaining 3 tablespoons olive oil in a large skillet over medium-low heat. Add garlic, shallots, and scallions and cook for 2 to 3 minutes; do not let garlic brown. Add lentil mixture, cook for a minute, add salt and pepper to taste. Add 1 cup stock (or cooking liquid) and kale, cover, simmer until tender. (If stock evaporates, add more.) Cook pasta according to package directions. Divide soba among 4 plates. Top with lentil sauce, garnish with parsley, and serve immediately.

4 SERVINGS

Calories 457.9 • Protein 16.19 gm • Fat 17.93 gm • Percentage of calories from fat 33% • Cholesterol 0 mg • Dietary fiber 2.641 gm • Sodium 539.2 mg • Calcium 68.54 mg

Tahini Linguine

In addition to being high in protein, tahini is also loaded with calcium, making it a great alternative to both meat and dairy.

1 pound linguine
½ cup tahini
3 tablespoons low-sodium tamari

2 tablespoons chopped fresh
  parsley

Cook the linguine in a large pot of boiling salted water until tender but still firm, 10 to 12 minutes. Meanwhile, in a small bowl, whisk together tahini and tamari until well blended. Slowly drizzle in ¼ cup of water or more until a creamy consistency is reached. When linguine is done, drain and toss with sauce in a serving bowl. Sprinkle with parsley and serve.

4 TO 6 SERVINGS

Calories 443.7 • Protein 16.78 gm • Fat 17.79 gm • Percentage of calories from fat 36% • Cholesterol 0 mg • Dietary fiber 2.062 gm • Sodium 386 mg • Calcium 21.92 mg

Penne Pasta Primavera

Miso, a fermented soybean paste available at natural foods stores, imparts a savory richness to the sauce.

3 tablespoons corn or safflower oil
1 clove garlic, minced
¼ cup minced onion
2 cup broccoli florets, blanched
½ cup red bell pepper, cut into
   ¼-inch strips
1 cup carrots, cut into ¼-inch
   julienne, blanched
4 scallions, minced
1 cup yellow squash cut into half
   moons, blanched

¼ cup minced fresh parsley
2 tablespoons chopped fresh basil
2 cups milk
8 ounces soft tofu
½ teaspoon salt
¼ teaspoon ground white pepper
1½ tablespoons cornstarch
1 tablespoon mellow white miso
1 pound penne or other tubular
   pasta

Heat oil in large skillet. Sauté garlic, onion, broccoli, bell pepper, and carrots for 2 minutes. Add scallions, squash, parsley, and basil and sauté for 5 minutes. In a bowl, slowly stir the milk with the tofu, blending to make a creamy consistency. Sprinkle in salt and white pepper. Slowly add the milk mixture to the skillet. Simmer for a few minutes. Dissolve the cornstarch in 2 tablespoons water. Add it to mixture in the skillet, stirring constantly to create a smooth sauce. Adjust seasonings. Add miso, diluted in 2 tablespoons of the sauce. In the meantime, cook penne in a large pot of boiling water until tender but still firm, 10 to 12 minutes. Drain well and put in a serving bowl. Spoon vegetables and sauce over pasta and serve.

4 TO 6 SERVINGS

Calories 543.5 • Protein 21.08 gm • Fat 13.05 gm • Percentage of calories from fat 21% • Cholesterol 7.2 mg • Dietary fiber 5.36 gm • Sodium 449.9 mg • Calcium 205.2 mg

Linguine with Pesto Sauce

Make this aromatic pesto when fresh basil is plentiful and at its peak. It is best made a day ahead of time, so the flavor intensifies.

3 cups fresh basil leaves, firmly packed
2 cloves garlic, halved
½ cup pine nuts
¼ cup grated Pecorino Romano cheese
½ teaspoon salt
⅛ teaspoon freshly ground black pepper
¾ cup olive oil
1 pound artichoke or other linguine

In a food processor place the basil, garlic, pine nuts, cheese, salt, and pepper and pulse to combine. With the machine running, stream in olive oil and process until well blended. If sauce is too thick, add a little water or olive oil.

Cook linguine in a large pot of boiling, salted water until tender but still firm, 10 to 12 minutes. Drain. To serve, toss ½ cup (or more, according to taste) of the sauce with the linguine. If making sauce ahead of time, store in refrigerator in a tightly covered container, topped with a thin layer of olive oil to seal. Pesto can also be frozen this way. Bring it to room temperature before serving.

4 TO 6 SERVINGS

Calories 644.7 • Protein 14.68 gm • Fat 44.33 gm • Percentage of calories from fat 59% • Cholesterol 4.632 mg • Dietary fiber 2.228 gm • Sodium 288.3 mg • Calcium 59.28 mg

Rotini with Tofu and Napa Cabbage

Napa cabbage is also know as Chinese cabbage. Its leaf is tall, firm, and frilly at the edge.

3 tablespoons olive oil
1 clove garlic, minced
2 shallots, minced
3 scallions, minced
½ pound firm tofu, cut into ½-inch cubes
2 cups napa cabbage thinly sliced on the diagonal, lightly steamed

¾ teaspoon salt
¼ teaspoon freshly ground black pepper
1 pound whole-wheat rotini or other rotini
2 tablespoons minced fresh parsley

Heat oil in a large skillet over medium heat. Add garlic, shallots, and scallions; sauté 2 minutes. Add tofu and steamed cabbage. Season with salt and pepper. Cook for 5 to 8 minutes until flavors combine. In the meantime, cook rotini in a large pot of boiling salted water until tender but still firm, 10 to 12 minutes. Drain. Combine pasta with tofu and cabbage in a serving bowl. Adjust seasonings. Garnish with parsley.

4 TO 6 SERVINGS

Calories 383.2 • Protein 18.83 gm • Fat 10.73 gm • Percentage of calories from fat 22% • Cholesterol 0 mg • Dietary fiber 12.14 gm • Sodium 374.3 mg • Calcium 67.67 mg

Seitan and Soba with Root Vegetables

Mirin is a sweet Japanese rice wine, available in natural foods stores. If you can't find it, use white wine or sherry.

8 ounces soba (buckwheat) noodles
1 tablespoon dark sesame oil
1 cup each: carrots, parsnips, and rutabaga, cut into 3-inch strips
2 tablespoons corn oil
8 ounces seitan (see page 11), cut into ¼-inch strips

1 leek, chopped (white part only)
1 tablespoon low-sodium tamari
1 tablespoon mirin
Salt and freshly ground black pepper
2 tablespoons minced fresh parsley

Cook soba according to package directions. Drain, rinse with cold water, and toss with sesame oil. Set aside. Blanch carrot, parsnip, and rutabaga strips. Set aside. Heat corn oil in a large skillet over medium-high heat. Add seitan and brown lightly on all sides; then add leek and sauté 3 to 4 minutes. Add tamari and mirin. Add vegetables and soba and toss lightly. Add salt and pepper to taste. Garnish with parsley.

4 SERVINGS

Calories 600.3 • Protein 23.78 gm • Fat 11.02 gm • Percentage of calories from fat 15% • Cholesterol 0 mg • Dietary fiber 3.79 gm • Sodium 439.5 mg • Calcium 83.77 mg

Pasta la Vista

A healthy alternative to meat sauce for pasta. If you don't want to use TVP, sautéed ground seitan or tempeh can be substituted.

2 tablespoons olive oil
1 cup minced onions
2 large cloves garlic, minced
¼ cup minced green bell pepper
½ cup diced carrots
1 6-ounce can tomato paste
1 cup TVP granules, combined
  with 1 cup water
1 14-ounce can tomatoes,
  chopped, with liquid
2 cups Basic Vegetable Stock (see
  page 10)

½ cup minced fresh parsley
⅛ teaspoon cayenne
1 teaspoon dried basil
½ teaspoon dried oregano
½ teaspoon salt
⅛ teaspoon freshly ground black
  pepper
1 pound artichoke or other
  linguine, freshly cooked

Heat the oil in a large skillet over medium heat, add onions, garlic, bell pepper, and carrots, and sauté them for 5 minutes. Add tomato paste to skillet. Sauté, stirring, 2 more minutes. Add TVP, tomatoes, stock, parsley, cayenne, basil, oregano, salt, and pepper to skillet. Cover and simmer 1 hour over low heat, stirring occasionally. If sauce becomes too thick, add more stock. To serve, divide hot pasta among individual serving plates and top with sauce, or place pasta in a serving bowl and top with sauce. Serve immediately.

6 SERVINGS

Calories 388.4 • Protein 23.03 gm • Fat 7.442 gm • Percentage of calories from fat 16% • Cholesterol 0 mg • Dietary fiber 8.483 gm • Sodium 419.6 mg • Calcium 130.7 mg

Fusilli with Broccoli, Seitan, and Pine Nuts

1 pound broccoli, trimmed
⅓ cup olive oil
8 ounces seitan (see page 11), cut into ¼-inch cubes
2 large cloves garlic, minced
2 pounds tomatoes, peeled (see page 375) and chopped

¾ teaspoon salt
⅓ cup raisins
⅓ cup pine nuts
1 pound fusilli or other curly pasta
¼ cup minced fresh Italian parsley

Cut broccoli florets into ½-inch pieces. Peel broccoli stems and cut into ½-inch pieces. Steam broccoli until just tender, about 5 minutes, then run under cold water to stop cooking process. Drain and pat dry. Reserve. Heat oil in a large skillet over medium heat. Add seitan and cook until browned, about 5 minutes. Add garlic and cook about 1 minute. Add tomatoes and salt to skillet, reduce heat to medium-low, and cook 10 minutes, stirring occasionally. Add raisins and pine nuts and cook 5 minutes. Add broccoli and toss until heated through. Meanwhile, cook fusilli in a large pan of boiling salted water, stirring occasionally, until just tender, about 12 to 14 minutes. Drain well and transfer to a large serving bowl. Add sauce and parsley and toss to combine. Serve immediately.

4 TO 6 SERVINGS

Calories 729.5 • Protein 25.13 gm • Fat 20.97 gm • Percentage of calories from fat 25% • Cholesterol 0 mg • Dietary fiber 12.72 gm • Sodium 489.8 mg • Calcium 100.1 mg

4

Casseroles, Gratins, and Risottos

Perfect for party buffets or do-ahead dinners, casseroles and gratins provide tasty alternatives for the busy cook. Most of the casseroles and gratins can be put together several hours before they are needed, so that you can come home from a busy day and simply pop dinner in the oven. What could be easier, and more delicious, than sitting down to a Tofu and Artichoke Gratin or a casserole of Baked Ziti with Seitan and Olives, served with a simple green salad and some warm bread?

Savory Tofu Bread Pudding

If the sweet Vidalia onion is unavailable, substitute ordinary yellow onions. This is a perfect do-ahead dish, making it a great choice for party buffets. Your guests will love it.

2 tablespoons corn oil
1 clove garlic, minced
1 pound Vidalia onions (about 4), chopped
4 ounces Jarlsberg cheese, shredded
1 pound soft tofu, crumbled

1½ cups milk
2 teaspoons Dijon mustard
1 teaspoon dried sage
¾ teaspoon salt
⅛ teaspoon freshly ground black pepper
4 cups whole-wheat bread cubes

Heat oil in a large skillet over low heat. Add garlic and onions, cover, and cook gently for 5 minutes. Uncover and continue cooking until liquid evaporates, stirring occasionally. In a bowl, combine cheese with tofu, ½ cup of the milk, mustard, sage, salt, and pepper and mix well. Stir in onion mixture, then remaining 1 cup milk. Lightly oil a large shallow baking dish and place bread cubes in it. Pour tofu mixture over bread, using fork to distribute onions evenly. Let soak until liquid is absorbed, about 30 minutes. Recipe may be made ahead to this point and refrigerated. Bring to room temperature before proceeding. Preheat oven to 325 degrees. Bake bread pudding 45 minutes. Increase temperature to 400 degrees and continue baking until puffy and well browned, about 10 minutes more. Let stand 10 minutes. Serve warm.

8 SERVINGS

Calories 363.6 • Protein 17.47 gm • Fat 12.12 gm • Percentage of calories from fat 30% • Cholesterol 16.35 mg • Dietary fiber 2.906 gm • Sodium 729.2 mg • Calcium 291.6 mg

Baked Ziti with Seitan and Olives

This hearty casserole may be assembled early in the day and popped in the oven later for no-fuss entertaining. Serve with a salad, crusty Italian bread, and a good Chianti.

2 tablespoons olive oil
1 large onion, minced
1 pound seitan (see page 11),
  finely chopped
1 clove garlic, minced
1 28-ounce can Italian peeled
  tomatoes, crushed, with liquid
½ cup dry red wine
½ cup Basic Vegetable Stock (see
  page 10)
¼ cup chopped fresh parsley
1 tablespoon chopped fresh basil
  or 1 teaspoon dried

1 teaspoon minced fresh marjoram
  or ½ teaspoon dried
½ teaspoon salt
¼ teaspoon freshly ground black
  pepper
1 pound ziti or other tubular pasta
12 oil-cured olives, pitted and
  chopped
½ cup grated Pecorino Romano
  cheese
8 ounces mozzarella cheese,
  shredded

Heat oil in a large skillet over medium-high heat, add onion, seitan, and garlic, and sauté for 5 to 7 minutes, or until onions are soft and seitan is browned. Add the tomatoes with their juice, wine, stock, parsley, basil, marjoram, salt, and pepper. Simmer until liquid is reduced by half. In a large pot of boiling salted water, cook the ziti, stirring occasionally, until al dente, about 10 minutes. Drain immediately. Preheat the oven to 375 degrees. In a large bowl, combine ziti with seitan mixture, olives, Romano cheese, and half the mozzarella. Spoon the mixture into a large baking dish and sprinkle with remaining mozzarella. Recipe can be prepared ahead of time to this point and refrigerated. Bring to room temperature before baking. Bake until the top is browned and the cheese has melted throughout, about 45 minutes.

6 TO 8 SERVINGS

Calories 644.6 • Protein 29.65 gm • Fat 14.2 gm • Percentage of calories from fat 20% • Cholesterol 25.49 mg • Dietary fiber 10.52 gm • Sodium 870.3 mg • Calcium 363.2 mg

Tempeh Cabbage Casserole

4 shiitake mushrooms, trimmed
1 pound poached tempeh (see
  page 12), coarsely chopped
2 tablespoons mirin, white wine,
  or sherry
2 tablespoons cornstarch
3 tablespoon minced scallions
½ teaspoon salt

2 teaspoons minced fresh ginger
1½ teaspoons dark sesame oil
6 cups Basic Vegetable Stock (see
  page 10)
4 tablespoons corn oil
1 head napa cabbage, trimmed,
  cut into 1-inch strips
1 tablespoon low-sodium tamari

Mince mushrooms and transfer to a medium bowl. Add chopped tempeh along with 1 tablespoon of the mirin, 1 tablespoon of the cornstarch, 1 tablespoon of the scallions, ¼ teaspoon of the salt, the ginger, and the sesame oil. Stir until ingredients are evenly distributed, then shape mixture into 4 large oval patties. Refrigerate, covered, until needed.

Preheat oven to 375 degrees. In a large bowl, combine the stock, remaining 1 tablespoon mirin, and remaining ¼ teaspoon salt; set aside. Heat 2 tablespoons of the corn oil in a large skillet or wok over medium-high heat. Add cabbage and stir-fry until coated with oil. Continue stir-frying, adding 2 to 3 tablespoons of the stock, until cabbage is wilted, about 3 minutes. Add remaining stock and heat to boiling. Reduce heat to low; simmer, uncovered, until cabbage is tender, about 10 minutes. Stir in remaining 2 tablespoons scallions and remove from heat. Transfer cabbage and stock to a large casserole. Stir together remaining 1 tablespoon cornstarch, the tamari, and 1 tablespoon water in small bowl until smooth. Dip tempeh patties in tamari mixture, using fingers to coat evenly. Heat remaining 2 tablespoons corn oil in a large skillet over medium-high heat, add tempeh patties, and fry until golden brown on both sides, about 5 minutes. Remove patties and arrange over cabbage. Pour any remaining coating mixture into casserole. Bake, covered, for 30 minutes.

6 SERVINGS

Calories 291.2 • Protein 14.89 gm • Fat 16.17 gm • Percentage of calories from fat 49% • Cholesterol 0 mg • Dietary fiber 5.015 gm • Sodium 549.9 mg • Calcium 94.89 mg

Terrine of Pasta with Tofu and Vegetables

This lovely terrine does not require a sauce, but a light fresh tomato sauce would make a suitable accompaniment.

3 fennel bulbs, trimmed and outer
  layer discarded
1 bunch broccoli, trimmed and
  stems peeled
5 tablespoons olive oil
1 large onion, minced
½ cup tomato paste
½ teaspoon salt

1 cup dried bread crumbs
8 ounces firm tofu, cut into ¼-inch
  dice
1 cup grated Romano cheese
¼ teaspoon freshly ground black
  pepper
1 pound ziti or other tubular pasta
Grated Romano cheese

Quarter fennel bulbs lengthwise, then cut into thin slices. Cut center stalk into ¼-inch pieces. Cut broccoli florets off stems. Slice broccoli stems thinly. Lightly steam broccoli and reserve. Heat 3 tablespoons of the olive oil in a large saucepan over medium-high heat. Add the onion and sauté about 2 minutes. Add the tomato paste and cook 2 minutes. Mix in 1 cup water. Add fennel and enough water to cover fennel by two thirds. Add the salt. Cover, reduce heat, and simmer until fennel is tender, about 15 minutes. Uncover, increase heat to high and stir until liquid is reduced by half. Transfer to a large pot or bowl. Add steamed broccoli to fennel, reserving 1 cup florets for garnish.

Preheat oven to 325 degrees. Heat last 2 tablespoons of the oil in a large skillet over medium heat. Add ⅓ cup of the bread crumbs and the tofu and stir until crumbs turn golden brown, about 2 minutes. Remove from heat and continue stirring 2 minutes. Add to vegetables. Mix in 1 cup Romano and pepper. Add pasta to large pot of boiling salted water. Cook until just tender but al dente, about 10 minutes. Drain well and add to vegetable mixture. Brush baking dish or springform pan with oil. Coat with remaining ⅔ cup bread crumbs. Transfer vegetable-ziti mixture to pan, packing down well. Terrine may be prepared in advance to this point. Bring to room temperature before baking. Bake about 45 minutes. When casserole is done, invert onto platter to serve. Garnish with reserved broccoli florets. Serve immediately, passing cheese separately.

6 TO 8 SERVINGS

Calories 520.7 • Protein 19.8 gm • Fat 18.21 gm • Percentage of calories from fat 31% • Cholesterol 14.47 mg • Dietary fiber 4.738 gm • Sodium 719.1 mg • Calcium 241.1 mg

Baked Tofu with Basil Pistou

The intriguing combination of basil and mint provides an aromatic contrast to the delicate tofu.

2 large cloves garlic
¼ teaspoon salt
2 cups lightly packed fresh basil leaves, plus additional for garnish
¼ cup lightly packed fresh mint leaves
½ cup plus 2 tablespoons olive oil
¼ cup grated Pecorino Romano cheese
¼ cup shredded Jarlsberg cheese

2 medium shallots, chopped
1 pound firm tofu, cut in ¼-inch slices
Salt and freshly ground black pepper
½ teaspoon ground allspice
¼ cup hot Basic Vegetable Stock (see page 10)
2 large tomatoes, seeded and diced

Preheat oven to 400 degrees. In a food processor, mince garlic and salt to paste. Add 2 cups basil and the mint and coarsely chop. With machine running, slowly add ½ cup of the oil through feed tube. Mix in cheeses using quick pulses. Heat 2 tablespoons of the oil in a large skillet over medium-high heat. Add shallots and cook for 3 minutes. Add tofu slices. Sprinkle with salt, pepper, and allspice. Cook tofu for 2 minutes on each side. Transfer tofu with a spatula to an oiled gratin dish. Add hot stock to basil-mint mixture and blend briefly. Drizzle mixture over tofu. Top with tomatoes. Bake for 15 minutes. Garnish with basil leaves and serve immediately.

6 SERVINGS

Calories 277.8 • Protein 8.294 gm • Fat 25.46 gm • Percentage of calories from fat 79% • Cholesterol 4.101 mg • Dietary fiber 0.626 gm • Sodium 200.4 mg • Calcium 103.3 mg

Layered Polenta

Fennel seeds may be ground in a pepper mill or with a mortar and pestle.

3 tablespoons olive oil
1 small onion, finely chopped
1 28-ounce can Italian peeled
 tomatoes, drained and chopped
2½ teaspoons salt
¼ teaspoon freshly ground black
 pepper
1½ cups cornmeal

1 cup grated Pecorino Romano
 cheese
1 pound ground seitan (see
 page 8)
½ teaspoon fennel seeds, ground
½ teaspoon ground allspice
½ pound mozzarella cheese,
 shredded

In a large saucepan, heat 1 tablespoon of the oil. Add the onion and cook over moderate heat until translucent, about 5 minutes. Add the tomatoes, ½ teaspoon of the salt, and the pepper. Bring to a boil, partially cover, and simmer, stirring occasionally, until the sauce thickens, about 45 minutes.

While sauce is cooking, bring 5 cups water to a boil in a large saucepan, add the remaining 2 teaspoons salt, and gradually whisk in the cornmeal in a slow stream, stirring constantly to avoid lumps. Cook over moderate heat, stirring, until the polenta begins to pull away from the sides of the pan, about 20 minutes. Remove from the heat and stir in the ⅓ cup of the Romano cheese. Transfer to a large lightly oiled baking dish. Smooth the surface with a wet spatula. Set aside.

Preheat the oven to 375 degrees. Heat remaining 2 tablespoons of the oil in a large skillet. Add seitan, fennel, allspice, salt, and pepper. Cook and stir until browned, about 10 minutes. Set aside.

To assemble, spread a layer of the tomato sauce over the polenta. Sprinkle half the mozzarella over the tomato sauce. Top with all of the seitan. Spread a layer of tomato sauce, sprinkle with the remaining mozzarella and Romano cheeses. Bake the polenta for 30 minutes, or until heated through.

6 TO 8 SERVINGS

Calories 478.9 • Protein 23.53 gm • Fat 16.33 gm • Percentage of calories from fat 30% • Cholesterol 15.54 mg • Dietary fiber 10.21 gm • Sodium 1814 mg • Calcium 335.3 mg

Brown Rice Baked with Mushrooms and Monterey Jack Cheese

Save time by starting with 4 cups of cooked rice.

1 teaspoon salt
1½ cups brown rice
2 tablespoons corn oil
⅓ cup minced onion
6 ounces mushrooms, chopped
1 clove garlic, minced
Salt and freshly ground black
 pepper

1 cup soft tofu
1 tablespoon Worcestershire
 sauce
1½ tablespoons fresh lemon juice
½ teaspoon Tabasco sauce
1 cup grated Monterey Jack
 cheese

In a large saucepan bring 2 quarts of water to a boil with 1 teaspoon salt and stir in the rice; keep stirring until the water returns to a boil and then boil it for 45 minutes. Drain the rice in a large sieve and rinse it. Heat oil in a large skillet and cook the onion, mushrooms, and garlic over moderate heat, stirring, for 5 minutes. Add salt and pepper to taste and remove the skillet from the heat.

Preheat oven to 375 degrees. In a large bowl combine the tofu, Worcestershire sauce, lemon juice, Tabasco, and ⅓ cup of the cheese. Gently stir in the rice and the mushroom mixture; then, turn the mixture into a large baking dish and bake it, covered, for 20 minutes. Remove from oven, top with the remaining cheese, return to oven, and bake uncovered for 10 minutes, or until cheese is melted and bubbly.

4 SERVINGS

Calories 266.9 • Protein 12.57 gm • Fat 14.4 gm • Percentage of calories from fat 48% • Cholesterol 15.72 mg • Dietary fiber 2.051 gm • Sodium 713.7 mg • Calcium 176.9 mg

Oven-Baked Winter Vegetables and Seitan

1 pound small new potatoes, halved
½ pound tomatoes, cut into eight wedges
1 pound butternut squash, peeled and cut into 1-inch dice
2 medium onions, cut into ¼-inch slices
½ pound green beans, trimmed, halved crosswise, and blanched
½ pound zucchini, cut into ½-inch slices
½ pound carrots, cut into ½-inch pieces

½ cup minced fresh parsley
2 cloves garlic, minced
1 teaspoon sweet paprika
½ teaspoon salt
⅛ teaspoon freshly ground black pepper
¼ cup olive oil (or more), plus 2 tablespoons
1 pound seitan (see page 11), cut into ½-inch slices
1 cup Basic Brown Sauce (see page 13)

Preheat the oven to 400 degrees. In a large baking dish combine the potatoes, tomatoes, squash, onions, green beans, zucchini, carrots, parsley, garlic, paprika, salt, and pepper and toss the mixture gently. Sprinkle with ¼ cup of the olive oil and bake the vegetables, covered, for 1 hour. Heat the 2 tablespoons of oil in a skillet over medium-high heat. Add the seitan and brown well on both sides, about 5 minutes. Season with salt and pepper to taste. Uncover vegetables, add seitan, and bake for 10 minutes more. Serve with Basic Brown Sauce.

6 SERVINGS

Calories 474.6 • Protein 16.59 gm • Fat 10.94 gm • Percentage of calories from fat 20% • Cholesterol 0 mg • Dietary fiber 14.45 gm • Sodium 500.1 mg • Calcium 127.8 mg

Kasha with Mushrooms and Kale

Kasha, also called buckwheat groats, is available in natural foods stores and most supermarkets. The deep earthy flavors in this dish will make it a welcome addition to your winter recipes.

8 large kale leaves, trimmed
2 tablespoons corn oil
1 medium onion, chopped
½ pound mushrooms, sliced
Salt and freshly ground black
  pepper

2 cups Basic Vegetable Stock (see
  page 10)
1 cup whole kasha

Remove ribs from kale leaves. Halve ribs lengthwise and slice thinly cross-wise. Chop leaves. Heat the oil in a medium saucepan over medium-low heat. Add onion and kale ribs and cook until onion is tender, stirring occasionally, about 10 minutes. Add mushrooms and shredded kale leaves. Season with salt and pepper. Stir until mushrooms soften, about 5 minutes. Add stock and bring to a boil. Turn off heat. Heat a large skillet over medium-high heat. Add kasha and stir until kernels separate, about 3 minutes. Reduce heat to low. Add stock-vegetable mixture. Cover and cook until kasha is tender and liquid is absorbed, about 20 minutes. Toss well with a fork before serving.

4 SERVINGS

Calories 270.1 • Protein 8.97 gm • Fat 8.796 gm • Percentage of calories from fat 27% • Cholesterol 0 mg • Dietary fiber 7.86 gm • Sodium 136.8 mg • Calcium 77.76 mg

Peach Pilaf

A light and refreshing dinner choice for a warm summer evening. As pretty as it is delicious.

2 tablespoons slivered almonds
2 tablespoons corn oil
1 pound firm tofu, cut into ½-inch dice
1 fresh peach, peeled, pitted, and diced
1 scallion, chopped

1 teaspoon minced fresh ginger
1 cup basmati rice
1 teaspoon grated lemon zest
1 teaspoon minced fresh mint
1 tablespoon minced fresh parsley
Salt and freshly ground black pepper

Preheat the oven to 325 degrees. Spread the nuts in a shallow baking pan and toast, stirring once, until lightly browned, about 5 minutes. Cool. Heat 1 tablespoon of the oil in a saucepan over medium heat. Add the tofu and peach and sauté, gently stirring, about 2 minutes. Remove and reserve. In the same pan, add the remaining 1 tablespoon oil and the scallion and sauté, stirring, until softened, about 2 minutes. Add the ginger and cook 1 minute longer. Add the rice, stirring to coat with the oil, and cook 1 minute. Stir in 2 cups of water and lemon zest. Bring the liquid to a boil over high heat. Lower heat, cover, and simmer until the liquid is absorbed and the rice is tender, about 30 minutes. Stir in the toasted almonds, tofu-peach mixture, mint, and parsley. Season to taste with salt and pepper and serve.

4 SERVINGS

Calories 340 • Protein 13.32 gm • Fat 11.42 gm • Percentage of calories from fat 30% • Cholesterol 0 mg • Dietary fiber 0.694 gm • Sodium 73.9 mg • Calcium 57.83 mg

Cassoulet

Tempeh and seitan join with the white beans in this meatless version of the French country classic.

2 tablespoons corn oil
1 cup poached tempeh (see page 12), cut in ½-inch dice
1 cup seitan (see page 11), cut in ¼-inch strips
2 cloves garlic, minced
3 cups cooked Great Northern beans
½ cup pearl onions, boiled
2½ cups tomato sauce

1 tablespoon chopped fresh parsley
½ teaspoon salt
⅛ teaspoon freshly ground black pepper
1 bay leaf
½ teaspoon minced fresh thyme or ¼ teaspoon dried
1 cup dry bread crumbs, lightly sauteéd in oil

Preheat oven to 350 degrees. Heat oil in a large skillet over medium-high heat. Add tempeh and seitan and cook until browned, about 5 minutes. Add garlic and sauté 1 minute. Combine all ingredients, except bread crumbs, in large casserole. Cover and bake 45 minutes. Remove cover and sprinkle bread crumbs on top. Bake uncovered another 15 minutes, until crumbs are golden brown.

4 TO 6 SERVINGS

Calories 361.9 • Protein 19.04 gm • Fat 9.919 gm • Percentage of calories from fat 24% • Cholesterol 0 mg • Dietary fiber 8.801 gm • Sodium 1146 mg • Calcium 173.4 mg

Tofu Florentine

3 tablespoons corn oil
1 medium onion, minced
3 cups packed fresh trimmed
  spinach, cooked and drained
1 pound firm tofu
¾ teaspoon salt
⅛ teaspoon freshly ground black
  pepper

Pinch nutmeg
½ cup milk
3 cups cooked pasta shells or
  similar pasta
1 cup shredded mozzarella cheese

Preheat the oven to 350 degrees. Heat oil in a large skillet over medium-high heat. Add onion and cook until translucent, about 5 minutes. Chop cooked spinach, stir into onions, and set aside. In a food processor, combine tofu, salt, pepper, and nutmeg. Add milk. Process to blend. Combine tofu mixture with spinach mixture. Then combine with cooked pasta and adjust seasonings. Spoon mixture into oiled baking dish. Top with cheese and bake for 40 minutes.

4 TO 6 SERVINGS

Calories 393.3 • Protein 24.45 gm • Fat 18.52 gm • Percentage of calories from fat 42% • Cholesterol 27.35 mg • Dietary fiber 3.157 gm • Sodium 736 mg • Calcium 405.6 mg

Tofu-Tahini Casserole

2 tablespoons corn oil
1 medium onion, minced
3 cups cooked brown rice
1 cup chopped, steamed broccoli
1 pound firm tofu, crumbled
2 tablespoons tahini
½ teaspoon salt

¼ teaspoon freshly ground black
  pepper
1 teaspoon lemon juice
1 teaspoon low-sodium tamari
1 teaspoon Dijon mustard
1 cup milk

Preheat oven to 375 degrees. Heat oil in a large skillet over medium-high heat. Add onion and sauté for 5 minutes. Stir in rice and broccoli; set aside.

In a food processor, combine tofu, tahini, salt, pepper, lemon juice, tamari, and mustard. Slowly pour in milk, blending until smooth. Taste for desired flavor: if milder flavor is desired, add more tahini; if saltier flavor is desired, add more lemon juice or tamari. Combine mixture with rice and broccoli, transfer to oiled baking dish, and bake for 30 minutes. This casserole can be assembled ahead of time and refrigerated. Bring to room temperature before baking.

6 SERVINGS

Calories 233.6 • Protein 11.69 gm • Fat 10.88 gm • Percentage of calories from fat 41% • Cholesterol 3 mg • Dietary fiber 2.52 gm • Sodium 311.7 mg • Calcium 117.8 mg

Quinoa-Seitan Pilaf

Called "the mother grain" by the Incas, quinoa is an ancient South American grain that supplies essential amino acids, making it a complete protein. If quinoa is unavailable, this dish is also delicious with brown rice.

½ cup sliced almonds
2 tablespoons corn oil
4 ounces seitan (see page 11), finely chopped
2 scallions, sliced diagonally
4 cups cooked quinoa (see page 5)

1 cup fresh or frozen green peas, blanched
½ cup grated carrot, blanched
Salt and freshly ground black pepper
1 tablespoon minced fresh parsley

Preheat the oven to 325 degrees. Spread almonds in baking pan and toast, stirring once, until lightly browned, about 5 minutes. Let cool. Heat oil in a large skillet over medium-high heat. Add seitan and cook until browned, about 5 minutes. Add scallions and cook 1 minute. Add quinoa, peas, carrot, and salt and pepper to taste. Stir to combine, then stir in almonds and parsley. Adjust seasonings.

4 SERVINGS

Calories 469 • Protein 16.07 gm • Fat 21.21 gm • Percentage of calories from fat 39% • Cholesterol 0 mg • Dietary fiber 9.177 gm • Sodium 281.3 mg • Calcium 100.5 mg

Turkish Pilaf

Aromatic and flavorful, this pilaf is sure to become a favorite. Meatless sausage is available under a variety of brand names in health food stores and supermarkets. Experiment until you find the one you like best.

½ cup chopped dried apricots
2 tablespoons corn oil
¼ cup chopped almonds
1 small yellow onion, minced
4 ounces meatless sausage, chopped
1 cup basmati rice

¼ cup raisins
1 teaspoon ground cinnamon
½ teaspoon salt
Freshly ground black pepper
2 cups hot Basic Vegetable Stock (see page 10)

Cover apricots with boiling water and let stand 10 minutes. Drain and set aside. Heat oil in a large skillet or heavy pot, add almonds, and sauté over medium heat until lightly browned, about 2 minutes. Remove from skillet and reserve. Add onion and meatless sausage to skillet and sauté over medium-low heat about 5 minutes, until onion softens and sausage browns. Add rice and sauté until grains are translucent, about 1 minute. Stir in apricots, raisins, cinnamon, salt, pepper, and hot stock. Bring to a boil. Do not stir rice. Cover pan tightly. Cook on top of stove over very low heat for 20 minutes. Add reserved almonds. Fluff rice with a fork before serving.

4 SERVINGS

Calories 461.7 • Protein 13.16 gm • Fat 17.12 gm • Percentage of calories from fat 32% • Cholesterol 0 mg • Dietary fiber 4.559 gm • Sodium 652.2 mg • Calcium 109.2 mg

Low Country Pilaf

I created this satisfying dish while working as a chef in the "low country" of Charleston, South Carolina.

2 tablespoons olive oil
½ pound tempeh bacon, finely diced
1 large Vidalia onion, finely chopped
2 cups brown rice
4 cups Basic Vegetable Stock (see page 10)
3 medium tomatoes, peeled (see page 375), seeded and finely chopped

2 teaspoons fresh lemon juice
2 teaspoons Worcestershire sauce
¾ teaspoon salt
¼ teaspoon freshly ground black pepper
¼ teaspoon cayenne
2 cups cooked black-eyed peas
¼ cup minced fresh parsley

Preheat oven to 350 degrees. Heat oil in a large skillet over medium-high heat. Add tempeh bacon and onion and cook until browned, about 5 minutes, then transfer to a large casserole dish. Add the rice to the casserole dish and stir to coat with the oil. In a saucepan, bring stock to a boil and pour over rice in casserole. Add tomatoes, lemon juice, Worcestershire sauce, salt, black pepper, and cayenne. Cover tightly and transfer the casserole to the oven. Bake for 45 minutes. Remove from oven and stir in black-eyed peas and parsley. Adjust seasonings and serve immediately.

A quick stove-top version can be made by using cooked rice. Eliminate the stock, add the cooked rice to the skillet after cooking the onions, and proceed by adding remaining ingredients.

6 SERVINGS

Calories 494.6 • Protein 15.1 gm • Fat 18.25 gm • Percentage of calories from fat 32% • Cholesterol 0 mg • Dietary fiber 11 gm • Sodium 947.6 mg • Calcium 67.75 mg

Barley and Mushroom Pilaf

2 tablespoons corn oil
1½ cups barley
1 medium yellow onion, minced
4 ounces seitan (see page 11),
  finely chopped

4 ounces mushrooms, sliced
2½ cups Basic Vegetable Stock
  (see page 10)

Preheat the oven to 350 degrees. Heat the oil in a large skillet over medium heat. Add the barley and sauté until golden and toasted, 6 to 8 minutes. Add onion and seitan and cook until onion is soft and seitan browns, about 5 minutes. Stir in the mushrooms, cook 1 minute. Transfer to 2-quart baking dish and pour in stock. Cover and bake until all the liquid is absorbed, about 1 hour.

4 TO 6 SERVINGS

Calories 354 • Protein 11.79 gm • Fat 7.308 gm • Percentage of calories from fat 18% • Cholesterol 0 mg • Dietary fiber 12.26 gm • Sodium 196.2 mg • Calcium 47.68 mg

Bulgur Pilaf with Adzuki Beans, Pine Nuts, and Raisins

Bulgur is a hearty grain, making this pilaf a warming choice after a busy day of winter activities. The orange zest and raisins add a pleasing sweetness.

2 tablespoons pine nuts
½ cup finely chopped onion
2 tablespoons corn oil
1 cup bulgur
1 teaspoon freshly grated orange zest
¼ cup golden raisins
2 cups Basic Vegetable Stock (see page 10)

¼ teaspoon salt
⅛ teaspoon freshly ground black pepper
¼ cup cooked adzuki beans
¼ cup minced scallions
¼ cup minced fresh parsley

Lightly toast the pine nuts in a small skillet over medium-low heat, for 5 minutes, shaking the pan several times. Set the pine nuts aside. In a small saucepan cook the onion in the oil over medium-low heat, stirring, for 5 minutes. Stir in the bulgur and orange zest and cook, stirring, for 2 minutes. Add the raisins, stock, salt, and pepper, bring the liquid to a boil, and cook, covered, over low heat for 15 minutes, or until the liquid is absorbed. Fluff the pilaf with a fork and stir in the adzuki beans, scallions, pine nuts, and parsley.

4 SERVINGS

Calories 285.8 • Protein 8.12 gm • Fat 10.04 gm • Percentage of calories from fat 29% • Cholesterol 0 mg • Dietary fiber 10.68 gm • Sodium 271.7 mg • Calcium 49.85 mg

Spiced Couscous with Tempeh

¼ cup unsalted cashews
¼ cup corn oil
4 ounces poached tempeh (see page 12), chopped fine
¼ teaspoon ground cinnamon
¼ teaspoon ground cardamom
⅛ teaspoon ground allspice
2¼ cups Basic Vegetable Stock (see page 10)
½ cup golden raisins
1 cup couscous
½ teaspoon salt

Preheat the oven to 325 degrees. Spread the cashews in a baking pan and toast, stirring once, until lightly browned, about 5 minutes. Let cool.

Heat oil in medium saucepan over low heat. Add tempeh and cook until browned, about 5 minutes. Add cinnamon, cardamom, and allspice and cook 2 minutes, stirring occasionally, to release the flavor of the spices. Add stock and raisins, bring to a boil, and stir in couscous. Cover and remove from heat; let stand 5 minutes. Fluff with fork, season with salt, add cashews, and stir gently. Transfer couscous to a bowl and serve immediately.

4 SERVINGS

Calories 469.3 • Protein 13.19 gm • Fat 20.23 gm • Percentage of calories from fat 38% • Cholesterol 0 mg • Dietary fiber 10.16 gm • Sodium 420 mg • Calcium 62.26 mg

Tofu and Artichoke Gratin

The artichokes add flavor and elegance to this simple gratin. Add hot rolls and a crisp green salad, and dinner is served.

¼ cup corn oil
½ cup minced scallions
¼ cup all-purpose flour
2 tablespoons minced fresh
  parsley
2 garlic cloves, minced
½ cup Basic Vegetable Stock (see
  page 10)
2 cans artichoke hearts, drained
  and chopped
1 pound firm tofu, cut into ½-inch
  dice

2 tablespoons fresh lemon juice
2 tablespoons Worcestershire
  sauce
¼ teaspoon Tabasco
½ teaspoon salt
⅛ teaspoon freshly ground black
  pepper
2 tablespoons grated Pecorino
  Romano cheese
½ cup bread crumbs

Water Chestnuts.
Sliced cooked carrots.

Preheat the oven to 375 degrees. Heat oil in a large skillet and cook the scallions over medium heat, stirring, for 1 minute. Stir in the flour and cook the roux over medium-low heat, stirring, for 2 minutes. Add the parsley and garlic and cook, stirring, for 1 minute. Add the stock and bring to a boil; then cook the mixture, stirring, for 3 minutes. Stir in the artichoke hearts, tofu, lemon juice, Worcestershire sauce, Tabasco, salt, and pepper. Cook over low heat for 5 minutes, then spoon into a large gratin dish. Sprinkle with the cheese and bread crumbs and bake for 20 minutes, or until hot and lightly browned on top.

6 SERVINGS

Calories 228.8 • Protein 8.936 gm • Fat 14.51 gm • Percentage of calories from fat 54% • Cholesterol 2.127 mg • Dietary fiber 1.882 gm • Sodium 507.6 mg • Calcium 89.31 mg

Indian-Style Rice and Split Pea Pilaf

¼ cup corn oil
1 medium onion, chopped
1 clove garlic, finely minced
1½ cups basmati rice, rinsed and
  drained
2 cups Basic Vegetable Stock (see
  page 10)

½ cup dried green split peas,
  soaked 3 hours
3 tablespoons fresh lemon juice
½ teaspoon ground cinnamon
Salt and freshly ground black
  pepper

Heat oil in a large saucepan and cook the onion over medium-low heat, stirring, for 5 minutes. Add the garlic and rice and cook, stirring, until the rice is coated with the oil. Stir in the stock, split peas, lemon juice, cinnamon, and salt and pepper to taste. Bring the liquid to a boil, reduce heat, and simmer, covered, over low heat for 25 minutes, or until the rice and peas are tender. Let the pilaf stand, covered, for 5 minutes, and fluff with a fork before serving.

6 SERVINGS

Calories 298.2 • Protein 5.528 gm • Fat 9.573 gm • Percentage of calories from fat 29% • Cholesterol 0 mg • Dietary fiber 2.419 gm • Sodium 89.26 mg • Calcium 33.57 mg

Rice and Lentil Pilaf

3 tablespoons olive oil
1 large bunch spinach, washed and
  chopped
1 clove garlic, minced
1 cup cooked lentils
2 cups cooked brown rice

1 tablespoon minced fresh parsley
¼ teaspoon ground coriander
¼ teaspoon ground cumin
¼ teaspoon salt
⅛ teaspoon freshly ground black
  pepper

Heat 2 tablespoons of the oil in a large skillet over medium-high heat. Add the spinach and garlic and cook until spinach is wilted, about 5 minutes.

Add lentils, rice, parsley, coriander, cumin, salt, and pepper and stir until just heated through; do not overcook.

4 SERVINGS

Calories 266.8 • Protein 8.317 gm • Fat 11.4 gm • Percentage of calories from fat 38% • Cholesterol 0 mg • Dietary fiber 5.287 gm • Sodium 172.9 mg • Calcium 66.67 mg

Radicchio and Tofu Pilaf

3 tablespoons olive oil
1 large clove garlic, crushed
1 medium onion, chopped
1 pound radicchio, cored and chopped
Salt and freshly ground black pepper

2 cups Arborio rice
5 cups Basic Vegetable Stock (see page 10)
8 ounces firm tofu, cut into ¼-inch dice
¾ cup grated Parmesan cheese

Heat oil in a large skillet over medium heat. Add garlic and stir until golden, then discard it. Add onions and cook over medium heat until golden, stirring frequently, about 5 minutes. Add all but 1 cup chopped radicchio and stir until wilted, about 1 minute. Season with salt and pepper. Add rice and stir 2 minutes. Mix in stock. Bring to a boil over medium-high heat. Reduce heat to low, cover, and simmer until rice is tender and all liquid is absorbed, about 20 minutes. Add remaining 1 cup radicchio and the tofu and cook for 5 minutes or until heated through. Stir in the cheese. Taste and adjust seasonings.

6 SERVINGS

Calories 448.4 • Protein 15.31 gm • Fat 12.03 gm • Percentage of calories from fat 24% • Cholesterol 9.875 mg • Dietary fiber 1.914 gm • Sodium 486.3 mg • Calcium 232.2 mg

Tofu and Potato Gratin

Serve a bright green vegetable such as steamed green beans or broccoli with this satisfying gratin.

4 cups Basic Vegetable Stock (see page 10)
1 large clove garlic, halved
5 tablespoons olive oil (approximately)
1 pound firm tofu, cut into ¼-inch slices

3 pounds baking potatoes, peeled and cut into ¼-inch crosswise slices
½ cup chopped fresh basil
Salt and freshly ground black pepper
½ cup shredded Jarlsberg cheese

Preheat oven to 400 degrees. Boil stock in a small saucepan until reduced to 2 cups. Rub bottom and sides of a large gratin dish with garlic. Brush with 1 tablespoon of the oil. Arrange a layer of slightly overlapping tofu and potatoes in the prepared dish. Sprinkle with some basil, salt, pepper, and 2 teaspoons of the oil. Continue layering, topping last layer of potatoes with salt, pepper, and oil. Pour stock over gratin. Bake uncovered until potatoes are easily pierced with knife, about 1 hour, basting potatoes and tofu with stock every 10 minutes. Sprinkle with cheese and bake until melted, about 5 minutes.

6 SERVINGS

Calories 377.8 • Protein 15.46 gm • Fat 15.95 gm • Percentage of calories from fat 37% • Cholesterol 8.651 mg • Dietary fiber 5.247 gm • Sodium 249.6 mg • Calcium 162.6 mg

Tempeh and Spinach Gratin

3 tablespoons corn oil
1 pound poached tempeh (see
  page 12), cut in ¼-inch slices
1 medium onion, minced
2 10-ounce packages frozen
  spinach, cooked, drained, and
  squeezed dry
1 teaspoon minced fresh tarragon
  or ½ teaspoon dried
½ teaspoon salt

⅛ teaspoon freshly ground black
  pepper
1 cup milk
2 tablespoons Dijon mustard
¼ cup dry white wine
2 tablespoons minced fresh
  parsley
¼ cup fresh bread crumbs
¼ cup grated Pecorino Romano
  cheese

Preheat the oven to 350 degrees. Heat 2 tablespoons of the oil in a large skillet over medium heat. Add tempeh and sauté for 5 minutes, or until golden brown on both sides. Remove from pan and reserve. Heat the remaining 1 tablespoon oil in the same skillet over medium heat, add the onion, and cook until translucent, about 5 minutes. Add the spinach, tarragon, salt, and pepper and cook the mixture, stirring occasionally, for 5 minutes, or until dry. Add the milk and reduce it over moderately high heat, stirring occasionally, for 3 to 5 minutes, or until the mixture is thick. Spoon the mixture into a large oiled gratin dish. Arrange the tempeh slices over the spinach mixture. Combine the mustard, wine, and parsley and spread this mixture on tempeh slices. Sprinkle gratin with the bread crumbs and cheese. Bake for 30 minutes, or until the top is golden.

This gratin can be assembled in advance and refrigerated. Bring to room temperature before baking.

4 SERVINGS

Calories 427.3 • Protein 28.37 gm • Fat 22.76 gm • Percentage of calories from fat 47% • Cholesterol 10.65 mg • Dietary fiber 7.21 gm • Sodium 749.1 mg • Calcium 458.3 mg

Ratatouille Gratin

This recipe transforms the classic French vegetable melange into a satisfying dinner entrée. Serve with lots of crusty French bread.

1 large eggplant, stemmed, peeled, and cut crosswise into ¼-inch slices
Salt
6 tablespoons olive oil
1 large onion, thinly sliced
1 medium zucchini, cut into ¼-inch slices
1 green bell pepper, chopped
½ teaspoon minced fresh thyme or ¼ teaspoon dried

1 teaspoon minced fresh basil or ½ teaspoon dried
½ teaspoon salt
⅛ teaspoon freshly ground black pepper
¾ pound tomatoes, peeled (see page 375), seeded, and chopped
1 pound firm tofu, cut into ¼-inch thick slices
1 cup shredded mozzarella cheese

Sprinkle both sides of eggplant lightly with salt. Place in colander and top with a plate weighted down by a heavy can. Let eggplant drain 1 hour, turning slices after 30 minutes. Pat dry. Heat 1 tablespoon of the oil in a medium skillet over low heat. Add onion, zucchini, bell pepper, thyme, basil, salt, and pepper. Cook for 5 minutes, stirring frequently, until vegetables begin to soften. Add tomatoes and cook 5 minutes longer. Set aside.

Heat 1 tablespoon of the oil in a large skillet over medium-high heat, add tofu slices, and cook 5 minutes, or until golden brown on both sides. Remove from skillet with slotted spatula and set aside.

Heat 2 more tablespoons of the olive oil in large skillet over medium heat. Add eggplant slices in batches and cook until just tender, about 2 minutes on each side, adding oil to skillet before cooking each batch. Transfer to a large plate.

In an oiled gratin dish, alternately layer the prepared eggplant, tofu, and vegetable mixture. Top with cheese. Bake 15 to 20 minutes or until cheese is melted.

The eggplant and vegetable mixture may be prepared in advance and refrigerated. Bring to room temperature while you cook the tofu slices, and then assemble.

4 TO 6 SERVINGS

Calories 383.2 • Protein 21.99 gm • Fat 26.89 gm • Percentage of calories from fat 62% • Cholesterol 30.2 mg • Dietary fiber 2.024 gm • Sodium 1803 mg • Calcium 410.3 mg

Tofu Gratin with Rosemary and New Potatoes

3 tablespoons olive oil
8 to 10 new red potatoes (about 2 pounds), cut into ½-inch slices
1 pound soft tofu, cut into ¼-inch slices
1 tablespoon minced fresh rosemary or 1 teaspoon dried

2 cloves garlic, minced
Salt and freshly ground black pepper
1½ cups Basic Vegetable Stock (see page 10)

Preheat the oven to 375 degrees. Oil a large gratin dish with 1 tablespoon of the olive oil. Spread half the potatoes and half the tofu on the bottom of prepared dish, overlapping them as necessary. Sprinkle with half the rosemary and half the garlic. Season with salt and pepper and drizzle with 1 tablespoon of the oil. Make another layer using the remaining half of the potatoes and tofu and sprinkle with remaining rosemary and garlic. Season with salt and pepper and drizzle with remaining 1 tablespoon of the oil. Pour stock over all. Bake for about 1 hour and 20 minutes, or until potatoes are tender, the top layer is lightly browned, and the liquid is absorbed. Serve directly from the gratin dish.

6 SERVINGS

Calories 228.8 • Protein 10.24 gm • Fat 8.684 gm • Percentage of calories from fat 33% • Cholesterol 0 mg • Dietary fiber 3.18 gm • Sodium 116.7 mg • Calcium 52.49 mg

Tofu and Cabbage Gratin

This gratin may be assembled ahead of time and refrigerated overnight. Bring to room temperature before baking.

12 ounces green cabbage, cored and finely chopped
1¼ cups milk
¼ teaspoon ground nutmeg
½ teaspoon salt
⅛ teaspoon freshly ground black pepper

2 tablespoons corn oil
1 pound firm tofu, cut into ¼-inch slices
½ pound mushrooms, thinly sliced
2 tablespoons grated Pecorino Romano cheese

Preheat the oven to 400 degrees. In a pot of salted water, boil the cabbage for 5 minutes. Drain it in a colander, squeezing out the excess liquid. In a large saucepan combine the cabbage with 1 cup of the milk and simmer, uncovered, for 10 minutes, stirring, until the milk is absorbed. Stir in the nutmeg, salt, and pepper, and set aside.

Heat oil in a large skillet and sauté the tofu slices 2 minutes on each side. Remove tofu with spatula and reserve. Reheat skillet and sauté the mushrooms over moderately high heat, stirring, for 4 minutes. Add the remaining ¼ cup milk, and simmer, stirring, for 3 minutes, or until the milk is absorbed; add salt and pepper to taste.

Spoon the mushroom mixture into an oiled gratin dish and layer the tofu slices over it. Spoon the cabbage on top of the tofu. Sprinkle with the Romano cheese and bake for 10 minutes, or until heated through. Place the gratin under a preheated broiler about 5 inches from the heat for 1 to 2 minutes, or until cheese is golden.

4 SERVINGS

Calories 214.1 • Protein 14.89 gm • Fat 11.99 gm • Percentage of calories from fat 48% • Cholesterol 8.816 mg • Dietary fiber 2.199 gm • Sodium 432 mg • Calcium 213 mg

Broccoli and Tofu Gratin

1 pound broccoli, cooked until just tender

4 tablespoons corn or safflower oil

½ pound firm tofu, cut into ¼-inch slices

2 tablespoons all-purpose flour

2 cups hot milk

½ cup freshly grated Parmesan cheese

½ cup grated Swiss cheese

Salt and freshly ground black pepper

1 cup dry bread crumbs

Preheat the oven to 375 degrees. Coarsely chop the broccoli and set aside. In a large skillet, heat 1 tablespoon of the oil over medium-high heat, add tofu slices, and cook until golden on each side, about 5 minutes. Remove tofu with slotted spatula to a plate and set aside. Add 2 more tablespoons of the oil to the skillet and heat over medium-low heat, add the flour, and cook the roux, stirring, for 3 minutes. Add the milk, in a stream, whisking. Bring the sauce to a boil, whisking, and simmer, stirring, for 5 minutes. Stir in the Parmesan and Swiss cheeses, add the salt and pepper to taste, and cook the sauce briefly. In a large, well-oiled gratin dish layer the tofu and broccoli and pour the sauce over all. Sprinkle the bread crumbs over the top, drizzle with the remaining 1 tablespoon of oil, and bake for 30 minutes.

This gratin can be prepared ahead of time and refrigerated. Bring to room temperature then reheat in a warm oven.

6 SERVINGS

Calories 318.7 • Protein 16.67 gm • Fat 17.8 gm • Percentage of calories from fat 49% • Cholesterol 21.23 mg • Dietary fiber 2.567 gm • Sodium 420.1 mg • Calcium 395.6 mg

Seitan and Yam Gratin

What could be better than the exotic flavors of a curry combined with the ease and simplicity of a do-ahead casserole? And you should prepare this ahead of time, to give the flavors time to mingle. Bring the refrigerated gratin back to room temperature before baking.

3 tablespoons olive oil
1 cup chopped onions
1 clove garlic, minced
1 tablespoon curry powder
1 pound ground seitan (see page 8)
⅔ cup Basic Vegetable Stock (see page 10)
⅓ cup raisins

½ teaspoon ground allspice
1 teaspoon ground cinnamon
1 tablespoon tomato paste
Salt and freshly ground black pepper
1 teaspoon grated orange zest
2 pounds cooked yams, peeled

Preheat the oven to 400 degrees. Heat 2 tablespoons of the oil in a large skillet over medium heat, and cook the onions and the garlic, stirring, for 5 minutes. Stir in the curry powder and cook the mixture, stirring, for 1 minute. Add seitan and cook over moderate heat for 5 minutes. Add stock, raisins, allspice, cinnamon, tomato paste, and salt and pepper to taste and simmer mixture for 15 minutes, or until most of the liquid is evaporated. Transfer seitan mixture to a 2-quart gratin dish and stir in orange zest. Slice cooked yams into ½-inch slices. Layer on top of seitan mixture. Drizzle with the remaining 1 tablespoon oil, and bake for 20 minutes or until heated through.

6 SERVINGS

Calories 488.3 • Protein 14.53 gm • Fat 8.417 gm • Percentage of calories from fat 15% • Cholesterol 0 mg • Dietary fiber 14.11 gm • Sodium 247.6 mg • Calcium 93.12 mg

Risotto with Butternut Squash and Pine Nuts

2 tablespoons olive oil
2 cups grated butternut squash
½ cup finely chopped red bell pepper
3 cloves garlic, minced
1½ cups Arborio rice
½ cup dry white wine
5 cups hot Basic Vegetable Stock (see page 10)

Salt and freshly ground black pepper
¼ cup pine nuts
⅓ cup firmly packed fresh basil leaves, chopped
⅓ cup finely grated Parmesan cheese
1 tablespoon lemon juice

Heat olive oil in a large, heavy pot over medium heat (enameled cast-iron is best). Sauté squash, bell pepper, and garlic for 5 minutes, then add rice and stir to coat with oil. Add the wine and stir gently until liquid is absorbed. Add stock ½ cup at a time, stirring constantly. When the liquid is absorbed and the rice is tender, 20 to 30 minutes, add salt and freshly ground black pepper to taste. Toast pine nuts in a medium skillet over medium heat, shaking pan frequently, until lightly browned, about 5 minutes. Add to the rice along with the basil, Parmesan, and lemon juice. Adjust seasonings. Serve immediately.

8 SERVINGS

Calories 315 • Protein 8.104 gm • Fat 7.681 gm • Percentage of calories from fat 21% • Cholesterol 3.259 mg • Dietary fiber 2.929 gm • Sodium 273.7 mg • Calcium 118.7 mg

Tempeh Risotto with Red, Yellow, and Green Bell Peppers

Tri-colored peppers add flavor as well as color to this creamy risotto.

4 tablespoons olive oil
1 small red bell pepper, cut into
  ¼-inch squares
1 small yellow bell pepper, cut into
  ¼-inch squares
1 small green bell pepper, cut into
  ¼-inch squares
4 ounces poached tempeh (see
  page 12), chopped

5 cups Basic Vegetable Stock (see
  page 10)
1 small onion, minced
1½ cups Arborio rice
⅓ cup dry white wine
⅔ cup grated Pecorino Romano
  cheese
Salt and freshly ground black
  pepper

Heat 2 tablespoons of the oil in a large skillet over moderate heat and cook the bell peppers, stirring, until they are softened but still firm. Remove from skillet with a slotted spoon and reserve. Add tempeh to skillet and cook over moderate heat for 5 minutes or until browned. Set aside. In a saucepan bring the stock to a simmer. In a large, heavy saucepan heat the remaining 2 tablespoons of the oil over medium heat and cook the onion, until softened. Add the rice and stir to coat with oil. Add the wine and stir until the liquid is absorbed. Add the stock ½ cup at a time, stirring until liquid is absorbed before adding more stock. Simmer, stirring, until desired consistency is reached. Add the cheese, reserved peppers, and tempeh to rice and mix gently until heated through. Season with salt and pepper to taste and serve immediately.

4 SERVINGS

Calories 612.7 • Protein 18.51 gm • Fat 21.65 gm • Percentage of calories from fat 32% • Cholesterol 19.9 mg • Dietary fiber 4.624 gm • Sodium 558.6 mg • Calcium 278.2 mg

Risotto with Adzuki Beans and Butternut Squash

1 tablespoon corn or safflower oil
¼ cup finely chopped onion
1 cup diced butternut squash
3½ cups hot Basic Vegetable Stock
  (see page 10)
1 cup Arborio rice
1 cup cooked adzuki beans

Salt and freshly ground black
  pepper
Pinch ground nutmeg
3 tablespoons freshly grated
  Parmesan cheese plus additional
  grated cheese (optional)

Heat oil in a medium saucepan over medium heat. Add onion and cook until translucent, about 5 to 8 minutes. Stir in squash. Add just enough hot stock to cover. Cook, stirring occasionally, 10 minutes. Stir in rice and just enough additional stock to cover and continue cooking, uncovered, stirring occasionally, until liquid evaporates. Add remaining stock a little at a time, stirring, until rice is tender but still al dente, about 20 minutes. Add adzuki beans. Season to taste with salt, pepper, and nutmeg. Stir in cheese. Transfer to serving dish. Pass additional cheese separately, if desired.

4 SERVINGS

Calories 354.8 • Protein 11.07 gm • Fat 5.307 gm • Percentage of calories from fat 13% • Cholesterol 3.703 mg • Dietary fiber 5.512 gm • Sodium 285 mg • Calcium 114.9 mg

Risotto Marsala

5 cups Basic Vegetable Stock (see
  page 10)
Pinch saffron threads, crumbled
3 tablespoons olive oil
1/3 cup minced onion
2 tablespoons minced tempeh
  bacon

1½ cups Arborio rice
¼ cup dry Marsala wine
¼ cup freshly grated Parmesan
  cheese
½ teaspoon salt
¼ teaspoon freshly ground black
  pepper

In a medium saucepan, bring the stock and saffron to a simmer, and keep at a simmer over moderately low heat. In a large saucepan, heat the oil over medium heat, add the onion and tempeh bacon, and cook about 5 minutes. Add the rice and stir for 1 minute, until well coated with oil and slightly translucent. Add the Marsala and cook, stirring, until it evaporates. Add ½ cup of the simmering stock and cook, stirring constantly, until the rice has absorbed most of the liquid. Gradually add the stock, ½ cup at a time, and cook, stirring constantly, until rice is almost tender, about 25 minutes. Continue to cook, stirring and adding stock as necessary, until the rice is tender, about 5 minutes longer. Add the cheese and season with salt and pepper. Serve immediately.

4 TO 6 SERVINGS

Calories 380 • Protein 8.071 gm • Fat 11.18 gm • Percent of calories from fat 26% • Cholesterol 3.95 mg • Dietary fiber 1.916 gm • Sodium 615.6 mg • Calcium 102.5 mg

Tempeh-Apple Risotto

For a non-alcoholic version, apple cider may be substituted for the Calvados; although when you use spirits in cooking, the alcohol generally evaporates, leaving the flavor behind.

3 tablespoons corn oil
4 ounces poached tempeh (see page 12), crumbled
5 cups Basic Vegetable Stock (see page 10)
1 medium onion, chopped
1 Granny Smith apple, peeled and cut into ½-inch dice

1½ cups Arborio rice
2 tablespoons Calvados or applejack
⅓ cup freshly grated Parmesan cheese
¼ teaspoon salt
½ teaspoon freshly ground black pepper

Heat 1 tablespoon of the oil in a skillet over medium-high heat. Add the crumbled tempeh and cook until browned, about 5 minutes, then remove and reserve. In a medium saucepan, bring the stock to a simmer, and keep it simmering over moderately low heat. Heat the remaining 2 tablespoons of oil in a large saucepan over medium-high heat. Add the onions and cook until translucent, about 5 minutes. Add the apple and cook 2 minutes longer. Add the rice and cook 1 minute, until coated with the oil and slightly translucent. Add the Calvados, cooking for 3 minutes. Add ½ cup of the hot stock and cook, stirring constantly, until the rice has absorbed most of the liquid. Maintain a simmer, adjusting heat if necessary. Gradually add more stock, ½ cup at a time, stirring constantly, until the rice is almost tender but still al dente, 20 to 25 minutes. Continue to cook, stirring and adding remaining stock as necessary, ¼ cup at a time, until the rice has a creamy texture, about 5 minutes longer. Add reserved tempeh to the rice mixture. Add the cheese and season with the salt and pepper. Serve immediately.

4 TO 6 SERVINGS

Calories 441.7 • Protein 12.25 gm • Fat 12.48 gm • Percentage of calories from fat 26% • Cholesterol 5.214 mg • Dietary fiber 3.38 gm • Sodium 488.1 mg • Calcium 144.7 mg

Risotto with Asparagus and Pine Nuts

½ cup pine nuts
1 pound asparagus, trimmed
4 cups Basic Vegetable Stock (see page 10)
1 cup dry white wine
3 tablespoons olive oil
1 medium onion, finely chopped
1½ cups Arborio rice
½ cup grated Parmesan cheese
½ teaspoon salt
⅛ teaspoon freshly ground black pepper

Toast pine nuts in a medium skillet over medium heat, shaking pan frequently, until lightly browned, about 5 minutes. Remove from heat and reserve. Pare asparagus stalks up to tips with vegetable parer. Cut stalks into diagonal ½-inch pieces; leave tips whole. Reserve. Heat the stock and the wine in a medium saucepan over low heat to simmering.

Meanwhile, heat oil in second medium saucepan over medium heat. Add onion and sauté, stirring frequently, until lightly browned, about 5 minutes. Add rice and stir until coated with oil. Add just enough of the hot stock-wine mixture to cover rice. Simmer uncovered, stirring frequently, until liquid is almost absorbed. Gradually add remaining liquid, ½ cup at a time, until rice is tender but firm and mixture is thick and creamy, about 25 minutes. About 10 minutes before rice is finished, stir in asparagus. When rice is finished, remove from heat; stir in pine nuts and cheese. Season with salt and pepper and serve immediately.

4 SERVINGS

Calories 647.4 • Protein 19.92 gm • Fat 25.32 gm • Percentage of calories from fat 34% • Cholesterol 9.875 mg • Dietary fiber 3.854 gm • Sodium 774.4 mg • Calcium 237 mg

5
Stir-Fries

The original "fast food," stir-fries are literally ready in minutes, especially when the cutting and chopping are done in advance. Treat your taste buds to Stir-Fry of Tempeh and Peanuts with Lemon Grass or Seitan and Fennel Stir-Fry with Sun-Dried Tomatoes. Many varieties of vegetables and high-protein, no-cholesterol meat alternatives make these stir-fries healthy yet satisfying meals that are quick and delicious.

Spicy Ginger Tempeh

3 tablespoons dry sherry

2 tablespoons cornstarch

⅔ cup Basic Vegetable Stock (see page 10)

1 pound poached tempeh (see page 12), cut into ½-inch dice

2 tablespoons canola or safflower oil

1 carrot, cut diagonally in ¼-inch slices

1 clove garlic, minced

2 teaspoons minced fresh ginger

¼ teaspoon hot red pepper flakes

¼ pound snow peas, trimmed and cut diagonally in ½-inch slices

3 tablespoons minced scallions

2 tablespoons low-sodium tamari

½ cup cashews

Combine 1 tablespoon each of the sherry, cornstarch, and stock in a shallow bowl. Add tempeh, coating thoroughly, and refrigerate at least 1 hour.

Dissolve the remaining tablespoon cornstarch in 2 tablespoons of the stock and set aside. Heat oil in a wok or large skillet over high heat and add carrot slices. Stir in the garlic, ginger, and red pepper flakes. Add tempeh, adding more oil if necessary, and stir-fry about 2 minutes. Add the snow peas and scallions and stir-fry about 30 seconds. Stir in the tamari, reserved cornstarch mixture, remaining 2 tablespoons sherry, and remaining stock and cook until liquid thickens. Sprinkle with cashews.

4 SERVINGS

Calories 399.7 • Protein 22.92 gm • Fat 23.42 gm • Percentage of calories from fat 52% • Cholesterol 0 mg • Dietary fiber 6.233 gm • Sodium 402.1 mg • Calcium 114.8 mg

Summer Garden Stir-Fry

Potatoes are a welcome surprise in this hearty Summer stir-fry.

1 large carrot, cut into matchstick julienne

3 small new red potatoes, halved, cut into ¼-inch slices

1 tablespoon cornstarch

3 tablespoons low-sodium tamari

2 tablespoons Basic Vegetable Stock (see page 10)

3 tablespoons corn oil

1 red bell pepper, seeded, cut into ½-inch squares

1 yellow bell pepper, seeded, cut into ½-inch squares

1 zucchini, cut into ¼-inch diagonal slices

½ pound seitan (see page 11), cut into ½-inch strips

1 large clove garlic, minced

2 minced scallions

2 teaspoons minced fresh ginger

Steam julienned carrot over boiling water about 2 minutes. Add potatoes to steamer, and cook another 2 minutes. Drain, rinse with cold water. Combine cornstarch with tamari and stock and set aside. Heat 2 tablespoons of the oil in a wok or large skillet over high heat. Add carrot and potatoes. Reduce heat to medium-high and add peppers and zucchini and stir-fry until beginning to soften, about 1 minute. Transfer to plate with slotted spoon. Return wok to medium-high heat and add remaining 1 tablespoon oil. Add seitan, garlic, scallions, and ginger and stir-fry until seitan browns, about 30 seconds. Stir cornstarch mixture and add to wok. Return the vegetables to the wok. Bring to simmer, stirring constantly, about 30 seconds.

4 SERVINGS

Calories 392 • Protein 12.53 gm • Fat 14.91 gm • Percentage of calories from fat 33% • Cholesterol 0 mg • Dietary fiber 8.01 gm • Sodium 623.9 mg • Calcium 52.36 mg

Hoisin Tempeh with Cashews

Hoisin sauce is a flavorful condiment that adds an exotic sweetness to any stir-fry. It can be found in Asian food stores or the gourmet section of most supermarkets.

6 tablespoons hoisin sauce
2 tablespoons low-sodium tamari
2 tablespoons Basic Vegetable
  Stock (see page 10) or water
1 tablespoon sake or white wine
3 tablespoons corn or safflower oil
1 pound poached tempeh (see
  page 12), cut into ¼-inch cubes

2 cups broccoli florets
1 tablespoon minced fresh ginger
1½ tablespoons minced scallions
¼ teaspoon hot red pepper flakes
½ cup unsalted cashews
Freshly cooked rice

Mix hoisin, tamari, stock or water, and sake in a small bowl and set aside. Heat 2 tablespoons of the oil in a wok or large skillet over high heat. Add tempeh and stir-fry quickly to brown on all sides. Remove immediately with slotted spoon. Reheat wok or skillet over medium-high heat with remaining 1 tablespoon oil. Add broccoli, ginger, scallions, and red pepper flakes and stir about 10 seconds, lowering heat to medium. Add hoisin mixture and simmer, stirring. Add tempeh and stir until heated through, 10 to 15 seconds. Garnish with cashews and serve over rice.

4 SERVINGS

Calories 531.2 • Protein 27.97 gm • Fat 35.46 gm • Percentage of calories from fat 60% • Cholesterol 0 mg • Dietary fiber 7.293 gm • Sodium 346.3 mg • Calcium 121.9 mg

Seitan and Fennel Stir-Fry with Sun-Dried Tomatoes

The stir-fry is an intriguing way to prepare these Mediterranean ingredients; one taste will convince you.

1 pound seitan (see page 11), cut into ½-inch strips
1 teaspoon tomato paste
1 teaspoon sugar or a natural sweetener
¾ teaspoon salt
2 tablespoons olive oil
2 tablespoons corn oil
1 tablespoon minced fresh parsley
1 tablespoon minced onion

2 medium cloves garlic, minced
¼ teaspoon hot red pepper flakes
1 fennel bulb, thinly sliced and cut into ¼-inch strips
1 cup chopped arugula
1 tablespoon drained, minced sun-dried tomatoes packed in olive oil
⅛ teaspoon freshly ground black pepper

In a medium bowl, combine the seitan with the tomato paste, sugar, ½ teaspoon salt, and olive oil; toss to mix well. Cover and refrigerate at least 1 hour. In a wok or large skillet, heat 1 tablespoon of the corn oil, add the seitan and its marinade, and stir-fry until seitan starts to brown, about 2 minutes. Remove with slotted spoon and set aside. In the same pan, heat the remaining 1 tablespoon of corn oil over medium-high heat. Add the parsley, onion, garlic, and red pepper flakes. Cook, stirring, about 10 seconds. Add the fennel, sprinkle with the remaining ¼ teaspoon salt, and toss until crisp-tender, about 2 minutes. Return seitan to the wok and stir-fry until heated through, about 30 seconds. Add the arugula, sun-dried tomatoes, and black pepper and stir-fry to blend the flavors, about 30 seconds, and serve.

4 TO 6 SERVINGS

Calories 384.1 • Protein 13.74 gm • Fat 12.58 gm • Percentage of calories from fat 28% • Cholesterol 0 mg • Dietary fiber 9.953 gm • Sodium 576.3 mg • Calcium 54.34 mg

Tofu Stir-Fry with Spinach and Red Peppers

Delicious over cooked pasta or rice. Either way, it's a quick and easy supper.

1 tablespoon mirin, white wine, or sherry
1 tablespoon cornstarch
1 teaspoon low-sodium tamari
1 pound firm tofu, cut into 1-inch cubes
2 tablespoons corn oil
1 tablespoon minced onion

1 clove garlic, minced
⅛ teaspoon hot red pepper flakes
1 large red bell pepper, cut into ¼-inch strips
½ teaspoon salt
1 cup chopped fresh spinach
1 teaspoon capers
Freshly ground black pepper

In a medium bowl, whisk together the mirin, cornstarch, and tamari. Add the tofu and combine well. Cover and refrigerate at least 1 hour. Heat corn oil in a wok or large skillet over high heat. Add the onion, garlic, and red pepper flakes all at once. Cook, stirring, about 10 seconds; do not let the garlic brown. Add the bell pepper strips to the wok. Sprinkle with the salt and stir-fry until crisp-tender, about 2 minutes. Add the tofu to the wok and toss over heat until warmed through, about 30 seconds. Add the spinach, capers, and black pepper, and toss another 30 seconds.

4 SERVINGS

Calories 152.2 • Protein 9.932 gm • Fat 9.341 gm • Percentage of calories from fat 54% • Cholesterol 0 mg • Dietary fiber 0.842 gm • Sodium 430.2 mg • Calcium 62.64 mg

Spicy Ginger-Seitan Stir-Fry

2 tablespoons corn oil
¼ cup thinly sliced onion
1 teaspoon minced garlic
1 teaspoon minced fresh ginger
4 ounces shiitake mushrooms,
  trimmed and sliced

2 cups chopped bok choy
½ teaspoon hot red pepper flakes
1 pound seitan (see page 11) cut
  into ½-inch strips
2 tablespoons low-sodium tamari
Freshly cooked rice

Heat oil in a large skillet over medium heat. Add onion, garlic, ginger, mushrooms, bok choy, and red pepper flakes and stir-fry for 2 minutes. Add seitan and tamari and stir-fry 3 minutes more. Serve immediately over rice.

4 TO 6 SERVINGS

Calories 348 • Protein 14.82 gm • Fat 7.026 gm • Percentage of calories from fat 17% • Cholesterol 0 mg • Dietary fiber 10.62 gm • Sodium 490.6 mg • Calcium 60.17 mg

Stir-Fry of Tempeh and Peanuts with Lemon Grass

The allspice and lemon grass mingle to create an aromatic stir-fry that is delicious over rice. Lemon grass is available in Asian food markets. If you can't find it, substitute 1 tablespoon grated lemon peel.

1 pound poached tempeh (see page 12), cut into ¼-inch slices
3 tablespoons minced fresh lemon grass
2 tablespoons safflower or canola oil
2 cloves garlic, mashed to a paste
2 teaspoons low-sodium tamari

1 teaspoon ground allspice
½ teaspoon arrowroot or cornstarch
1 large onion, chopped
½ teaspoon sugar or a natural sweetener
3 tablespoons chopped dry-roasted peanuts

In a bowl, combine tempeh with the lemon grass, 1 tablespoon of the oil, the garlic, 1 teaspoon of the tamari, the allspice, and arrowroot. In a medium skillet heat the remaining 1 tablespoon oil and the remaining 1 teaspoon tamari over high heat until hot. Add the onion and sauté for 5 minutes, or until golden brown. Transfer the onion with a slotted spoon to a plate. Add the tempeh mixture to the skillet, sprinkle with the sugar, and sauté for 1 to 2 minutes, or until just cooked. Transfer the mixture to a heated platter, top it with the onions, and sprinkle with the peanuts.

4 SERVINGS

Calories 306.4 • Protein 20.6 gm • Fat 18.89 gm • Percentage of calories from fat 54% • Cholesterol 0 mg • Dietary fiber 4.555 gm • Sodium 166.6 mg • Calcium 98.35 mg

Sesame Seitan and Broccoli

A meat-alternative variation on the popular Chinese restaurant dish Beef with Broccoli.

½ cup sesame seeds
2 tablespoons low-sodium tamari
2 tablespoons tomato paste
2 tablespoons mirin
1½ tablespoons toasted sesame oil
1½ tablespoons hoisin sauce
1 tablespoon sugar or a natural sweetener

1 tablespoon rice wine vinegar
2 tablespoons safflower or canola oil
1 pound seitan (see page 11), cut into ¼-inch slices
2 cups broccoli florets, blanched
2 scallions, minced

Toast the sesame seeds in a medium skillet over medium heat, stirring frequently for 5 minutes. Grind all but 1 tablespoon of the sesame seeds in a food processor, using short pulses. Place ground seeds in a bowl, add the tamari, tomato paste, mirin, sesame oil, hoisin sauce, sugar, and rice wine vinegar, plus the reserved tablespoon of sesame seeds. Combine well. Heat oil in a large skillet, add seitan, and stir-fry until browned, about 5 minutes. Add broccoli and scallions and stir-fry another minute. Add sauce, turning to coat seitan and broccoli.

6 SERVINGS

Calories 398.4 • Protein 14.62 gm • Fat 14.96 gm • Percentage of calories from fat 32% • Cholesterol 0 mg • Dietary fiber 11.6 gm • Sodium 416.1 mg • Calcium 162 mg

Spicy Seitan Stir-Fry

3 tablespoons safflower or canola oil
2 cloves garlic, minced
2 green serrano chili peppers, seeded and slivered
3 scallions, minced
1 teaspoon minced fresh ginger
1 pound seitan (see page 11), cut into 2- × ½-inch strips

1 tablespoon fresh lime juice
1 tablespoon low-sodium tamari
1 teaspoon sugar or a natural sweetener
Freshly cooked brown rice
1 tablespoon minced fresh cilantro

Heat oil in a wok or large skillet over medium-high heat. Add garlic and stir-fry until lightly golden, 1 to 2 minutes. Add chilies, scallions, and ginger and stir-fry 1 minute. Add seitan and stir-fry until just browned, about 1 minute. Add lime juice, tamari, and sugar; toss to mingle. Serve over rice and garnish with cilantro.

4 SERVINGS

Calories 443.8 • Protein 17.04 gm • Fat 12.05 gm • Percentage of calories from fat 23% • Cholesterol 0 mg • Dietary fiber 12.47 gm • Sodium 465.6 mg • Calcium 47.61 mg

Tofu with Garlic-Cilantro Sauce

The tofu absorbs the flavor of the pungent sauce, creating a dazzling taste sensation.

1 tablespoon minced fresh cilantro
1 clove garlic, minced
1 scallion, minced
¼ teaspoon hot red pepper flakes
2 tablespoons low-sodium tamari
2 tablespoons mirin, white wine, or sherry

1 teaspoon hoisin sauce
1 teaspoon toasted sesame oil
2 tablespoons safflower or canola oil
1 pound firm tofu, cut into ½-inch strips
Freshly cooked rice

Combine the cilantro, garlic, scallion, pepper flakes, tamari, mirin, hoisin sauce, and sesame oil in a bowl. In a large skillet, heat the safflower oil over medium-high heat. Stir-fry tofu until golden brown on both sides, 2 to 3 minutes. Add sauce, lightly stir-frying to coat tofu. Simmer about 2 minutes. Serve over rice.

4 SERVINGS

Calories 155.1 • Protein 10.11 gm • Fat 10.39 gm • Percentage of calories from fat 59% • Cholesterol 0 mg • Dietary fiber 0.102 gm • Sodium 378 mg • Calcium 48.63 mg

Stir-Fry with Spinach and Tofu

Served on a bed of freshly cooked rice, this light and easy stir-fry makes a quick yet nourishing supper. Try it with Kirin, the rich, aromatic Japanese beer.

3 tablespoons low-sodium tamari
1 tablespoon red wine vinegar
1 teaspoon toasted sesame oil
3 tablespoons sliced almonds
2 tablespoons safflower or canola oil

1 tablespoon minced fresh ginger
1 pound firm tofu, cut into ½-inch slices
1 pound spinach, washed well, cut into ½-inch strips
4 cups freshly cooked rice

In a small bowl, combine tamari, vinegar, and sesame oil and mix well. Set aside.

Heat a wok or large skillet over medium-high heat. Add almonds and stir-fry until they turn golden, about 45 seconds. Transfer to a plate. Heat oil in the same pan. Add ginger and stir-fry about 30 seconds; remove with slotted spoon and discard. Add tofu to wok in batches and fry until golden, about 2 minutes each side. Keep tofu warm in a 275-degree oven. Add spinach and stir-fry until just wilted, about 3 minutes. Drizzle with tamari mixture. To serve, divide rice among 4 plates and top with spinach. Place tofu slices on top of the spinach and sprinkle with almonds. Serve immediately.

4 SERVINGS

Calories 451.4 • Protein 19.18 gm • Fat 13.95 gm • Percentage of calories from fat 28% • Cholesterol 0 mg • Dietary fiber 3.44 gm • Sodium 619.1 mg • Calcium 175.5 mg

Seitan and Leek with Hoisin-Chili Sauce

1 pound seitan (see page 11), cut into 2- × ¼-inch strips
4 tablespoons safflower or canola oil
1 tablespoon low-sodium tamari
¾ teaspoon cornstarch
⅛ teaspoon freshly ground black pepper
2 tablespoons hoisin sauce
½ teaspoon hot Oriental chili sauce

½ teaspoon sugar or a natural sweetener
1 leek, cut into ½-inch julienne
1 red bell pepper, cut into ½-inch julienne
½ teaspoon hot red pepper flakes
¼ teaspoon salt
1 teaspoon minced fresh ginger
1 clove garlic, minced

Combine seitan, 1 tablespoon of the oil, the tamari, cornstarch, and pepper in a shallow bowl. Cover and refrigerate at least 1 hour. Combine hoisin, chili sauce, and sugar; set aside.

Heat 1 tablespoon of the oil in a wok or large skillet over medium-high heat. Add leek and stir-fry 3 minutes. Add bell pepper, red pepper flakes, and salt and stir-fry 1 minute. Transfer to a plate.

Heat last 2 tablespoons of the oil in the pan over medium-high heat. Add ginger and garlic and stir-fry 30 seconds. Add marinated seitan and stir-fry 1 minute. Add hoisin sauce mixture, return vegetables to the pan, and stir-fry 1 minute. Serve immediately.

4 SERVINGS

Calories 511.8 • Protein 17.82 gm • Fat 15.64 gm • Percentage of calories from fat 26% • Cholesterol 0 mg • Dietary fiber 12.99 gm • Sodium 596.4 mg • Calcium 66.77 mg

Tofu with Thai Sauce

This recipe lends itself well to vegetables that are stir-fried in addition to the tofu. Prepare the sauce in advance to allow the flavors to blend. This will allow you to get dinner on the table in minutes.

½ cup rice wine vinegar
½ cup sugar or a natural
  sweetener
½ cup golden raisins
1 clove garlic, chopped
½ teaspoon salt
1 teaspoon hot red pepper flakes

1 teaspoon minced fresh ginger
2 tablespoons safflower or canola
  oil
1 pound firm tofu, cut into ½-inch
  strips
Freshly cooked rice

Combine vinegar, sugar, raisins, garlic, salt, pepper flakes, ginger, and oil in a saucepan and bring to a boil over high heat. Reduce heat and simmer until raisins are soft, about 15 to 20 minutes. Remove from heat and cool. Transfer mixture to food processor and mix until smooth, adding water if too thick.

Heat oil in a wok or large skillet over medium-high heat. Add tofu and stir-fry until golden brown, about 3 minutes. Add enough sauce to coat tofu slices. Simmer about 2 minutes. Serve over rice with remaining sauce on the side.

4 SERVINGS

Calories 282.4 • Protein 9.773 gm • Fat 9.339 gm • Percentage of calories from fat 28% • Cholesterol 0 mg • Dietary fiber 0.952 gm • Sodium 346.5 mg • Calcium 55.44 mg

Shiitake-Tofu Stir-Fry

1 tablespoon low-sodium tamari
1 tablespoon cornstarch
1 tablespoon sake
1 pound firm tofu, cut into ½-inch dice
3 tablespoons corn oil
2 dried red chili peppers
1 teaspoon minced fresh ginger
1 teaspoon minced garlic

½ pound shiitake mushrooms, stemmed
1 red bell pepper, cut into ¼-inch julienne strips
2 tablespoons thinly sliced scallion
½ cup bamboo shoots, cut into julienne strips
2 tablespoons hoisin sauce

Combine tamari, cornstarch, and sake in a small bowl. Add tofu pieces, turning to coat them, and let stand 5 minutes. Then drain off and discard marinade. Heat oil in a wok or large skillet over medium-high heat. Add chilies and stir about 30 seconds, then discard. Add ginger and garlic and stir just until garlic is golden. Add tofu and stir 2 minutes; transfer to a plate with a slotted spoon. Add mushrooms, bell pepper, scallion, bamboo shoots, and hoisin sauce to wok and stir until vegetables are crisp-tender, about 1 minute. Return tofu to the pan and stir 30 seconds. Serve immediately.

4 SERVINGS

Calories 224.4 • Protein 10.95 gm • Fat 12.88 gm • Percentage of calories from fat 49% • Cholesterol 0 mg • Dietary fiber 2.084 gm • Sodium 240.4 mg • Calcium 53.26 mg

Kung Pao Seitan

Black bean sauce can be found in Asian markets or the gourmet section of many supermarkets.

2 tablespoons black bean sauce
1 clove garlic, minced
1 tablespoon hoisin sauce
1 tablespoon rice vinegar
2 teaspoons sherry
1 teaspoon sugar or a natural
  sweetener

2 tablespoons corn oil
½ cup raw unsalted peanuts
1 teaspoon hot red pepper flakes
1 pound seitan (see page 11), cut
  into ½-inch strips
Freshly cooked brown rice

Mix black bean sauce, garlic, hoisin sauce, vinegar, sherry, and sugar, plus 2 tablespoons water, in a small bowl. Set sauce aside. Heat oil in a wok or large skillet over medium-high heat. Add peanuts and red pepper flakes and cook until peanuts are golden brown, about 1 minute. Remove with slotted spoon and set aside. Increase heat to high. Add seitan and stir-fry until browned, about 1 to 2 minutes. Reduce heat to medium, return peanuts to pan, add sauce, and stir. Cook, stirring, until heated through, about 2 minutes. Serve over freshly cooked rice.

4 SERVINGS

Calories 524.3 • Protein 21.6 gm • Fat 17.65 gm • Percentage of calories from fat 29% • Cholesterol 0 mg • Dietary fiber 13.86 gm • Sodium 324.3 mg • Calcium 59.62 mg

Green Bean and Seitan Stir-Fry

Reduce the amount of red pepper flakes and ginger for a less "hot and spicy" version.

2 tablespoons low-sodium tamari
1 tablespoon mirin, white wine, or sherry
½ teaspoon salt
1 teaspoon sugar or a natural sweetener
1 tablespoon toasted sesame oil
3 tablespoons corn oil

1½ pounds green beans, trimmed
1 tablespoon minced garlic
2 teaspoons hot red pepper flakes
1 tablespoon minced fresh ginger
½ pound ground seitan (see page 8)
3 tablespoons minced scallions

In a small bowl stir together the tamari, mirin, salt, sugar, and sesame oil. In a wok or large skillet heat 2 tablespoons of the corn oil over high heat. Stir-fry the beans, a handful at a time, for 30 seconds, transferring them as they are fried with a slotted spoon to paper towels to drain. When finished cooking beans, add remaining 1 tablespoon oil to pan and stir-fry the garlic, red pepper flakes, and ginger for 10 seconds. Add the seitan and stir-fry for 2 minutes, or until browned. Add all the beans and stir-fry for 30 seconds. Add the tamari sauce and scallions and stir-fry for 30 seconds, or until the beans are heated through and coated with the sauce.

4 TO 6 SERVINGS

Calories 276.3 • Protein 8.816 gm • Fat 11.85 gm • Percentage of calories from fat 37% • Cholesterol 0 mg • Dietary fiber 6.599 gm • Sodium 586.8 mg • Calcium 60.23 mg

Stir-Fry Thai

The tofu soaks up this pungent marinade to create a fragrant stir-fry that is a feast for the nose as well as the palate. Tofu that has been frozen has a meatier texture, but regular firm tofu may also be used.

1 pound firm tofu, frozen and thawed
2 tablespoons low sodium tamari
2 tablespoons minced lemon grass (see page 175) or 2 teaspoons
2 small dried red chili peppers, sliced in half crosswise
2 tablespoons minced fresh cilantro
⅓ cup fresh orange juice
1 tablespoon fresh lime juice

2 tablespoons light sesame oil
2 cloves garlic, minced
1 large carrot, cut into matchstick julienne
½ pound green beans, trimmed and halved diagonally
½ pound mushrooms, thinly sliced
2 scallions, minced
1 tablespoon arrowroot or cornstarch, dissolved in 2 tablespoons water

Squeeze thawed tofu gently to remove excess water. Cut tofu into ¼-inch strips. Combine tamari, lemon grass, chilies, cilantro, orange juice, and lime juice. Toss mixture with tofu in a small bowl and reserve. Heat sesame oil in a large skillet over medium heat. Sauté the garlic, carrot, green beans, mushrooms, and scallions 3 minutes, then add ½ cup water and immediately cover. Steam until vegetables are tender, about 7 minutes. Pour in the tofu with marinade, stir, and sauté until tofu is hot, about 5 minutes. Stir arrowroot mixture into tofu and vegetables. Continue to cook for 1 minute. Serve immediately.

4 TO 6 SERVINGS

Calories 159 • Protein 10.23 gm • Fat 7.787 gm • Percentage of calories from fat 41% • Cholesterol 0 mg • Dietary fiber 2.039 gm • Sodium 310.3 mg • Calcium 70.43 mg

Seitan Fried Rice

Add a little grated carrot or minced red bell pepper for a splash of color in this quick and satisfying dish.

2 tablespoons safflower or canola oil
½ cup minced scallions
½ cup minced celery
8 ounces ground seitan (see page 8)

1 cup sliced mushrooms
4 cups cooked brown rice
2 tablespoons low-sodium tamari
1 teaspoon toasted sesame oil

Heat safflower oil in a wok or large skillet over medium-high heat, add scallions and celery, and stir-fry 3 minutes. Add seitan and mushrooms; stir-fry 3 minutes. Add rice, tamari, and sesame oil and stir-fry 5 minutes on medium heat. Pass extra tamari separately.

6 SERVINGS

Calories 294.1 • Protein 8.757 gm • Fat 8.284 gm • Percentage of calories from fat 25% • Cholesterol 0 mg • Dietary fiber 6.218 gm • Sodium 312.6 mg • Calcium 34.36 mg

Citrus Tofu Stir-Fry

This unusual combination is ideally suited for a hot summer day. It is light, refreshing, and quick to prepare. Serve with basmati rice.

2 tablespoons safflower or canola oil
1 small onion, minced
2 teaspoons minced fresh ginger
1 fresh green chili pepper, seeded and finely chopped
1 pound firm tofu, cut into ½-inch cubes

¼ cup fresh orange juice
2 tablespoons fresh lemon juice
1 tablespoon low-sodium tamari
2 tablespoons chopped fresh cilantro

Heat the oil in a wok or deep skillet over medium-high heat. Add the onion and stir-fry 1 minute, then add the ginger and chili. Stir-fry 30 seconds, then add the tofu. Stir-fry 3 minutes, then add the orange and lemon juice and tamari. Stir-fry 1 minute, then add the cilantro and toss well.

4 SERVINGS

Calories 161.4 • Protein 10.22 gm • Fat 9.327 gm • Percentage of calories from fat 51% • Cholesterol 0 mg • Dietary fiber 1.121 gm • Sodium 283.8 mg • Calcium 56.7 mg

Stir-Fried Tofu Italian Style

A delightful mingling of East and West. Tofu is as well suited to Italian cuisine as it is to Asian cookery. This dish is delightful served over rice or pasta.

2 tablespoons olive oil
1 clove garlic, minced
1 teaspoon hot red pepper flakes
1 pound firm tofu, cut into ½-inch cubes
1 tablespoon capers
10 black oil-cured olives, halved and pitted

10 cherry tomatoes, halved
½ cup dry white wine
1 tablespoon fresh lemon juice
1 tablespoon chopped fresh parsley
½ teaspoon salt
⅛ teaspoon freshly ground black pepper

Heat the oil in a wok or large skillet over medium heat. Add the garlic and red pepper flakes and sauté 2 minutes. Add the tofu to the hot oil and sauté for 2 minutes. Add the capers, olives, and tomatoes and cook for 1 minute. Add the wine, lemon juice, parsley, salt, and pepper. Simmer for 1 minute and serve.

4 SERVINGS

Calories 177.3 • Protein 10.04 gm • Fat 11.07 gm • Percentage of calories from fat 53% • Cholesterol 0 mg • Dietary fiber 1.24 gm • Sodium 478.3 mg • Calcium 61.29 mg

6

Burgers, Loaves, and Savory Pies

This collection of culinary delights will stimulate your imagination. Try an old-fashioned pot pie brimming with savory chunks of tofu, or seitan and vegetables in a creamy sauce. A "pizza with everything" takes on new meaning when you add seitan sausage and your favorite vegetable toppings.

There's no need to shy away from A Quiche Is Still a Quiche (see page 212)—it contains no eggs, using protein- and calcium-rich tofu instead, and is every bit as delicious as its cholesterol-laden counterpart. Make a better burger using grains, nuts, and vegetables instead of ground meat. These recipes will tempt even the most finicky eater, and the terrine and loaf recipes make great family dinners as well as wonderful additions to a party buffet table.

Peanut Burgers

A favorite with the kids. They think it's so much fun to have peanut butter in their burgers that they don't even notice they're getting a healthy portion of squash as well!

4 tablespoons corn or safflower oil
½ cup chopped onions
1 cup grated zucchini or yellow squash
½ cup cooked brown rice
1 cup finely chopped peanuts
2 tablespoons peanut butter
⅔ cup dried bread crumbs
2 scallions, finely minced
1 teaspoon minced fresh parsley
½ teaspoon salt
⅛ teaspoon freshly ground black pepper

Heat 2 tablespoons of the oil in a large skillet over medium heat. Add the onion and squash and sauté 5 minutes. Remove from heat and transfer squash mixture to a mixing bowl. Add the rice, peanuts, peanut butter, bread crumbs, scallions, parsley, salt, and pepper to the bowl. Mix well, then shape the mixture into 6 patties. Place burgers in an oiled pan and bake at 400 degrees for 30 minutes, turning once, or heat the remaining 2 tablespoons of oil in a large skillet over medium heat, add burgers, and cook until well browned on both sides, about 5 minutes per side.

6 SERVINGS

Calories 323.9 • Protein 9.971 gm • Fat 24.58 gm • Percentage of calories from fat 65% • Cholesterol 0 mg • Dietary fiber 2.738 gm • Sodium 313.5 mg • Calcium 61.73 mg

Three-Bean Burgers

If there's a three-bean salad, why not a three-bean burger? This is a healthful and delicious alternative to the hamburger.

4 tablespoons corn oil
½ cup finely chopped onions
1 clove garlic, minced
½ cup Basic Vegetable Stock (see page 10)
1 cup cooked kidney beans
½ cup cooked black beans
½ cup cooked lentils

2 tablespoons tomato purée
½ teaspoon minced fresh basil
1 teaspoon minced fresh chives
½ teaspoon paprika
½ teaspoon salt
⅛ teaspoon freshly ground black pepper
2 tablespoons all-purpose flour

In a large skillet, heat 2 tablespoons of the oil over medium heat and sauté the onions and garlic about 5 minutes. Add the stock and bring to a boil. Stir in beans, lentils, tomato purée, basil, chives, paprika, salt, and pepper. Simmer until the liquid has evaporated. Allow to cool, then mash and mold into 6 burgers. Coat burgers lightly in the flour and chill. Heat remaining 2 tablespoons oil in the skillet over medium-high heat. Add the burgers to skillet and brown 4 to 6 minutes on each side.

6 SERVINGS

Calories 174.9 • Protein 5.685 gm • Fat 9.451 gm • Percentage of calories from fat 47% • Cholesterol 0 mg • Dietary Fiber 4.221 gm • Sodium 349 mg • Calcium 27.37 mg

Ground Seitan Patties with Mustard-Wine Sauce

The delectable mustard-wine sauce elevates these patties to almost-haute cuisine.

1 pound ground seitan (see page 8)
1 teaspoon finely minced scallion
1 tablespoon plus 1 teaspoon Dijon mustard
¼ teaspoon salt
⅛ teaspoon freshly ground black pepper

2 tablespoons corn oil
2 tablespoons minced shallot
⅓ cup dry white wine
⅓ cup Basic Vegetable Stock (see page 10)
Salt and freshly ground black pepper

Crumble seitan into a bowl. Add scallion, 1 teaspoon of the mustard, salt, and pepper and mix lightly. Shape into 4 patties, each about 1 inch thick. Refrigerate 30 minutes. Heat oil in a large skillet over medium heat. Add patties and fry about 5 minutes. Turn them, fry until second side is browned, about 5 more minutes. Remove to a heated platter. Add shallots to skillet and sauté about 2 minutes. Add wine, stock, and remaining 1 tablespoon mustard; heat to boiling, scraping up brown bits that cling to pan. Boil until sauce is reduced by half, about 3 minutes. Taste for seasoning, adding salt and pepper if necessary. Spoon sauce over patties and serve hot.

4 SERVINGS

Calories 427.5 • Protein 16.97 gm • Fat 8.964 gm • Percentage of calories from fat 18% • Cholesterol 0 mg • Dietary fiber 12.42 gm • Sodium 581.1 mg • Calcium 46.92 mg

White Bean and Vegetable Cutlets

These versatile cutlets lend themselves to a variety of sauces, from a fruity chutney or spicy salsa to a hot peanut or tomato sauce.

1 cup cauliflower florets, steamed
1 cup peeled, diced potatoes,
  boiled
1 cup sliced carrots, steamed
2 cups cooked Great Northern
  beans
1 teaspoon salt

½ teaspoon freshly ground black
  pepper
2 tablespoons minced fresh
  parsley
1 cup dried bread crumbs
¼ cup corn oil

Purée the cooked cauliflower, potatoes, and carrots with the beans in a food processor with the salt, pepper, and parsley. Shape about ½ cup of the vegetable mixture into a ball. Flatten into oval cutlet about ½ inch thick. Set on baking sheet. Repeat with remaining mixture. Coat evenly with bread crumbs. Refrigerate for 30 minutes. Heat oil in large skillet over medium heat. Fry cutlets in batches until brown, about 2 minutes per side, adding more oil as necessary. Drain cutlets on paper towels and serve.

4 TO 6 SERVINGS

Calories 293.4 • Protein 9.891 gm • Fat 12.35 gm • Percentage of calories from fat 37% • Cholesterol 0 mg • Dietary fiber 5.634 gm • Sodium 588.1 mg • Calcium 89.6 mg

Grilled Tempeh Burgers with Creole Sauce

Make the sauce ahead of time to allow the flavors to bloom. If a hotter sauce is desired, add more Tabasco sauce or a dash of cayenne.

1 ripe tomato, seeded and finely chopped
2 tablespoons minced green bell pepper
2 tablespoons minced scallion
1 tablespoon minced celery
¼ cup prepared horseradish
1 tablespoon minced fresh parsley
½ teaspoon salt

2 tablespoons fresh lemon juice
1 teaspoon Tabasco sauce
¼ cup olive oil
3 tablespoons corn oil
1 pound poached tempeh (see page 12), cut into 4 equal pieces
1 tablespoon chopped fresh parsley

Mix tomato, bell pepper, scallion, celery, horseradish, parsley, salt, lemon juice, and Tabasco sauce in a medium bowl. Whisk in olive oil in a thin stream. Adjust seasonings. Heat corn oil in a large skillet over medium-high heat, add tempeh slices, and cook until golden brown, about 5 minutes on each side. Arrange on plates. Top with sauce, garnish with chopped parsley, and serve. Pass extra sauce.

4 SERVINGS

Calories 406.7 • Protein 18.75 gm • Fat 32.43 gm • Percentage of calories from fat 70% • Cholesterol 0 mg • Dietary fiber 4.246 gm • Sodium 294.9 mg • Calcium 97.07 mg

Whole-Grain Burgers

A new incarnation for leftover rice and beans. Sauté some mushrooms and onions along with the burgers for added flavor.

2½ cups cooked brown rice
½ cup cooked adzuki beans
¼ cup minced fresh parsley
¾ teaspoon salt
⅛ teaspoon freshly ground black pepper

1 tablespoon tahini
2 tablespoons minced scallions
½ cup dried bread crumbs, plus more if desired
2 tablespoons corn oil

Combine all ingredients except oil. Shape ingredients into 4 patties. Coat with additional bread crumbs on both sides (optional). Heat oil in a large skillet over medium heat. Add burgers and cook until browned, about 5 minutes on each side.

4 SERVINGS

Calories 296.8 • Protein 7.474 gm • Fat 9.388 gm • Percentage of calories from fat 28% • Cholesterol 0 mg • Dietary fiber 3.934 gm • Sodium 669.4 mg • Calcium 70.78 mg

Kabocha Squash Patties with Peanut Sauce

If kabocha squash is unavailable, substitute any sweet winter squash, such as butternut or turban.

2 tablespoons peanut butter
2 tablespoons low-sodium tamari
1 tablespoon sugar or a natural
  sweetener
2 drops Chinese hot oil
2 cups steamed kabocha squash
  pulp

2 cups cooked couscous
2 scallions, finely minced
½ teaspoon salt
⅛ teaspoon freshly ground black
  pepper
All-purpose flour for dredging
2 tablespoons corn oil

In a bowl, combine peanut butter, tamari, sugar, and 1 tablespoon water, stirring until smooth. Add hot oil and set aside. In a separate bowl combine squash pulp with couscous, scallions, salt, and pepper. Shape into 8 patties. If mixture is too wet, add some flour to bind. Otherwise, dredge patties in flour. Heat oil in a large skillet and fry patties in batches on each side until golden brown, about 2 minutes each side. Patties can be kept warm in oven until ready to serve. Serve peanut sauce on the side.

4 SERVINGS

Calories 325.9 • Protein 8.823 gm • Fat 11.21 gm • Percentage of calories from fat 30% • Cholesterol 0 mg • Dietary fiber 6.97 gm • Sodium 617.4 mg • Calcium 75.71 mg

Curried Vegetable Loaf

This is "meat loaf" as you've never had it, loaded with an intriguing combination of ingredients that are as nutritious as they are flavorful.

2 tablespoons safflower oil
4 medium carrots, cut into ¼-inch dice
1 medium onion, cut into ¼-inch dice
2 red bell peppers, seeded and cut into ¼-inch squares
1 rib celery, cut into ¼-inch dice
2 cups chopped broccoli florets
1 tablespoon curry powder

1 clove garlic, minced
⅛ teaspoon cayenne
2 medium tomatoes, peeled (see page 375) and chopped
1½ teaspoons salt
2 cups cooked chick-peas, mashed
2 tablespoons peanut butter
2 tablespoons soft tofu
1 teaspoon lemon juice

Preheat oven to 375 degrees. Heat oil in large skillet over medium heat until hot. Add carrots, onion, bell peppers, and celery. Sauté until onion begins to brown, about 5 minutes. Add broccoli, curry powder, garlic, and cayenne to skillet; toss to mix. Cook, stirring occasionally, 2 minutes. Add tomatoes, ½ cup water, and salt; reduce heat. Simmer, covered, until vegetables are tender, about 15 minutes. Remove from heat and stir in chick-peas, peanut butter, tofu, and lemon juice. Combine well. Transfer to an oiled 4-cup loaf pan, pack down, and smooth out top. Bake 30 minutes.

4 SERVINGS

Calories 392.8 • Protein 14.01 gm • Fat 19.57 gm • Percentage of calories from fat 42% • Cholesterol 0 mg • Dietary fiber 12.45 gm • Sodium 1200 mg • Calcium 118.2 mg

Hazelnut Kasha Loaf

Add variety to your repertoire by substituting different grains and nuts for the kasha and hazelnuts each time you make this loaf.

1 cup medium kasha
2 cups boiling Basic Vegetable
  Stock (see page 10)
4 tablespoons corn oil
½ teaspoon salt
⅛ teaspoon freshly ground black
  pepper
½ cup minced scallions
4 ounces fresh mushrooms, cut
  into ¼-inch dice

½ cup diced tempeh bacon
¼ cup hazelnuts, hulled and
  chopped
2 cups fresh whole-grain bread
  crumbs
¼ cup minced fresh parsley
2 tablespoons tahini

Preheat oven to 350 degrees. Combine kasha and 1 tablespoon water in large saucepan. Heat over medium-high heat, stirring constantly, until mixture is dry, about 2 minutes. Stir in boiling stock, 2 tablespoons of the oil, salt, and pepper. Reduce heat to medium-low. Cook, covered, until moisture is absorbed, about 20 minutes. Remove from heat; fluff kasha with fork and reserve.

Heat remaining 2 tablespoons oil in large heavy skillet over medium-high heat. Add scallions, mushrooms, and tempeh bacon. Sauté, stirring frequently, about 10 minutes. Remove from heat and stir in hazelnuts, bread crumbs, parsley, and tahini. Combine mushroom mixture and reserved kasha in large bowl. Adjust seasonings. Transfer to an oiled 4-cup loaf pan and bake for 30 minutes.

4 SERVINGS

Calories 630.6 • Protein 17.28 gm • Fat 30.49 gm • Percentage of calories from fat 41% • Cholesterol 0 mg • Dietary fiber 8.702 gm • Sodium 1120 mg • Calcium 138.1 mg

Southern Italian Rice Loaf

The raisins and pine nuts add texture and flavor to this savory loaf. Chopped almonds or walnuts can make great stand-ins for the pine nuts.

¼ cup golden raisins
2 tablespoons pine nuts
3 tablespoons corn oil
1 medium onion, minced
1 pound ground seitan (see page 8)
1 teaspoon ground fennel seed
½ teaspoon hot red pepper flakes
½ teaspoon ground allspice
½ teaspoon salt
⅛ teaspoon freshly ground black pepper
2 cups cooked brown rice
¼ cup minced fresh parsley
1 cup fresh bread crumbs
3 tablespoons grated Parmesan cheese

Heat oven to 350 degrees. Place raisins in a small heatproof bowl and cover with boiling water. Let stand until raisins are plump, about 15 minutes. Meanwhile, toast pine nuts in a small skillet over low heat, stirring, until evenly browned, about 5 minutes. Remove pine nuts from heat and reserve. Drain raisins and reserve.

Heat oil in a large skillet over medium heat. Add onion and seitan and sauté, stirring frequently, until onion is soft and seitan is browned, about 5 minutes. Add fennel seed, red pepper flakes, allspice, salt, and pepper. Remove from heat and reserve. Combine cooked rice, raisins, pine nuts, seitan mixture, parsley, bread crumbs, and Parmesan in a large bowl; stir until blended. Stir in 3 to 4 tablespoons water to moisten. Adjust seasonings. Transfer mixture to an oiled loaf pan and bake for 30 minutes.

6 SERVINGS

Calories 442.2 • Protein 15.95 gm • Fat 11.67 gm • Percentage of calories from fat 23% • Cholesterol 2.469 mg • Dietary fiber 10.26 gm • Sodium 482.3 mg • Calcium 105.3 mg

Tempeh-Bulgur Fruit Loaf

1½ cups bulgur
8 dried apricots, quartered
½ cup golden raisins
1 cup Basic Vegetable Stock (see page 10)
1 teaspoon minced fresh mint
1 Granny Smith apple, peeled, cored, and quartered

2 teaspoons fresh lemon juice
2 tablespoons corn oil
1 large onion, minced
4 ounces poached tempeh (see page 11)
Salt
Freshly ground black pepper
½ cup dried bread crumbs

Pour 3 cups boiling water over bulgur in a medium heat-proof bowl; stir. Let stand at room temperature 30 minutes. Combine apricots and raisins in second heat-proof bowl. In small, heavy saucepan, heat stock and mint to boiling. Remove from heat and pour liquid over fruits. Let stand at room temperature until fruits are softened, about 30 minutes.

Meanwhile, preheat oven to 350 degrees. Cut apple into ½-inch dice. Toss in large bowl with the lemon juice and reserve.

Heat oil in a large skillet over medium heat, add onion, and sauté until softened, about 5 minutes. Remove onion from pan with slotted spoon and add to bowl containing apples. Finely chop tempeh. Reheat oil in skillet over medium-high heat, add tempeh, and cook until lightly browned, stirring frequently, about 5 minutes. Add to bowl containing apples and onions. Drain bulgur thoroughly; toss with mixture in bowl. Add apricots and raisins, with soaking liquid, to bowl with other ingredients. Mix well, add salt and pepper to taste, and stir in bread crumbs. Turn into an oiled loaf pan and bake for 30 minutes.

4 SERVINGS

Calories 483.9 • Protein 14.96 gm • Fat 10.74 gm • Percentage of calories from fat 19% • Cholesterol 0 mg • Dietary fiber 16.93 gm • Sodium 202.1 mg • Calcium 111.8 mg

Wheat Loaf with Sautéed Mushrooms

A satisfying alternative to meat loaf. Serve with Basic Brown Sauce and a generous helping of mashed potatoes for comfort food at its best.

½ cup soft tofu
¼ cup milk
1 cup fresh bread crumbs
1 teaspoon salt
¼ teaspoon freshly ground black pepper
½ teaspoon ground allspice
2 tablespoons corn oil
8 ounces white mushrooms, finely chopped

¼ cup grated carrot
¼ cup minced onion
2 cloves garlic, minced
1 pound ground seitan (see page 8)
1 tablespoon Dijon mustard
1½ cups Basic Brown Sauce (see page 13)

Heat oven to 375 degrees. Combine tofu and milk in a food processor and process until smooth. Combine bread crumbs, salt, pepper, and allspice in a large bowl. Pour tofu mixture over crumbs, stir, and let soak 10 minutes. While crumbs are soaking, heat the oil in large skillet over medium heat. Add mushrooms and sauté, stirring frequently, until softened, about 2 minutes. Increase heat to medium-high and cook, uncovered, until liquid has evaporated, about 3 minutes. Add carrot, onion, and garlic; sauté, stirring, until vegetables are tender, about 4 minutes. Remove from heat. Add sautéed vegetables and oil left in skillet to crumb mixture; add seitan. Mix gently with hands to blend—mixture will be very soft at first. Spoon mixture into shallow loaf pan; smooth surface, and carefully spread surface of mixture with the mustard. Bake loaf about 45 minutes. Remove from oven and let stand 10 minutes. Serve with Basic Brown Sauce.

4 TO 6 SERVINGS

Calories 435.5 • Protein 20.35 gm • Fat 10.18 gm • Percentage of calories from fat 20% • Cholesterol 0.9 mg • Dietary fiber 11.82 gm • Sodium 969.7 mg • Calcium 131.4 mg

Shepherdess Pie

Leave it to the shepherdess to make a great Shepherd's Pie—just as satisfying and flavorful as the original but without the meat.

3 tablespoons corn oil
1 large onion, chopped
¼ cup chopped walnuts
1 cup TVP granules combined with
 1 cup water
½ teaspoon ground coriander
¼ teaspoon dried thyme
¼ teaspoon freshly ground black
 pepper

½ cup frozen green peas, thawed
Juice of ½ large lemon
1 tablespoon low-sodium tamari
4 large potatoes, peeled and
 cubed
½ cup milk
¼ teaspoon salt
2 cups Basic Brown Sauce (see
 page 13)

Heat 2 tablespoons of the oil in a large skillet over medium-high heat. Add onion and cook until translucent, about 5 minutes. Stir in walnuts, TVP, coriander, thyme, and pepper. Cook over medium heat, stirring, about 2 minutes or until ingredients are heated. Add peas, lemon juice, and tamari. Cover, remove from heat, and set aside.

Preheat oven to 350 degrees. Boil potatoes until tender. Drain them and mash with milk and salt. Spread TVP mixture over bottom of a lightly oiled baking dish. Spoon Basic Brown Sauce over TVP and cover with the mashed potatoes. Drizzle surface of potatoes with remaining 1 tablespoon oil and bake 15 to 20 minutes or until top is golden.

4 SERVINGS

Calories 480.6 • Protein 28.05 gm • Fat 16.03 gm • Percentage of calories from fat 29% • Cholesterol 2.25 mg • Dietary fiber 11.56 gm • Sodium 593.2 mg • Calcium 191.5 mg

Pizza de Résistance

The meaty Portobello mushroom makes this pizza hard to resist. Add some hot red pepper flakes and ground fennel seed to the sautéed mushrooms for a sausagelike flavor. For the diehard pepperoni lover, add some spicy meatless pepperoni and dig in.

1¼ teaspoons active dry yeast
1½ cups all-purpose flour
½ teaspoon salt
3 tablespoons olive oil
1 cup tomato sauce
½ teaspoon minced fresh basil or
   ¼ teaspoon dried
¼ teaspoon minced fresh oregano
   or ¼ teaspoon dried

¼ pound grated mozzarella
   cheese
1 cup sliced Portobello
   mushrooms
½ cup chopped shallots
1 tablespoon capers
2 ounces meatless pepperoni
   (optional)

Dissolve yeast in ⅔ cup warm water. In a food processor, mix flour and salt. Pour in the dissolved yeast while the machine is running and pulse it on and off a few times until the mixture is like coarse cornmeal. With machine running, add 2 tablespoons of the olive oil and mix for a few more seconds. If the dough is too moist, add 1 or 2 tablespoons flour. Process until dough forms a ball. Lightly oil a large bowl and place the dough in the bowl, turning to coat all sides. Let the dough rise, covered tightly with plastic wrap, in a warm place until doubled in size, about 1 hour.

When dough is ready, preheat oven to 450 degrees. Punch down dough. Place the dough on a floured surface and knead gently about 1 minute. Flatten into a circle. Using a floured rolling pin, roll out until about 6 inches across. Pick it up and drape it over your closed fist. Transfer the dough from one fist to another, tossing it back and forth, until it is approximately 12 inches in diameter. Lay it on a cookie sheet or pizza pan. Spread tomato sauce over the pizza and sprinkle with basil, oregano, and cheese.

To prepare toppings, heat remaining 1 tablespoon olive oil in a medium skillet over medium-high heat. Add mushrooms and shallots, and sauté 2 minutes, or until mushrooms are tender. Add capers. Distribute topping mixture evenly over pizza. (If using meatless pepperoni, sauté it in skillet for 1 minute on each side and place on the pizza.) Place pizza on the lowest oven rack and bake for 25 to 30 minutes.

4 SERVINGS

Calories 372.9 • Protein 13.88 gm • Fat 15.35 gm • Percentage of calories from fat 36% • Cholesterol 15.97 mg • Dietary fiber 2.536 gm • Sodium 852.7 mg • Calcium 256 mg

You'll-Never-Miss-the-Meat Loaf

This loaf may be prepared in advance and refrigerated. Just bring to room temperature before baking. Leftovers make great sandwiches.

2 cups cooked lentils
1 tablespoon corn oil
½ cup chopped onion
1 garlic clove, minced
1 tablespoon minced fresh basil or
  1 teaspoon dried
1 tablespoon minced fresh parsley

½ pound whole-grain bread,
  cubed
½ cup ground walnuts
⅛ teaspoon cayenne
1 tablespoon low-sodium tamari
1 teaspoon salt
2 tablespoons tahini

Preheat oven to 350 degrees. Mash lentils with a fork or purée in a food processor. Set aside. Heat oil in a large skillet. Sauté onion over medium heat for 5 minutes, then add garlic, basil, and parsley and sauté 1 minute. Stir in bread and walnuts, then lentil purée. Continue sautéing over low heat and season with cayenne, tamari, and salt. Cook for 10 minutes. Remove from heat and stir in tahini. Pour mixture into an oiled loaf pan and bake for 25 minutes or until top has a golden crust. Cool loaf, then run a knife around the edges of the pan, invert, and remove it. Allow to stand 5 minutes before cutting in slices to serve.

4 TO 6 SERVINGS

Calories 278.9 • Protein 15.9 gm • Fat 9.956 gm • Percentage of calories from fat 28% • Cholesterol 0 mg • Dietary fiber 8.289 gm • Sodium 629.5 mg • Calcium 170.6 mg

Whole-Wheat Three-Pepper Pizza

A pepper lover's delight. If you can find meatless pepperoni, use it in place of the meatless sausage for a real taste treat. Banana peppers are so named because they are similar in shape and color to unripe bananas. If these are unavailable, substitute yellow bell pepper.

1 ¼ teaspoon active dry yeast
3 tablespoons olive oil
¾ teaspoon salt
½ cup whole-wheat flour
1 cup all-purpose flour, plus flour
  for dusting
1 cup tomato sauce
¼ pound grated mozzarella
  cheese

½ cup sliced red bell pepper
¼ cup seeded and chopped
  jalapeño peppers
¼ cup sliced sweet banana pepper
4 ounces meatless sausage,
  crumbled

Dissolve yeast in ⅔ cup warm water in a medium bowl, and let stand 5 minutes. Stir 2 tablespoons of the olive oil, salt, whole-wheat flour, and 1 cup of the all-purpose flour into yeast mixture to form a ball. Turn out onto lightly floured surface and knead dough about 4 minutes, adding flour as necessary to make a soft, slightly sticky dough. Lightly oil a large bowl. Place dough in the bowl, turning to coat all sides with oil. Let rise, covered tightly with plastic wrap, in a warm place until doubled in size, about 1 hour.

When dough is ready, preheat oven to 450 degrees. Punch dough down. Roll out on lightly floured surface with floured rolling pin to make a 12-inch circle. If dough is too sticky, flour hands heavily a couple of times and give dough a light dusting. If dough seems too elastic, let it rest a few minutes and then try shaping it again. Lay dough on a cookie sheet or pizza pan. Spread tomato sauce on top within ½ inch of the edge. Sprinkle on cheese.

Heat remaining 1 tablespoon oil in a medium skillet over moderate heat. Add peppers and cook 5 to 8 minutes or until soft. Remove with slotted spoon and reserve. Reheat pan and add meatless sausage. Cook for 5 minutes or until brown. Remove from pan and chop fine. Sprinkle on pizza and top with reserved peppers. Bake on lowest oven rack for 25 to 30 minutes.

4 SERVINGS

Calories 456.6 • Protein 20.81 gm • Fat 22.35 gm • Percentage of calories from fat 42% • Cholesterol 15.97 mg • Dietary fiber 4.517 gm • Sodium 1275 mg • Calcium 262.2 mg

Tempeh-Mushroom Turnovers

I like to serve these hearty turnovers with a zesty chutney. Try one of the chutney recipes in this book (see index) or use a store-bought brand.

2 tablespoons corn oil
1 medium onion, minced
8 ounces poached tempeh (see page 12)
2 cups chopped mushrooms
¼ cup milk
1½ cups cooked brown rice
½ teaspoon salt

⅛ teaspoon cayenne
¼ cup toasted almonds (see page 142)
¼ cup minced fresh parsley
1 tablespoon chopped fresh tarragon or 1 teaspoon dried
12 4-inch squares commercial puff pastry dough

Preheat oven to 350 degrees. In a large skillet, heat oil and sauté onions and tempeh until onions are soft and tempeh is lightly browned, about 5 minutes. Remove from heat and stir in mushrooms, milk, rice, salt, cayenne, almonds, parsley, and tarragon. Place a heaping tablespoon of mixture in center of each pastry square. Fold points of pastry into center and overlap each point. Press lightly to seal. Bake on a cookie sheet for 30 minutes until puffed and golden. Serve immediately.

6 SERVINGS

Calories 727 • Protein 17.01 gm • Fat 46.7 gm • Percentage of calories from fat 57% • Cholesterol 0.75 mg • Dietary fiber 3.23 gm • Sodium 425.2 mg • Calcium 89.61 mg

Chick-pea Pot Pie

The exotic flavors of coriander and chick-peas jazz up the down-home goodness of this satisfying dish.

For filling:

½ cup diced cooked carrots
½ cup cooked chopped onions
½ cup cooked chick-peas
½ cup TVP granules combined
  with ½ cup water
2 tablespoons minced fresh
  parsley
2 tablespoons corn oil

3 tablespoons all-purpose flour
1 cup milk
1 cup Basic Vegetable Stock (see
  page 10)
¼ teaspoon salt
⅛ teaspoon freshly ground black
  pepper

For crust:

1½ cups all-purpose flour
1 teaspoon salt
½ teaspoon ground coriander

½ cup puréed cooked chick-peas
½ cup corn oil

For filling:

Place carrots, onions, chick-peas, TVP, and parsley in a lightly oiled casserole dish. Heat oil in a medium saucepan. Stir in flour and cook, stirring constantly, 3 minutes. Gradually add milk and stock to saucepan, stirring until smooth. Bring sauce to a boil, stirring. Then remove from heat. Add salt and pepper. Pour sauce over TVP and vegetables in casserole dish. Reserve.

For crust:

Preheat oven to 350 degrees. Mix flour, salt, and coriander in medium bowl. Add chick-pea purée with pastry cutter until mixture is flaky. Slowly pour oil and 3 tablespoons water into flour mixture, tossing with fork until well mixed. Knead briefly on lightly floured surface. Roll out dough ⅛ inch thick. Cut pastry into shape 1 inch larger all around than top of casserole. Carefully place crust over filled casserole, crimping edges. Bake pie for 40 minutes or until crust is lightly browned.

4 TO 6 SERVINGS

Calories 551.3 • Protein 16.4 gm • Fat 31.9 gm • Percentage of calories from fat 51% • Cholesterol 0 mg • Dietary fiber 6.574 gm • Sodium 850 mg • Calcium 177.7 mg

Vegetable-Nut Burgers

Nuts are easily ground in a food processor. Be sure to use a series of short pulses, however, or you may end up with nut butter.

1 cup cooked lentils, mashed
1 cup cooked brown rice
½ cup ground almonds or pecans
¼ cup grated carrot, lightly
  steamed for 1 minute
¼ cup grated onion

½ teaspoon salt
1 teaspoon chili powder
⅛ teaspoon cayenne
¾ cup dry bread crumbs
2 tablespoons corn oil

In a large bowl, combine all ingredients except the bread crumbs and oil. Shape mixture into 6 patties. Coat patties with the bread crumbs. Heat oil in a large skillet over medium-high heat. Cook the patties about 4 minutes per side, until golden brown. Add more oil to the skillet as needed.

6 SERVINGS

Calories 239.5 • Protein 7.895 gm • Fat 11.45 gm • Percentage of calories from fat 42% • Cholesterol 0 mg • Dietary fiber 3.61 gm • Sodium 216.1 mg • Calcium 74.48 mg

Seitan Pot Pie

The classic comfort food is updated here with seitan, but, if you prefer, TVP or ground tempeh work just as well.

For filling:

2 cups ground seitan (see page 8)
1 cup diced cooked carrots
1 cup frozen peas, thawed
½ cup cooked chopped onions
1 tablespoon minced fresh parsley
2 tablespoons corn oil
3 tablespoons all-purpose flour

1 cup Basic Vegetable Stock (see page 10)
1 cup milk
¼ teaspoon salt
⅛ teaspoon freshly ground black pepper

For crust:

¾ cup all-purpose flour
¼ teaspoon salt

¼ cup (½ stick) margarine
2 tablespoons ice water

For filling:

Place seitan, carrots, peas, onions, and parsley in a lightly oiled casserole dish. Heat oil in a medium saucepan. Stir in flour and cook, stirring constantly, 3 minutes. Gradually add stock and milk, stirring until smooth. Bring sauce to a boil, stirring, then remove from heat. Add salt and pepper. Pour sauce over seitan and vegetables in casserole dish. Reserve.

For crust:

Preheat oven to 350 degrees. Combine flour and salt in a food processor, using steel blade. Add margarine, processing until mixture resembles coarse crumbs. Slowly add water, processing to blend. Roll dough on lightly floured surface to ¼ inch thickness, shaped to size of casserole dish. Carefully place crust over top of filled casserole, crimping edges. Bake for 40 minutes or until crust is lightly browned.

6 SERVINGS

Calories 247.2 • Protein 5.547 gm • Fat 13.3 gm • Percentage of calories from fat 48% • Cholesterol 3 mg • Dietary fiber 3.016 gm • Sodium 650.1 mg • Calcium 100.1 mg

Grain Loaf

This recipe easily adapts to whatever grains you have on hand. You may substitute TVP or ground seitan for some of the grains in order to achieve a meatier texture.

2 tablespoons corn oil
1 small onion, grated
1 rib celery, minced
1 tablespoon minced fresh parsley
¼ teaspoon ground sage
¼ teaspoon dried thyme
¼ teaspoon salt
¼ teaspoon freshly ground black
  pepper

2 cups cooked millet
2 cups cooked brown rice
3 slices whole-grain bread, cubed
2 tablespoons soft tofu
1 cup Basic Brown Sauce (see
  page 13)

Preheat oven to 350 degrees. Heat oil in a large skillet over medium-high heat. Add onion, celery, parsley, sage, thyme, salt, and pepper. Cook for 5 minutes or until onion is translucent. Place mixture in a large bowl. Add millet, rice, bread, and tofu. Mix well; adjust seasonings. Transfer to a well-oiled loaf pan and bake for 30 minutes. Serve with Basic Brown Sauce.

4 TO 6 SERVINGS

Calories 299.3 • Protein 7.166 gm • Fat 7.522 gm • Percentage of calories from fat 22% • Cholesterol 0 mg • Dietary fiber 7.249 gm • Sodium 235.5 mg • Calcium 39.92 mg

A Quiche Is Still a Quiche

The tofu stands in for the eggs and cream, and soy bacon bits add a hint of smoky flavor to this healthful version of an old favorite.

For crust:

½ cup all-purpose flour
¼ cup whole-wheat pastry flour
¼ teaspoon salt

¼ cup (½ stick) margarine
2 tablespoons ice water

For filling:

1 pound fresh spinach
2 tablespoons corn oil
¼ cup minced onion
¼ cup chopped mushrooms
1 pound firm tofu
¼ teaspoon dried basil

¼ teaspoon dried thyme
½ teaspoon salt
¼ teaspoon ground nutmeg
⅛ teaspoon cayenne
2 tablespoons soy bacon bits
½ cup grated mozzarella cheese

For crust:

Sift flours together into a bowl with salt. Divide margarine into 4 pieces and use a pastry cutter to cut pieces into flour mixture until crumbly. Add 2 table-spoons of the ice water slowly, stirring to form mixture into a ball. Wrap in waxed paper and refrigerate for 1 hour. Remove from refrigerator and bring to room temperature for 15 minutes. Roll out on a floured board into a circle large enough to line a 9-inch pie pan. Place dough in pan, fitting against sides and bottom. Trim off any extra dough. Crimp edge of dough with fingers.

Preheat oven to 350 degrees.

For filling:

Trim, wash, drain, and chop the spinach. Heat oil in a large skillet over medium heat. Add onion and sauté for 5 minutes. Add spinach and mushrooms and cover, cooking for 5 minutes or until spinach is wilted. Remove cover and continue cooking, stirring, until all liquid evaporates. Place the spinach mixture in a large bowl and set aside.

Place the tofu in a food processor with the basil, thyme, salt, nutmeg, and cayenne and blend until smooth and creamy. Scrape the sides of the food processor with a rubber spatula to combine well. Add the tofu mixture and the soy bacon bits to the cooked spinach and mix well. Fold in the grated cheese and fill the pie crust with the spinach-tofu mixture. Bake for 40 minutes or until the crust is brown and the filling is firm. Cool for 5 to 10 minutes before slicing.

4 TO 6 SERVINGS

Calories 348.1 • Protein 17.61 gm • Fat 21.74 gm • Percentage of calories from fat 56% • Cholesterol 0 mg • Dietary fiber 3.962 gm • Sodium 683.1 mg • Calcium 238.5 mg

Seitan Burgers

Serve on whole-grain rolls with all the trimmings and you'll have to remind yourself that you're not eating meat. Chick-pea flour is available in natural foods stores.

1 pound ground seitan (see page 8)
6 tablespoons chick-pea flour
3 tablespoons whole-wheat flour
1 tablespoon minced fresh parsley
1 tablespoon paprika

½ teaspoon salt
¼ teaspoon freshly ground black pepper
1½ tablespoons low-sodium tamari
2 tablespoons corn oil

In a large bowl, combine well all the ingredients except the oil. Form this mixture into 6 patties. Heat the oil in a large skillet over medium heat. Add the burgers and cook about 5 minutes per side, until browned.

6 SERVINGS

Calories 303 • Protein 13.29 gm • Fat 6.213 gm • Percentage of calories from fat 17% • Cholesterol 0 mg • Dietary fiber 9.369 gm • Sodium 531.3 mg • Calcium 42.68 mg

Tofu Pot Pie With Sweet Potato Crust

1 pound firm tofu, cut into ½-inch dice
1 cup diced cooked carrots
½ cup cooked chopped onions
1 tablespoon minced fresh parsley
2 tablespoons plus ¼ cup corn oil
3 tablespoons plus 2 cups all-purpose flour
1 cup milk
1 cup Basic Vegetable Stock (see page 10)
½ teaspoon salt
⅛ teaspoon freshly ground black pepper
1 teaspoon baking powder
1 cup cold mashed sweet potatoes

Preheat oven to 350 degrees. Place tofu, carrots, onions, and parsley in a lightly oiled casserole dish. Heat the 2 tablespoons oil in a medium saucepan. Stir in the 3 tablespoons flour and cook, stirring constantly, 3 minutes. Gradually add milk and stock, stirring until smooth. Bring sauce to a boil, stirring, then remove from heat. Add ¼ teaspoon of the salt and the pepper. Pour sauce over tofu and vegetables in casserole dish. Reserve.

Combine the 2 cups flour, baking powder, and remaining ¼ teaspoon salt in a food processor, using steel blade. Add the ¼ cup oil, processing until mixture resembles coarse crumbs. Add sweet potatoes, processing to blend. Roll dough on lightly floured surface to ¼ inch thickness, shaped to the size of the casserole dish. Carefully place crust over casserole, crimping edges over edge of dish. Bake at 350 degrees for 40 minutes or until crust is lightly browned.

6 SERVINGS

Calories 596.2 • Protein 19.79 gm • Fat 24.9 gm • Percentage of calories from fat 37% • Cholesterol 4.5 mg • Dietary fiber 5.198 gm • Sodium 731.7 mg • Calcium 280.8 mg

7

Under Wraps, Stuffed, and Skewered

From the simple goodness of a stuffed baked potato to the spectacular Roast Seitan with Pear-Walnut Stuffing (a showpiece that is stuffed, rolled, roasted, and then sliced for serving) this chapter explores a wide variety of recipes.

Using ground seitan or a combination of grains and beans you can stuff peppers, eggplant, and cabbage and never miss the ground meat. A tempting array of skewered recipes proves that there's more to life than beef chunks. Dazzle your dinner guests with Seitan Roulades with Apricot Stuffing, Stuffed Summer Squash Florentine, or a seitan roast with one of several delectable stuffings. This chapter is "fun food" at its finest.

Seitan Roulades with Apricot Stuffing

Serve with basmati rice and asparagus with lemon butter for a light yet elegant dinner.

½ cup dried apricots
3 tablespoons corn oil
1 small onion, minced
2 slices tempeh bacon, chopped
¼ pound mushrooms, minced
⅔ cup fresh bread crumbs
¼ teaspoon salt

1 pound seitan (see page 11), cut
 in 6 x 3 x ¼ inch slices
1 shallot, chopped
¼ teaspoon freshly ground black
 pepper
¼ cup brandy
1 tablespoon apricot jam

Pour 1 cup boiling water over apricots in a small heatproof bowl. Allow to stand for several minutes to soften. Drain off water and reserve apricots. In a small skillet, heat 1 tablespoon of the oil over moderately low heat. Add minced onion and cook until softened, 3 to 4 minutes, then add tempeh bacon and mushrooms. Sauté 2 minutes and set aside. Chop the apricots in a food processor, add the onion mixture, and pulse to combine. Transfer to a bowl, add bread crumbs and salt and toss to combine.

Preheat the oven to 375 degrees. Lay the seitan slices next to one another on a surface. Spread the stuffing evenly on top of each slice. With your fingers, starting at a short end, roll each seitan slice into a roulade. Secure with kitchen twine. Heat remaining 2 tablespoons oil in a large skillet over medium-high heat. Add the seitan rolls and shallot, sprinkle with pepper, and cook 15 to 20 minutes, turning carefully, to brown on all sides. In a small bowl, combine brandy with jam. When roulades are browned, add brandy mixture, turning roulades to coat them. Serve immediately.

4 SERVINGS

Calories 636 • Protein 21.1 gm • Fat 15.34 gm • Percentage of calories from fat 21% • Cholesterol 0 mg • Dietary fiber 14.62 • Sodium 699.3 mg • Calcium 104 mg

Seitan Roulades with Tomato-Basil Sauce

Using seitan as the meat alternative in this updated version of Italian braciola *makes it taste even better than it did when my mom made it with round steak.*

2 red bell peppers
1½ pounds seitan (see page 11),
  cut into 6 slices, each ¼ inch thick
1 cup dry red wine
2 tablespoons red wine vinegar
4 tablespoons olive oil
1 large clove garlic, minced
½ teaspoon freshly ground black
  pepper
½ teaspoon dried thyme
1 bay leaf

4 medium carrots, cut into ¼-inch
  strips
½ pound fresh spinach, washed
  and trimmed
2 tablespoons capers, chopped
Salt and freshly ground black
  pepper
2 cups Basic Vegetable Stock (see
  page 10)
Tomato-Basil Sauce (recipe
  follows)

Roast peppers directly over a gas flame or under the broiler until the skin is charred, about 5 minutes. Place in tightly closed paper bag or covered bowl and allow steam to build for 10 minutes. Rub off the skin, remove stems and seeds, and discard. Cut into ¼-inch strips and reserve. Combine seitan with wine, vinegar, 2 tablespoons of the olive oil, garlic, pepper, thyme, and bay leaf in a non-aluminum pan. Marinate in refrigerator 1 hour or overnight, turning occasionally. Drain seitan, reserving marinade. Lay seitan pieces out on a surface, lining them up next to one another. Lightly steam carrot strips until crisp-tender. Layer each piece of seitan with a layer of spinach leaves, then a row of carrots arranged horizontally at one end. Alongside the carrots, line roasted pepper strips, and sprinkle the chopped capers over all the vegetables. Sprinkle with salt and pepper. Roll up tightly, starting at the vegetable edge. Tie roulades securely with kitchen twine, at 1-inch intervals. Roulades may be prepared ahead of time to this point and refrigerated overnight in the marinade. Heat remaining 2 tablespoons olive oil in a large pot over medium-high heat. Add roulades and cook until browned on all sides, turning carefully. Combine stock and reserved marinade and pour over roulades. Bring liquid to a boil, then simmer over low heat, uncovered, for 20 minutes. Transfer roulades to a serving plate. Boil liquid until reduced to about 1½ cups if using in place of tomato-basil sauce. Remove twine from roulades. Serve with reduced cooking liquid or Tomato-Basil Sauce.

4 TO 6 SERVINGS

Calories 192.6 • Protein 3.02 gm • Fat 11.23 gm • Percentage of calories from fat 49% • Cholesterol 0 mg • Dietary fiber 3.876 gm • Sodium 315.1 mg • Calcium 82.22 mg

Tomato-Basil Sauce

2 tablespoons olive oil
1 medium onion, minced
1 large clove garlic, minced
1 tablespoon chopped fresh basil
  or 1 teaspoon dried, crumbled
⅛ teaspoon dried oregano,
  crumbled

3 cups tomato purée
1 tablespoon tomato paste
Salt and freshly ground black
  pepper

Heat olive oil in a large skillet over low heat. Add onion, cover, and cook slowly, about 15 minutes, stirring occasionally. Uncover, increase heat to medium, add garlic, basil, and oregano, and stir 30 seconds. Blend in tomato purée and tomato paste with salt and pepper to taste. Bring to a boil and continue boiling until thickened slightly, about 5 minutes. Reduce heat to low and simmer about 30 minutes, stirring occasionally.

MAKES 4 CUPS

Calories 158.2 • Protein 3.819 gm • Fat 7.07 gm • Percentage of calories from fat 37% • Cholesterol 0 mg • Dietary fiber 5.223 gm • Sodium 41.93 mg • Calcium 42.35 mg

Eggplant Roulades

These delicious roulades may be prepared several hours in advance and re-frigerated. Bring to room temperature before baking. Serve with a crisp green salad and warm garlic bread for a light, casual supper.

2 large eggplants, cut lengthwise
   into ¼-inch slices (about 8 slices
   per eggplant)
1½ teaspoons salt
3 tablespoons olive oil, plus
   additional for brushing
2 large onions, minced
¾ pound mushrooms, sliced
¼ teaspoon freshly ground black
   pepper
1 pound firm tofu, crumbled
¾ cup grated Pecorino Romano
   cheese

3 chopped scallions
2 tablespoons chopped fresh basil
   or 2 teaspoons dried
½ teaspoon chopped fresh
   oregano or ⅛ teaspoon dried
1 large clove garlic, minced
⅛ teaspoon dried marjoram
3 cups tomato purée
1 cup shredded mozzarella cheese

Place eggplant slices in colander and sprinkle lightly with ½ teaspoon of the salt. Set aside 30 minutes to drain. Rinse under running water; pat dry with paper towels. Preheat oven to 475 degrees.

Brush large baking sheet with oil and lightly brush 1 side of eggplant slices with oil. Arrange eggplant slices oiled side down on prepared baking sheet. Bake until softened, about 5 minutes.

Heat 1 tablespoon of the oil in a large skillet over low heat. Add half of the minced onions, cover, and cook about 5 minutes, stirring occasionally. Increase heat to medium-high, add mushrooms, and sauté until lightly browned. Let cool. Season to taste with ¼ teaspoon of the salt and ⅛ teaspoon of the pepper. Combine tofu, cheese, scallions, 1 tablespoon basil, and oregano in a large bowl and mix well. Blend in cooled mushroom mixture.

For sauce, heat remaining 2 tablespoons oil in a large skillet over low heat. Add remaining minced onion, cover, and cook 15 minutes, stirring occasionally. Uncover, increase heat to medium, add garlic, remaining basil, and marjoram, and stir 30 seconds. Blend in tomato purée with remaining ¾ teaspoon salt and ⅛ teaspoon pepper. Bring to a boil. Let sauce boil until thickened slightly, about 5 minutes.

Preheat oven to 375 degrees. Lightly oil a large, shallow baking dish. Spread about 2 tablespoons filling over each piece of eggplant, leaving about 1 inch border at thickest end. Starting at narrower end, roll eggplant up "jelly roll" style. Transfer to prepared baking dish. Spread sauce over eggplant rolls and sprinkle with shredded mozzarella. Bake until heated through, about 45 minutes. Serve immediately.

6 SERVINGS

Calories 380.5 • Protein 25.26 gm • Fat 18.94 gm • Percentage of calories from fat 43% • Cholesterol 36.02 mg • Dietary fiber 5.092 gm • Sodium 952.9 mg • Calcium 482.3 mg

Roast Seitan with Feta–Pine Nut Stuffing

1-pound piece raw, unpoached
  seitan (see page 11)
½ cup low-sodium tamari
5 tablespoons olive oil
1 pound mushrooms, thinly sliced
3 tablespoons pine nuts
1 clove garlic, minced
½ pound feta cheese, crumbled

2 cups cooked brown rice
1 tablespoon minced fresh parsley
½ teaspoon salt
⅛ teaspoon freshly ground black
  pepper
3 tablespoons fresh lemon juice
1 teaspoon Dijon mustard

Marinate seitan in tamari at least 1 hour or overnight. Heat 2 tablespoons of the olive oil in a large skillet over medium-high heat. Add mushrooms, pine nuts, and garlic and stir until pine nuts are golden brown, about 5 minutes. Stir in feta, rice, and parsley. Season with salt and pepper. Set aside.

Preheat oven to 300 degrees. In a small bowl, combine remaining 3 tablespoons olive oil with lemon juice and mustard. Set aside. Remove seitan from marinade and reserve marinade. Roll out marinated raw seitan with a rolling pin until about ¼ inch thick. Spread surface with stuffing. Roll up in "jelly roll" fashion. Place seam side down in an oiled shallow baking pan. Pierce with a fork in several places. Combine tamari marinade with ½ cup water and pour over roast. Brush lemon-mustard mixture over roast, and baste with this mixture during the cooking. Roast uncovered for 30 to 40 minutes, basting every 10 minutes. The roast is done when surface is firm, browned, and glossy. Remove from oven and cut into ½-inch slices with a serrated knife (see note page 229).

6 SERVINGS

Calories 566.8 • Protein 23.21 gm • Fat 23.98 gm • Percentage of calories from fat 37% • Cholesterol 33.27 mg • Dietary fiber 10.31 gm • Sodium 1635 mg • Calcium 236.1 mg

Stuffed Curried Eggplant

2 medium eggplants, trimmed
1 teaspoon salt
4 tablespoons olive oil
1 clove garlic, minced
1 tablespoon curry powder
2 cups tomato purée
¼ teaspoon freshly ground black
  pepper

½ medium onion, minced
2 cups cooked brown rice
2 tablespoons currants
1 tablespoon chopped fresh
  coriander
½ cup slivered almonds

Preheat oven to 400 degrees. Halve eggplants lengthwise and arrange them cut side up in a lightly oiled baking dish. Sprinkle surfaces with ½ teaspoon of the salt and 1 tablespoon of the oil. Bake until eggplants are tender, about 25 minutes. Cool slightly. Scoop out eggplant pulp from shells with a spoon, being careful not to pierce the skin. Coarsely chop pulp and set aside.

Heat 1 tablespoon of the oil in a large saucepan over low heat. Add garlic and cook, stirring occasionally, about 30 seconds. Add curry powder and stir 30 seconds. Mix in tomato purée and ⅛ teaspoon pepper. Bring to a boil, reduce heat to low and simmer, stirring occasionally, about 20 minutes. Adjust seasonings and remove from heat.

Heat 1 tablespoon of the oil in a medium skillet over low heat. Add onion and cook about 10 minutes, stirring frequently. Add eggplant pulp, rice, currants, remaining ½ teaspoon salt and remaining ⅛ teaspoon pepper. Simmer for 10 minutes. Add fresh coriander. Adjust seasonings and remove from heat.

Preheat oven to 350 degrees. Heat last tablespoon of the oil in a small skillet over medium-low heat. Add almonds and stir until lightly browned, about 2 minutes. Stir into eggplant-rice mixture. Lightly oil a large baking dish. Place eggplants cut side up in dish. Spoon stuffing into eggplant shells. Bake about 15 minutes. Reheat sauce in medium saucepan, stirring frequently. To serve, spoon sauce over eggplant. Serve immediately.

4 SERVINGS

Calories 422.2 • Protein 10.94 gm • Fat 24.1 gm • Percentage of calories from fat 48% • Cholesterol 0 mg • Dietary fiber 7.333 gm • Sodium 566.4 mg • Calcium 111.2 mg

Nori Makis

(Japanese Rice Rolls)

Sushi means "rice sandwich" in Japanese. The filling doesn't need to include raw fish or any kind of meat. Try these tasty rolls made with seitan for a special treat. The nori sheets (dried seaweed), wasabi paste (hot Japanese horseradish, available as paste or powder), and pickled ginger can be purchased in Asian markets and in some supermarkets.

1 tablespoon light sesame oil
6 ounces seitan (see page 11), cut
  into ¼-inch strips
1 teaspoon low-sodium tamari
6 roasted 8 x 7-inch nori sheets
6 cups freshly cooked brown rice,
  cooled slightly

2 tablespoons wasabi paste
6 strips blanched carrot, ¼ inch
  thick x 4 inches long
6 strips cucumber, ¼ inch thick x 4
  inches long
Pickled ginger
Additional tamari for dipping

Heat sesame oil in a large skillet over medium-high heat. Add seitan strips and sauté until browned. Add 1 teaspoon tamari. Remove from heat and allow to cool. Place 1 sheet of nori on a bamboo sushi mat *(sudare)* or cloth napkin placed in front of you. Spread 1 cup rice evenly on nori, coming to edge on sides, leaving a ½-inch top and bottom margin. Closest to you, spread ½ teaspoon wasabi paste horizontally along length of rice. Place seitan strips in one length, end to end down rice on top of wasabi. Line 2 carrot strips end to end next to the seitan. Beginning at the end nearest you, start rolling up sushi mat, pressing firmly against nori to roll around ingredients, all the while keeping the end of the sushi mat from rolling into the sushi. Continue rolling slowly up to the top margin. Wet the end of exposed nori with a little water to seal the roll. Gently squeeze the mat around the sushi roll and remove mat. Using a sharp knife, cut across the center of the sushi roll, then cut each half into thirds, to create 6 round pieces. Arrange pieces on their sides to reveal the rice and vegetable pattern. Repeat with remaining nori sheets, rice, and fillings, using carrot strips in the first 3 rolls and cucumber strips in the remaining 3 rolls. Garnish sushi platter with pickled ginger, remaining wasabi, shaped into a small mound, and a small dipping bowl for tamari.

MAKES 6 ROLLS, OR 36 PIECES

Calories 53.53 • Protein 1.479 gm • Fat 0.71 gm • Percentage of calories from fat 12% • Cholesterol 0 mg • Dietary fiber 1.109 gm • Sodium 15.99 mg • Calcium 5.578 mg

Tempeh Tacos

Ground seitan or TVP also work well in this recipe in place of the tempeh.

2 tablespoons corn oil
1 onion, chopped
1 pound poached tempeh (see page 12), crumbled
1 ½ cups chunky salsa, homemade (see page 33) or purchased
2 tablespoons tomato paste

Salt and freshly ground black pepper to taste
12 taco shells
Grated cheese, shredded lettuce, and diced tomato as toppings (about 1 cup each)

Preheat the oven to 350 degrees. Heat oil in large skillet over medium-high heat. Add onion and tempeh and sauté until onion is soft and tempeh is golden brown. Stir in salsa and tomato paste and bring to a gentle boil. Season with salt and pepper if desired. Meanwhile, heat the tacos in the oven about 10 minutes. To serve, spoon hot filling into taco shells and serve topped with cheese, lettuce, and tomato.

6 SERVINGS

Calories 430.8 • Protein 24.31 gm • Fat 23 gm • Percentage of calories from fat 48% • Cholesterol 19.96 mg • Dietary fiber 3.761 gm • Sodium 380.6 mg • Calcium 107.2 mg

Eggplant Rolls with Tofu

These eggplant rolls are excellent with Tomato-Basil Sauce on page 219.

1 large eggplant, trimmed and
  peeled, cut lengthwise into 8
  slices, each ¼-inch thick
1½ teaspoons salt
8 ounces spinach, washed and
  trimmed
6 tablespoons corn oil
2 tablespoons all-purpose flour
1 cup scalded milk

1 bay leaf
⅛ teaspoon freshly ground black
  pepper
¼ cup minced onion
1 pound firm tofu, crumbled
1 cup grated Parmesan cheese
¼ cup heavy cream
¼ teaspoon freshly grated nutmeg

Sprinkle the eggplant slices with 1 teaspoon of the salt and let them drain on a rack, turning them once, for 1 hour. Cook the spinach. Squeeze liquid from spinach, coarsely chop, and set aside. Rinse the eggplant slices and pat them dry. In a saucepan, heat 2 tablespoons of the oil over moderate heat, stir in flour, and cook the roux over low heat, stirring, for 3 minutes. Remove the pan from the heat and add milk in a stream, whisking vigorously until the mixture is thick and smooth. Add the bay leaf, the remaining ½ teaspoon salt, and the pepper and simmer the sauce for 10 minutes; then discard the bay leaf and remove sauce from heat.

In a small skillet cook onion in 2 tablespoons of the oil over moderate heat until softened; add tofu, reserved spinach, ¼ cup of the Parmesan, cream, nutmeg, and salt and pepper to taste. Combine the mixture well.

Preheat oven to 350 degrees. In a large skillet heat remaining 2 tablespoons oil over moderately high heat, add the eggplant slices in batches, and cook them over moderate heat, adding more oil if necessary, for 2 minutes on each side, or until they are softened. Transfer the slices as done to paper towels to drain. Put 2 tablespoons of the tofu mixture on a short end of each slice and, starting with the filled end, roll up the slices; arrange them seam side down in a large oiled baking dish. Pour sauce over the rolls, sprinkle them with remaining ¾ cup Parmesan, and bake them for 15 minutes, or until the cheese is lightly browned.

4 SERVINGS

Calories 329.4 • Protein 16.98 gm • Fat 24.53 gm • Percentage of calories from fat 65% • Cholesterol 27.67 mg • Dietary fiber 1.566 gm • Sodium 961.2 mg • Calcium 387.7 mg

Roast Seitan with Pear-Walnut Stuffing

I make this spectacular roast often for special dinner company. Choose a firm pear such as Anjou for the delectable stuffing. Rolling out the raw seitan requires a bit of patience, but the results are worth it.

1-pound piece raw, unpoached
  seitan (see page 11)
½ cup low-sodium tamari
4 tablespoons corn oil
4 pears, peeled, cored, and diced
1½ cups chopped walnuts
8 ounces ground poached seitan
  (see page 8)

1 cup golden raisins
2 cups fresh bread crumbs
½ cup grated Parmesan cheese
¼ teaspoon ground nutmeg
Salt and freshly ground black
  pepper
1½ cup Basic Brown Sauce (see
  page 13)

Marinate raw seitan in tamari at least 1 hour or overnight.

Preheat oven to 300 degrees. Heat oil in a large skillet over medium heat. Add pears, walnuts, and ground seitan. Cook for 5 minutes, stirring. Transfer mixture to a large bowl. Add all remaining ingredients but the Brown Sauce and blend well. Remove seitan from marinade and reserve marinade. Roll out marinated raw seitan with a rolling pin to ¼-inch thickness. Spread surface with stuffing. Roll up in "jelly roll" fashion. Place seam side down in oiled shallow baking pan. Pierce with fork in several places. Combine tamari marinade with ½ cup water and pour over roast for basting. Bake uncovered for 30 to 40 minutes, basting every 10 minutes. Roast is done when surface is firm, browned, and glossy. Remove from oven and cut into ½-inch slices with a serrated knife (see note page 229). Serve with Basic Brown Sauce.

6 TO 8 SERVINGS

Calories 821.7 • Protein 30.81 gm • Fat 28.61 gm • Percentage of calories from fat 30% • Cholesterol 5.643 mg • Dietary fiber 16.42 gm • Sodium 1416 mg • Calcium 216.4 mg

Roast Seitan with Apple Stuffing

A showpiece roast to rival any turkey or ham. Serve with pride at your next holiday dinner.

1-pound piece raw, unpoached
  seitan (see page 11)
½ cup low-sodium tamari
½ pound ground poached seitan
  (see page 8)
1 teaspoon salt
½ teaspoon freshly ground black
  pepper
1 teaspoon dried thyme, crumbled
1 teaspoon dried sage, crumbled
¼ teaspoon ground nutmeg

¼ teaspoon ground allspice
¼ cup brandy
6 cups cubed bread
2 tablespoons corn oil
2 cups chopped peeled Granny
  Smith apples
1 cup minced onion
½ cup minced celery
½ cup minced fresh parsley
1½ cups Basic Brown Sauce (see
  page 13)

Marinate raw seitan in tamari at least 1 hour or overnight. Place the ground seitan in a large bowl. Add ½ teaspoon of the salt, ¼ teaspoon of the pepper, ½ teaspoon of the thyme, ½ teaspoon of the sage, the nutmeg, and the allspice and mix well. Blend in brandy. Cover and refrigerate at least 1 hour.

Spread cubes of bread on 2 large baking sheets. Bake until brown and dry, stirring frequently, about 20 minutes. Let them cool, then transfer to a large mixing bowl. Heat 2 tablespoons oil in a large skillet over medium heat. Add apples, onion, and celery and cook until vegetables begin to soften, 5 to 7 minutes, stirring occasionally. Add reserved ground seitan mixture and parsley, and cook 3 more minutes. Add mixture to bread and toss gently. Blend in remaining ½ teaspoon salt, ¼ teaspoon pepper, ½ teaspoon thyme, and ½ teaspoon sage. Taste and adjust seasonings. Cool completely. Then refrigerate at least 30 minutes before using.

Preheat oven to 300 degrees. Remove seitan from marinade and reserve marinade. Roll out marinated raw seitan with a rolling pin until about ¼ inch thick. Spread surface with stuffing. Roll up in "jelly roll" fashion. Place seam side down in oiled shallow baking pan. Pierce with fork in several places. Combine tamari marinade with ½ cup water and pour over roast for basting. Roast uncovered 30 to 40 minutes, basting every 10 minutes. Roast is done when surface is firm, browned, and glossy. Remove from oven and slice in ½-inch slices with serrated knife (see note). Serve with Basic Brown Sauce.

8 SERVINGS

Calories 395.6 • Protein 17.62 gm • Fat 5.412 gm • Percentage of calories from fat 11% • Cholesterol 0 mg • Dietary fiber 12.33 gm • Sodium 1265 mg • Calcium 137.1 mg

Note: Roast seitan cuts more easily when allowed to rest for 5 to 10 minutes before slicing. I have also had success with roasting it in advance, allowing it to cool completely, and refrigerating overnight. On the serving day, I simply slice the roast, sprinkle with 1 tablespoon of water (to create steam), wrap loosely in foil, and bake at 375 degrees for 15 minutes, until heated through.

Sicilian Stuffed Peppers

4 green bell peppers, tops cut off, seeded
1 large carrot, grated
¼ cup minced onion
¼ cup chopped walnuts
1 tablespoon grated Pecorino Romano cheese
¼ cup raisins

4 tablespoons corn oil
¼ cup dry bread crumbs
¼ teaspoon salt
⅛ teaspoon freshly ground black pepper
¼ cup shredded mozzarella cheese

Cook peppers in large saucepan of boiling water for 5 minutes. Rinse under cold water and drain. Preheat oven to 350 degrees. Lightly oil a baking dish large enough to hold the peppers. Combine carrot, onion, walnuts, Romano cheese, raisins, 2 tablespoons of the oil, 2 tablespoons of the bread crumbs, salt, and pepper in a large bowl and mix well. Arrange peppers in prepared dish and divide stuffing among them. Top each with mozzarella and remaining bread crumbs. Drizzle with remaining oil. Bake 30 minutes or until heated through. Serve immediately.

4 SERVINGS

Calories 290.8 • Protein 5.991 gm • Fat 20.59 gm • Percentage of calories from fat 61% • Cholesterol 5.46 mg • Dietary fiber 3.222 gm • Sodium 266 mg • Calcium 114.8 mg

Stuffed Eggplant

The capers and olives add a piquant flavor to this savory dish. Advance preparation makes this a no-fuss dinner on a busy evening. If prepared ahead, bring to room temperature before baking.

2 large eggplants
1 onion, chopped
1 red bell pepper, chopped
4 tablespoons olive oil
2 tablespoons capers
½ cup chopped green olives
1 cup cooked brown rice
½ cup TVP combined with ½ cup water

½ cup grated Pecorino Romano cheese
2 tablespoons minced fresh parsley
2 tablespoons minced fresh basil
1 teaspoon salt
½ teaspoon freshly ground black pepper

Halve eggplants lengthwise. Scoop out centers and chop. Place eggplant shells on large steamer rack over boiling water, cover, and steam for 5 minutes. Remove from heat and allow to cool. Preheat oven to 400 degrees. In a large skillet cook the onion and bell pepper in 2 tablespoons of the oil over moderate heat, stirring, for 5 minutes; then transfer to a large bowl. Heat remaining 2 tablespoons oil in the skillet over moderately high heat, and sauté the chopped eggplant, stirring, until tender. Transfer the eggplant to the onion mixture and stir in the capers, olives, rice, TVP, cheese, parsley, basil, salt, and pepper. Divide the stuffing among the eggplant halves. Arrange the eggplants in an oiled baking dish and bake them for 20 minutes, or until heated through.

4 SERVINGS

Calories 330 • Protein 15.23 gm • Fat 19.13 gm • Percentage of calories from fat 50% • Cholesterol 12.67 mg • Dietary fiber 3.688 gm • Sodium 989 mg • Calcium 223.3 mg

Kabocha Squash with Ginger-Peanut Stuffing

If kabocha squash is unavailable, substitute any sweet winter squash, such as butternut or acorn. The sweetness of the squash is enhanced by the array of aromatic spices. Serve with Basic Brown Sauce (see page 13) or Green Apple Chutney (see page 21).

1 large or 2 small kabocha squash
2 tablespoons corn oil
1 large onion, sliced
1 clove garlic, minced
2 cups sliced mushrooms
½ cup raisins
2 teaspoons minced fresh ginger
¼ teaspoon ground cardamom
¼ teaspoon ground cinnamon

¼ teaspoon freshly ground black pepper
⅛ teaspoon ground cloves
2 cups cooked brown rice
½ cup chopped unsalted roasted peanuts
½ cup Basic Vegetable Stock (see page 10)

Preheat oven to 375 degrees. Halve kabocha squash and scoop out seeds. Place squash halves face down in shallow baking dish, add ½ inch water, cover tightly, and bake for 30 minutes. Remove from oven and carefully turn squash over. Allow to cool slightly. Meanwhile, while squash is baking, heat oil in large skillet over medium heat. Add onion and garlic, cover, and cook, stirring occasionally, until onion is translucent, about 5 minutes. Add mushrooms, raisins, ginger, and spices and cook until mushrooms are soft, about 5 minutes. Remove from heat and stir in rice, peanuts, and stock. Cool stuffing briefly, then divide it among squash halves. Return baking dish to oven and bake uncovered for 20 minutes.

4 SERVINGS

Calories 433.6 • Protein 10.61 gm • Fat 17.05 gm • Percentage of calories from fat 34% • Cholesterol 0 mg • Dietary fiber 6.815 gm • Sodium 48.94 mg • Calcium 106.4 mg

Bulgur-Stuffed Cabbage Rolls with Tomato Chutney

The fragrantly spiced fruit and nuts are a delicious complement to the bulgur and cabbage. The tomato chutney is a tasty accompaniment, although these flavorful rolls are also great without it.

4 tablespoons corn oil
1 large onion, chopped
1 teaspoon ground coriander
1½ cups slivered almonds
1½ cup dried apricots, coarsely
 chopped
1½ cups raisins
4 cups cooked bulgur

2 teaspoons ground cinnamon
½ teaspoon ground cloves
½ teaspoon salt
⅛ teaspoon freshly ground black
 pepper
1 large green cabbage
Tomato Chutney (recipe follows)

Heat oil in a large skillet over medium heat. Add onion and coriander, cover, and cook, stirring occasionally, until onion is translucent, about 5 minutes. Add almonds, apricots, and raisins and cook uncovered, stirring occasionally, until almonds are golden. Transfer to a large bowl. Add bulgur, cinnamon, cloves, salt, and pepper and toss well. Cool briefly, then refrigerate stuffing at least 30 minutes before using.

Place steamer rack in a pot large enough to hold entire head of cabbage. Add water, place cabbage on steamer rack, and heat to boiling. Steam, covered, 5 minutes. Remove lid and take out cabbage. When cabbage is cool enough to handle, peel 3 or 4 leaves away as carefully as possible without tearing. When leaves have been removed, return cabbage to steamer. Cook cabbage for 5 more minutes; remove; peel leaves. Repeat process of cooking cabbage and peeling off leaves until 24 to 28 leaves have been removed.

Thoroughly stir stuffing. Place cabbage leaves, one at a time, on cutting surface with rib side down. Place a scant ¼ cup stuffing in center of rib end of cabbage leaf. Roll up cabbage leaf, folding in sides of leaf so stuffing will not spill out while cooking. Place rolled cabbage leaves, seam side down, on a platter. Repeat until all stuffing and cabbage leaves have been used. Arrange cabbage rolls tightly in a large saucepan or Dutch oven, layering if necessary. Add 2 cups water, sprinkle with salt and pepper, and cook, covered, over very low heat until tender, about 45 minutes. Uncover and continue to cook over low heat to reduce liquid, about 10 minutes. Remove cabbage rolls to platter. Serve with Tomato Chutney on the side.

6 TO 8 SERVINGS

Calories 524.2 • Protein 15.69 gm • Fat 22.6 gm • Percentage of calories from fat 35% • Cholesterol 0 mg • Dietary fiber 14.21 gm • Sodium 81.42 mg • Calcium 216.4 mg

Tomato Chutney

1 28-ounce can Italian plum
  tomatoes, with liquid
¾ cup red wine vinegar
½ cup sugar or a natural
  sweetener

1 teaspoon salt
½ teaspoon cayenne
1 tablespoon minced garlic
2 teaspoons minced fresh ginger
2 tablespoons golden raisins

Bring tomatoes and their liquid, vinegar, sugar, salt, and cayenne to a boil in a saucepan. Stir in garlic and ginger. Reduce heat, cover partially, and simmer gently about 1 hour, stirring occasionally. Uncover and continue simmering, stirring frequently, about 10 minutes. Cool. Stir in raisins and adjust seasonings. Serve at room temperature.

MAKES 3 CUPS (⅓-CUP SERVING)

Calories 88.89 • Protein 1.76 gm • Fat 0.037 gm • Percentage of calories from fat 0% • Cholesterol 0 mg • Dietary fiber 1.75 gm • Sodium 791.1 mg • Calcium 6.322 mg

Barley-Stuffed Cabbage Rolls

Full of Old World flavor, these cabbage rolls are satisfying and delicious. Several years ago, a craving for this dish from my childhood prompted me to find my mother's old recipe and devise a meatless version.

2 tablespoons corn oil
1 cup minced onion, plus
  1 tablespoon grated
1 cup minced celery
1 cup minced carrot
3 cups tomato purée
¼ cup sugar or a natural
  sweetener
1 cup barley

1 large head green cabbage,
  trimmed and cored
1 pound ground seitan (see
  page 8)
1 teaspoon salt
¼ teaspoon freshly ground black
  pepper
2 tablespoons fresh lemon juice

Heat oil in a large saucepan over medium heat. Add minced onion, celery, and carrot and sauté, stirring often, until vegetables begin to soften, about 5 minutes. Cook vegetables, covered, over low heat until tender, about 10 minutes. Stir tomato purée and sugar into cooked vegetables. Cook this mixture, partially covered, over low heat about 10 minutes. Remove from heat.

Meanwhile, cook barley in 3 cups boiling water in a medium saucepan over medium heat, uncovered, 10 minutes. Drain and serve.

Place steamer rack in a pot large enough to hold entire head of cabbage. Add water, place cabbage on steamer rack, and heat to boiling. Steam, covered, 5 minutes. Remove lid, and take out cabbage from steamer. When cabbage is cool enough to handle, carefully peel off outer leaves. When 3 or 4 limp leaves have been removed, return cabbage to steamer. Cook cabbage for 5 minutes; remove; peel leaves. Repeat process of cooking cabbage and peeling off leaves until 24 to 28 leaves have been removed.

Place reserved cooked barley, ground seitan, the 1 tablespoon grated onion, salt, and pepper in a large bowl. Combine well. Place cabbage leaves, one at a time, on work surface, rib side down.

Place ¼ cup stuffing in center of rib end of cabbage leaf. Roll up cabbage leaf, folding in sides of leaf so stuffing mixture will not spill out. Place rolled cabbage leaves, seam side down, on a platter. Repeat until all stuffing and cabbage leaves have been used.

Stir lemon juice into tomato sauce; season with salt and pepper to taste. Arrange cabbage rolls in a large saucepan or Dutch oven, layering if necessary. Add tomato sauce and cook, covered, over very low heat until tender, about 45 minutes. Uncover and continue to cook over low heat until sauce thickens, about 15 minutes. Remove cabbage rolls to a serving platter. Spoon tomato sauce over cabbage rolls and serve immediately.

6 TO 8 SERVINGS

Calories 444.9 • Protein 17.54 gm • Fat 6.05 gm • Percentage of calories from fat 11% • Cholesterol 0 mg • Dietary fiber 18.07 gm • Sodium 551.1 mg • Calcium 139 mg

Stuffed Butternut Squash with Brown Sauce

1 butternut squash, halved and
seeded
2 tablespoons corn oil
1 medium onion, minced
1 rib celery, minced
¼ cup minced fresh parsley
½ teaspoon salt
⅛ teaspoon freshly ground black
pepper

⅛ teaspoon dried thyme
⅛ teaspoon dried sage
2 cups fresh bread cubes
½ cup TVP combined with ½ cup
water
1 cup cooked brown rice
¼ cup Basic Vegetable Stock (see
page 10), if needed
Basic Brown Sauce (see page 13)

Preheat oven to 350 degrees. Place squash halves in baking pan, cut side up. Set aside. Heat oil in a large skillet over medium-high heat, add onion and celery, and sauté for 5 minutes. Add parsley, salt, pepper, thyme, and sage. Sauté 3 minutes longer. Transfer onion mixture to a large bowl and add bread cubes, TVP, and rice, tossing well to combine. Taste to adjust seasonings. If additional moisture is needed, add stock to moisten. Fill squash cavities with stuffing. Add 1 inch water to baking pan, cover, and bake for 1 hour or until squash is tender. Uncover for last 5 minutes of cooking time to brown top. Serve with Brown Sauce.

2 SERVINGS

Calories 563.5 • Protein 26.6 gm • Fat 16.83 gm • Percent of calories from fat 25% • Cholesterol 0 mg • Dietary fiber 17.71 gm • Sodium 849.4 mg • Calcium 298.4

Stuffed Peppers Italian Style

¼ cup olive oil
½ cup minced onion
1 clove garlic, minced
½ teaspoon salt
¼ teaspoon freshly ground black
  pepper
1 20-ounce can tomato purée
½ cup minced celery
1 cup cooked brown rice
1 cup TVP combined with 1 cup
  water

1 tablespoon minced fresh parsley
1 teaspoon minced fresh basil or
  ½ teaspoon dried
1 cup dried bread crumbs
6 large green bell peppers, tops
  cut off, seeded
½ cup freshly grated Parmesan
  cheese

Preheat the oven to 350 degrees. Heat 2 tablespoons of the oil in a large skillet over medium-high heat. Add onion and sauté for 5 minutes. Add garlic, salt, pepper, tomato purée, and celery. Simmer uncovered for 20 minutes. Add cooked rice and TVP. Combine well and remove from heat.

Combine remaining olive oil, parsley, basil, and bread crumbs. Toss with a fork and set aside.

Place peppers in boiling water and cook for 5 minutes. Drain and cool. Stuff peppers with rice mixture and sprinkle with crumb mixture, topping all with Parmesan cheese. Place in a lightly oiled baking dish and bake for 30 minutes.

6 SERVINGS

Calories 358.7 • Protein 21.61 gm • Fat 13.27 gm • Percentage of calories from fat 31% • Cholesterol 6.583 mg • Dietary fiber 8.506 gm • Sodium 522 mg • Calcium 262.7 mg

Tofu-Stuffed Lasagne Spirals

Make this appealing dish when fresh tomatoes and basil are at their peak for a light, delicious change from regular lasagne.

8 ounces lasagne noodles
4 cups chopped ripe tomatoes
1 large clove garlic, minced
½ cup chopped fresh parsley
2 teaspoons minced fresh basil
½ teaspoon salt

¼ teaspoon freshly ground black pepper
1 pound firm tofu
1 cup chopped mushrooms
⅓ cup minced scallions

Place lasagne noodles in a large pot of boiling salted water and cook uncovered, stirring occasionally, until tender. While noodles are cooking, make a sauce by combining tomatoes, garlic, half the parsley, half the basil, half the salt, and half the pepper in a large skillet. Cover and cook over low heat for 20 minutes. Remove from heat and set aside.

Preheat oven to 350 degrees. Drain cooked noodles in a colander, rinse with cold water and separate, laying out each noodle on a flat surface. In a medium bowl, combine tofu, mushrooms, scallions, and the remaining ¼ cup parsley, 1 teaspoon basil, ¼ teaspoon salt, and ⅛ teaspoon pepper. Stir until blended. Spread mixture evenly over each noodle within ½ inch of each end and roll up. Meanwhile, place 1 cup tomato sauce in the bottom of a lightly oiled casserole dish. Set lasagne rolls upright in casserole. Pour remaining tomato sauce over and around rolls. Cover and bake for 30 minutes or until heated through.

4 SERVINGS

Calories 246 • Protein 15.85 gm • Fat 5.327 gm • Percentage of calories from fat 18% • Cholesterol 0 mg • Dietary fiber 5.335 gm • Sodium 374.8 mg • Calcium 75.21 mg

Stuffed Summer Squash Florentine

A bright sunny dish, perfect for a casual summer supper.

1 teaspoon corn oil
1½ cups cooked basmati rice
¼ cup minced fresh spinach
2 tablespoons minced onion
2 tablespoons minced green bell
  pepper
½ cup soft tofu blended with 1
  tablespoon milk
3 tablespoons freshly grated
  Parmesan cheese

¼ teaspoon salt
⅛ teaspoon cayenne pepper
3 medium yellow squash, halved
  lengthwise and seeded
½ cup sour cream, or ½ cup tofu
  mixed with 1 tablespoon lemon
  juice
Snipped fresh chives

Preheat oven to 350 degrees. Lightly oil a baking dish with the corn oil. In a large bowl, combine rice, spinach, onion, green pepper, tofu mixture, Parmesan, salt, and cayenne. Spoon into squash halves. Arrange squash halves in the prepared baking dish. Add ¼ cup water and cover tightly. Bake until squash is tender, about 30 minutes. Serve immediately, topped with sour cream or tofu mixture and chives.

6 SERVINGS

Calories 145.3 • Protein 5.65 gm • Fat 5.516 gm • Percentage of calories from fat 33% • Cholesterol 10.66 mg • Dietary fiber 0.198 gm • Sodium 161.2 mg • Calcium 116.2 mg

Pesto-Stuffed Potatoes

A recipe for pesto sauce is given on page 126, where it is paired with linguine.

4 large baking potatoes, well scrubbed

2 tablespoons pine nuts

2 tablespoons Pesto Sauce (see page 126)

¼ cup soft tofu

2 teaspoons olive oil

2 tablespoons grated Parmesan cheese

Preheat oven to 375 degrees. Prick potatoes with a fork and bake for about 1 hour, or until soft. Toast pine nuts in a small skillet over medium-low heat, shaking frequently until lightly browned, about 5 minutes. Carefully scoop out potato centers into a bowl, mash with pesto sauce, tofu, and olive oil, combine well. Replace stuffing in each of the potato skins and arrange potatoes in a broiler pan or baking dish. In a small bowl, combine Parmesan with pine nuts, sprinkle on the potatoes, and brown under the broiler.

4 SERVINGS

Calories 287.3 • Protein 9.994 gm • Fat 12.37 gm • Percentage of calories from fat 37% • Cholesterol 3.086 mg • Dietary fiber 4.159 gm • Sodium 101.7 mg • Calcium 89.39 mg

Seitan Kebabs

Especially delicious when cooked on the grill. Your guests will find it hard to believe they're not eating meat! A Cabernet Sauvignon complements the smoky flavor of the grilled food.

1 cup dry red wine
2 tablespoons red wine vinegar
4 tablespoons olive oil
1 large garlic clove, minced
½ teaspoon freshly ground black pepper
½ teaspoon dried thyme
8 ounces seitan (see page 11), cut into 1-inch cubes
2 tablespoons corn or safflower oil

1 onion, cut into wedges
1 red bell pepper, seeded and cut into 1-inch squares
8 mushroom caps
1 yellow squash, cut into ¼-inch rounds
8 cherry tomatoes, or 1 large tomato cut into wedges
Freshly cooked brown rice

Combine wine, vinegar, olive oil, garlic, pepper, and thyme in a bowl to make the marinade. Combine seitan with marinade in a shallow bowl. Marinate in refrigerator at least 1 hour or overnight, turning occasionally. Drain seitan, reserving marinade. Heat oil in a large skillet over medium-high heat. Add onion and pepper pieces and cook for 2 minutes. Add mushroom caps and squash slices; cook 2 more minutes. Remove from pan and set aside. Reheat skillet, add marinated seitan, and brown lightly. Allow to cool.

Assemble seitan, tomatoes, and partially cooked vegetables on skewers, alternating ingredients. Kebabs may now finish cooking on outdoor grill, basting with remaining marinade, or roasted in a 400-degree oven for 10 minutes. Reduce remaining marinade by one half and spoon over kebabs on a bed of brown rice. Serve immediately.

4 TO 6 SERVINGS

Calories 349.1 • Protein 8.127 gm • Fat 17.35 gm • Percentage of calories from fat 43% • Cholesterol 0 mg • Dietary fiber 6.389 gm • Sodium 156.5 mg • Calcium 41.49 mg

Seitan Satays with Peanut Dressing

Bamboo skewers are available in many supermarkets and specialty stores. Soak skewers in water for 30 minutes before using, to prevent them from burning.

1 onion, chopped
2 tablespoons lemon juice
3 tablespoons low-sodium tamari
2 tablespoons tomato paste
2 tablespoons sugar or a natural
  sweetener
8 tablespoons dark sesame oil
2 cloves garlic, chopped
¾ teaspoon salt
½ teaspoon ground coriander

½ teaspoon ground cinnamon
¼ teaspoon ground cloves
1 pound seitan (see page 11), cut
  into ½-inch strips
¼ cup rice vinegar
4 tablespoons safflower oil
1 head romaine lettuce, cut in
  ¼-inch strips (about 6 cups)
1 cup unsalted roasted peanuts
Peanut Dressing (recipe follows)

Blend onion, lemon juice, tamari, tomato paste, sugar, 2 tablespoons of the sesame oil, garlic, ½ teaspoon of the salt, coriander, cinnamon, and cloves in food processor until smooth. Transfer to a large bowl. Add seitan and toss to coat with mixture. Cover and marinate at least 1 hour at room temperature. Mix vinegar with remaining ¼ teaspoon salt in a small bowl. Whisk in remaining 6 tablespoons sesame oil and the 4 tablespoons safflower oil in thin steady stream.

Preheat broiler. Drain seitan, reserving marinade, then thread strips on soaked bamboo skewers, in an "S" pattern. Broil 3 inches from heat source until slightly browned, turning once and brushing with marinade.

Place romaine in a large bowl. Rewhisk sesame vinaigrette and add enough to romaine to season to taste. Toss to blend. Line serving plates with romaine, top with hot satay skewers, and sprinkle with chopped nuts. Serve immediately, passing Peanut Dressing separately.

6 SERVINGS

Calories 659 • Protein 19.64 gm • Fat 40.5 gm • Percentage of calories from fat 53% • Cholesterol 0 mg • Dietary fiber 11.46 gm • Sodium 781.2 mg • Calcium 86.95 mg

Peanut Dressing

1 cup peanut butter
¼ cup low-sodium tamari
2 tablespoons fresh lemon juice

1 large clove garlic
1 teaspoon hot chili oil

Blend ingredients in a food processor until smooth, stopping occasionally to scrape down sides of work bowl. With machine running, add just enough water (about ¼ to ½ cup) in thin steady stream to thin dressing to desired consistency. Adjust seasonings. Serve at room temperature.

MAKES ABOUT 2 CUPS (¼-CUP SERVING)

Calories 20.25 • Protein 8.79 gm • Fat 16.56 gm • Percentage of calories from fat 69% • Cholesterol 0 mg • Dietary fiber 2.04 gm • Sodium 456 mg • Calcium 14.85 mg

Mushroom-Tofu Stuffed Potatoes

4 large baking potatoes, well
  scrubbed
1 tablespoon olive oil
1 cup sliced mushrooms

1 tablespoon low-sodium tamari
4 ounces soft tofu, mashed
2 tablespoons grated Parmesan
  cheese

Preheat oven to 375 degrees. Prick potatoes with a fork and bake about
1 hour or until soft. Meanwhile, heat oil in a medium skillet over medium
heat. Add mushrooms and sauté for 2 minutes. Add tamari. Remove from
heat and set aside. Carefully scoop out the potato centers into a bowl and
mash with tofu, combining well. Fold in mushrooms, including pan juices.
Return stuffing to each of the potato skins and arrange potatoes in a baking
pan. Sprinkle potatoes with Parmesan and brown under the broiler.

4 SERVINGS

Calories 233.9 • Protein 9.914 gm • Fat 5.338 gm • Percentage of calories from fat
20% • Cholesterol 2.469 mg • Dietary fiber 4.324 gm • Sodium 235.4 mg • Calcium
76.62 mg

8

Sautéed, Seared, and Grilled

Take out your sauté pan and get ready to cook up delicious meals in minutes. All your favorite classic recipes are featured here, as Seitan Marsala, Tempeh Normandy, Tofu Grenoble, updated and reinterpreted, using delicious and healthful meat alternatives.

Experiment with flavors by trying out Tofu with Lime-Wasabi Marinade, Three-Mushroom Sauté with Seitan and Cognac Sauce, or Tempeh with Port and Ginger Sauce. Each recipe is simple to make, with spectacularly tasty results.

Seitan in Mustard-Cognac Sauce

This is a dish for a special occasion, and it deserves your best china and silver.

2 tablespoons corn oil
1 pound seitan (see page 11), cut into ¼-inch slices
2 cloves garlic, minced
2 tablespoons white wine vinegar
¾ cup dry white wine
1 tablespoon Cognac or brandy

2 tablespoons Dijon mustard
1 teaspoon tomato paste
1 cup heavy cream
Salt and freshly ground black pepper
1 tablespoon chopped fresh parsley

Preheat oven to 275 degrees. Heat oil in a large skillet over medium heat. Add seitan and garlic; sauté until seitan is lightly browned on both sides, about 5 minutes. Transfer seitan to ovenproof platter and keep warm in oven. Add vinegar to skillet and deglaze over medium-low heat, scraping up brown bits; pour liquid into a medium saucepan. Stir in wine, Cognac, mustard, and tomato paste. Boil over medium heat until reduced to ½ cup, about 5 minutes. Boil cream gently in a separate small saucepan over medium heat to reduce slightly, about 2 minutes. Gradually stir cream into wine mixture and heat for about 30 seconds; remove from heat. Season with salt and pepper to taste. Pour sauce over seitan and garnish with chopped parsley. Serve immediately.

4 SERVINGS

Calories 657.1 • Protein 18.27 gm • Fat 31.15 gm • Percentage of calories from fat 41% • Cholesterol 81.5 mg • Dietary fiber 12.34 gm • Sodium 514.4 mg • Calcium 87.25 mg

Tempeh with Madeira

1 tablespoon corn oil
1 shallot, minced
1 pound poached tempeh (see
   page 12), cut into ¼-inch slices
½ cup dry white wine
3 tablespoons Madeira

½ teaspoon tomato paste
½ cup heavy cream
¼ teaspoon salt
⅛ teaspoon freshly ground black
   pepper

Heat oil in a large skillet over medium heat and cook shallot and tempeh until tempeh is browned on both sides, about 4 minutes. Add white wine and bring to a boil. Reduce heat and simmer until reduced by half, about 5 minutes. Remove tempeh and keep warm. Add Madeira to skillet and cook 2 minutes. Whisk in tomato paste and cream. Bring sauce to a boil, then lower heat and simmer until slightly thickened, about 2 minutes. Season to taste with salt and pepper. Add tempeh to pan with sauce and heat about 1 minute. Put tempeh on plates and top with sauce.

4 SERVINGS

Calories 341.6 • Protein 18.81 gm • Fat 22.96 gm • Percentage of calories from fat 60% • Cholesterol 40.75 mg • Dietary fiber 3.34 gm • Sodium 197.1 mg • Calcium 103.2 mg

Barbecued Tofu Cutlets

This sauce is so tasty, you'll want to eat it with a spoon; but if you save some for the tofu, you won't be sorry.

1 onion, chopped
1 large clove garlic, chopped
¼ cup apple butter
1 teaspoon Chinese chili paste
¼ cup fresh lemon juice
3 tablespoons corn oil
1 tablespoon Worcestershire
  sauce

½ cup tomato sauce
2 teaspoons dry mustard
1 tablespoon sugar or a natural
  sweetener
½ teaspoon salt
1 pound firm tofu, cut into 8
  ½-inch cutlets
Freshly cooked brown rice

Place onion and garlic in a food processor and pulse until onion is finely chopped. Add apple butter, chili paste, and lemon juice; process until mixture is well blended. Add 1 tablespoon of the oil, the Worcestershire sauce, tomato sauce, mustard, sugar, and salt and process until combined. Transfer barbecue sauce to a saucepan and simmer, stirring occasionally, for 30 minutes.

Meanwhile, heat remaining 2 tablespoons oil in a large skillet over medium-high heat. Add tofu slices and cook until golden brown, about 3 minutes on each side. When browned, add enough barbecue sauce to coat well, and simmer tofu in sauce about 15 minutes. Serve over rice with extra sauce passed separately.

4 SERVINGS

Calories 244.3 • Protein 10.31 gm • Fat 13.14 gm • Percentage of calories from fat 47% • Cholesterol 0 mg • Dietary fiber 1.252 gm • Sodium 420.5 mg • Calcium 68.54 mg

Tempeh in Mustard Sauce

3 tablespoons corn oil
1 pound poached tempeh (see
 page 12), cut into ¼-inch slices
½ cup minced shallots
1 clove garlic, finely minced
½ cup dry white wine
½ cup heavy cream
4 tablespoons Dijon mustard

1 tablespoon fresh lemon juice
1 tablespoon minced fresh parsley
1 tablespoon minced fresh
 tarragon
½ teaspoon salt
⅛ teaspoon freshly ground black
 pepper

Heat 2 tablespoons oil in a large skillet over medium-high heat. Add tempeh and sauté on both sides until golden. Reduce heat to low, cover, and cook 5 minutes. Transfer tempeh to a platter and keep warm. Add remaining 1 tablespoon oil to the skillet over medium heat, add shallots, and cook 5 minutes or until soft. Add garlic and stir 1 minute. Increase heat to high, add white wine, and cook until reduced by half. Reduce heat to medium, add cream and mustard, and cook, stirring, until sauce is thick. Blend in lemon juice. Add parsley, tarragon, salt, and pepper. Spoon some sauce into center of each serving plate. Top with tempeh. Spoon more sauce over and serve.

4 SERVINGS

Calories 398.6 • Protein 20.27 gm • Fat 27.34 gm • Percentage of calories from fat 61% • Cholesterol 40.75 mg • Dietary fiber 3.463 gm • Sodium 667.6 mg • Calcium 116.8 mg

Ginger-Marinated Seitan

The pungent flavors of this simple marinade are absorbed into the seitan for a very tasty simple sauté.

1 clove garlic, minced
2 tablespoons minced fresh ginger
½ cup low-sodium tamari
4 tablespoons corn oil
1 teaspoon crushed black peppercorns

1 pound seitan (see page 11), cut into ¼-inch slices
⅛ teaspoon freshly ground black pepper
Freshly cooked brown rice

In a bowl, combine garlic, ginger, tamari, 3 tablespoons of the oil, and the peppercorns. Put seitan in a shallow bowl, cover with the mixture, and marinate for at least 1 hour or overnight. In a large skillet, heat remaining 1 tablespoon oil over medium-high heat. Brown seitan slices on both sides, about 2 minutes for each. Season seitan with pepper, add marinade, and cook 10 to 15 minutes, turning once and basting with the marinade. Serve over rice.

4 SERVINGS

Calories 496.1 • Protein 20.04 gm • Fat 15.48 gm • Percentage of calories from fat 27% • Cholesterol 0 mg • Dietary fiber 12.37 gm • Sodium 1647 mg • Calcium 55.67 mg

Tempeh with Pears

1 cup heavy cream
1½ cups Basic Vegetable Stock
 (see page 10)
2 tablespoons corn oil
2 firm pears, peeled and sliced
1 pound poached tempeh (see
 page 12), cut into 3- × 1- × ¼-inch
 bars

1 tablespoon brandy
1 teaspoon fresh lemon juice
Salt and freshly ground black
 pepper

Heat cream in medium saucepan over low heat to boiling. Boil slowly, stirring often, until reduced to ¾ cup, about 5 minutes. While cream is reducing, heat stock in separate saucepan to boiling; boil over medium heat until reduced to ¾ cup, about 5 minutes. When both liquids are reduced, pour stock into cream; cook over medium-low heat until reduced to 1 cup, about 5 minutes; reserve. Heat oil in medium skillet. Add pear slices; sauté over medium-high heat until lightly browned on both sides, about 5 minutes. Transfer pears with a slotted spatula to a warm platter; keep warm, covered. Add tempeh to skillet. Sauté over medium heat until heated through, about 3 minutes. Transfer tempeh to serving platter. Reheat sauce over medium heat. Add brandy and lemon juice; season with salt and pepper to taste. Pour over tempeh and serve immediately.

4 SERVINGS

Calories 541.6 • Protein 20.35 gm • Fat 37.92 gm • Percentage of calories from fat 61% • Cholesterol 81.5 mg • Dietary fiber 7.504 gm • Sodium 125.8 mg • Calcium 139.9 mg

Seitan Milanese

½ cup grated Parmesan cheese
⅓ cup dry bread crumbs
3 tablespoons corn oil
1 pound seitan (see page 11), cut
  into ¼-inch slices
½ teaspoon salt
⅛ teaspoon freshly ground black
  pepper

¼ cup all-purpose flour
2 tablespoons fresh lemon juice
1 lemon, cut into ¼-inch slices
2 tablespoons minced fresh
  parsley

In a small bowl, combine Parmesan and bread crumbs. Mix 1 tablespoon of the corn oil with 1 teaspoon water in a shallow bowl. Sprinkle seitan with salt and pepper and dredge in flour, shaking off excess. Then dip slices in oil mixture and coat with bread crumb mixture. Heat remaining 2 tablespoons of the oil in a large skillet over medium-high heat. Add seitan slices and cook, turning once, until golden brown, about 4 minutes each side. Splash with lemon juice. Garnish with lemon slices and minced parsley.

4 SERVINGS

Calories 555.8 • Protein 23.85 gm • Fat 16.37 gm • Percentage of calories from fat 25% • Cholesterol 9.875 mg • Dietary fiber 13.02 gm • Sodium 861.6 mg • Calcium 250.5 mg

Seitan with Four Peppers

A plethora of peppers will wake up your taste buds in this zesty, colorful sauté. Eliminate the jalapeño if you want to turn down the heat.

4 tablespoons olive oil
1 jalapeño pepper, seeded and minced
1 green bell pepper, seeded and cut into ¼-inch strips
1 red bell pepper, seeded and cut into ¼-inch strips

1 yellow bell pepper, seeded and cut into ¼-inch strips
Salt
1 pound seitan (see page 11), cut into ¼-inch slices
Freshly ground black pepper
1 tablespoon minced fresh parsley

Heat 2 tablespoons of the oil in a large skillet over low heat. Add jalapeño, bell peppers, and a pinch of salt and cook until tender, stirring frequently, about 15 minutes. Sprinkle seitan with salt and pepper. Heat remaining 2 tablespoons olive oil in another large skillet over medium-high heat. Add seitan and cook until brown, about 2 minutes per side. Reheat peppers over low heat, stirring constantly. On the dinner plates, spoon peppers around seitan. Sprinkle with parsley and serve.

4 SERVINGS

Calories 475.8 • Protein 16.88 gm • Fat 15.42 gm • Percentage of calories from fat 28% • Cholesterol 0 mg • Dietary fiber 13.24 gm • Sodium 404.9 mg • Calcium 46.33 mg

Tofu Cutlets with Tapenade Sauce

The neutral flavor of tofu provides the perfect vehicle for the piquant flavors of the tapenade sauce.

2 tablespoons capers
6 oil-cured olives, pitted
3 oil-packed sun-dried tomatoes,
  cut into pieces
¼ cup firmly packed fresh parsley
  leaves

2 tablespoons fresh lemon juice
¼ cup plus 2 tablespoons olive oil
1 pound firm tofu, cut into 8
  ½-inch slices

In a food processor blend capers, olives, tomatoes, parsley, and lemon juice until mixture is chopped fine. With the motor running add the ¼ cup olive oil in a stream and blend tapenade sauce until emulsified. In the meantime, heat remaining 2 tablespoons olive oil in a large skillet and cook the tofu until golden brown, about 2 minutes for each side. Serve tofu topped with tapenade sauce.

4 SERVINGS

Calories 263.9 • Protein 9.572 gm • Fat 24.03 gm • Percentage of calories from fat 79% • Cholesterol 0 mg • Dietary fiber 0.135 gm • Sodium 265.2 mg • Calcium 52.89 mg

Tarragon Tofu

1 pound firm tofu, cut into ¼-inch
  slices
Salt and freshly ground black
  pepper
2 tablespoons corn oil
2 cloves garlic, minced

¼ cup tarragon wine vinegar
1 cup Basic Vegetable Stock (see
  page 10)
1 tablespoon tomato paste
1 tablespoon minced fresh
  tarragon or 1 teaspoon dried

Preheat oven to 275 degrees. Sprinkle tofu with salt and pepper. Heat 1 tablespoon of the oil in a large skillet over medium-high heat. Add tofu and
cook until golden brown, about 1 minute per side. Arrange on ovenproof
platter and keep warm in oven. Heat remaining 1 tablespoon oil over low
heat. Add garlic and stir 30 seconds. Add vinegar, increase heat to medium-
high, and boil until reduced to 3 tablespoons, scraping up any browned
bits. Add stock and boil until reduced to ½ cup, stirring frequently, about 5
minutes. Transfer sauce to a small saucepan. Whisk in tomato paste and
bring to a simmer. Remove sauce from heat and stir in tarragon. Adjust seasonings, pour sauce over tofu, and serve.

4 SERVINGS

Calories 146.5 • Protein 9.794 gm • Fat 9.345 gm • Percentage of calories from
fat 54% • Cholesterol 0 mg • Dietary fiber 0.636 gm • Sodium 139.2 mg • Calcium
54.49 mg

Seitan with Piquant Mushroom Sauce

3 tablespoons olive oil
¼ cup minced onion
¼ cup finely chopped carrot
2 cloves garlic, minced
½ cup finely chopped mushrooms
½ cup chopped fresh tomato
½ cup dry red wine
2 cups Basic Vegetable Stock (see page 10)
¼ teaspoon dried thyme, crumbled

1 pound seitan (see page 11), cut into ¼-inch slices
1 teaspoon tomato paste
1 teaspoon Dijon mustard
⅓ cup red wine vinegar
1 cup sliced mushrooms
¼ teaspoon salt
⅛ teaspoon freshly ground black pepper
1 tablespoon minced fresh parsley

Heat 1 tablespoon of the olive oil in a medium saucepan over medium-high heat. Add onion, carrot, and garlic and cook 2 minutes, stirring. Add mushrooms and tomato and continue stirring 1 minute. Blend in wine, scraping bottom of saucepan. Add stock and thyme. Reduce heat to medium-low; cover and simmer until sauce is reduced to 2 cups, about 30 minutes.

In a large skillet, heat remaining 2 tablespoons olive oil over medium-high heat. Add seitan slices and cook until brown, about 2 minutes on each side. Remove seitan to an ovenproof plate and keep warm in a 275-degree oven.

Strain stock into the skillet, pressing on solids, which are then discarded. Simmer stock over medium-high heat; do not boil. Whisk in tomato paste and mustard. Cook until sauce is reduced to 1 cup, about 15 minutes. Meanwhile, reduce vinegar in a small saucepan over high heat to 2 tablespoons, about 5 minutes. Stir into sauce. Add mushrooms to sauce and cook until tender, about 2 to 3 minutes. Increase heat to high, add salt and pepper, and cook 1 minute. Reduce heat to medium-low. Return seitan to skillet. Cook until seitan is just heated through and coated with sauce, about 1 minute. Sprinkle with parsley and serve immediately.

4 SERVINGS

Calories 503.6 • Protein 18.54 gm • Fat 12.39 gm • Percentage of calories from fat 21% • Cholesterol 0 mg • Dietary fiber 14.32 gm • Sodium 754.4 mg • Calcium 70.87 mg

Seitan with Hazelnuts and Almonds

Reserve this elegant dish for special occasions, as the sauce is positively decadent. I once prepared a "meat" version of this recipe, which became a favorite among restaurant patrons.

½ cup shelled hazelnuts, blanched and skinned
¼ cup Frangelico (hazelnut liqueur)
2 tablespoons corn oil
1 pound seitan (see page 11), cut into ¼-inch slices
Salt and freshly ground black pepper

½ cup sliced almonds
1 cup heavy cream
¼ cup Basic Vegetable Stock (see page 10)
1 teaspoon Dijon mustard
1 tablespoon minced fresh mint

In a small bowl let the hazelnuts soak in the Frangelico for 1 hour and drain them, reserving the liqueur. Heat oil in a large skillet over medium-high heat and add seitan slices, seasoned with salt and pepper, cooking them in batches until browned, about 2 minutes for each side. Transfer seitan to a platter and keep warm, covered. Reheat skillet, add reserved Frangelico, and heat. Ignite it, shake skillet until flames go out, and pour liqueur over the seitan. Put in skillet the almonds, the hazelnuts, cream, stock, mustard, and salt and pepper to taste. Bring liquid to a boil, stirring, over moderately high heat and stir until sauce thickens slightly. Spoon sauce over seitan and garnish with mint.

6 SERVINGS

Calories 571.8 • Protein 16.27 gm • Fat 33.38 gm • Percentage of calories from fat 50% • Cholesterol 54.33 mg • Dietary fiber 10.68 gm • Sodium 246.7 mg • Calcium 111.1 mg

Tofu Cutlets with Warm Shallot Vinaigrette

3 shallots, minced
¼ cup plus 2 tablespoons minced
 fresh parsley
2 tablespoons fresh lemon juice
2 tablespoons balsamic vinegar
1 cup olive oil
Salt and freshly ground black
 pepper

3 tablespoons corn oil
1 cup fresh bread crumbs
1 tablespoon minced fresh
 marjoram or 1 teaspoon dried
1 pound firm tofu, cut into ¼-inch
 slices
All-purpose flour
Lemon wedges

Mix shallots, ¼ cup parsley, lemon juice, and vinegar in a small bowl. Whisk in olive oil in a thin stream. Season with salt and pepper and set the vinaigrette aside.

Combine 1 tablespoon of the corn oil with 1 teaspoon water in a shallow bowl. Combine bread crumbs, remaining 2 tablespoons parsley, and marjoram on a plate. Dust tofu with flour, brush with corn oil mixture, then dredge in crumbs, coating evenly.

Heat remaining 2 tablespoons corn oil in a large skillet over high heat. Add tofu in batches (do not crowd) and cook until golden brown, about 1 minute on each side. Transfer to an ovenproof platter and keep warm in a 275-degree oven. Pour vinaigrette into the skillet and bring to a boil, stirring up any browned bits. Reduce heat and simmer about 4 minutes. Season tofu with salt and pepper, spoon sauce on top, garnish with lemon wedges, and serve immediately.

4 SERVINGS

Calories 742.9 • Protein 12.81 gm • Fat 67.99 gm • Percentage of calories from fat 80% • Cholesterol 0 mg • Dietary fiber 0.935 gm • Sodium 260.6 mg • Calcium 89.96 mg

Tofu Teriyaki

1 pound firm tofu, cut into ¼-inch slices
1 garlic clove, minced
3 tablespoons fresh lemon juice
3 tablespoons low-sodium tamari

1 tablespoon honey or a natural sweetener
3 tablespoons toasted sesame oil
2 tablespoons corn oil

Place the tofu in a large, shallow dish. In a small bowl whisk together garlic, lemon juice, tamari, and honey; add sesame oil in a stream, whisking until marinade has emulsified. Pour marinade over tofu, turning slices to coat well, and let the tofu marinate, turning it occasionally, for at least 1 hour or overnight.

Remove tofu from marinade. Heat corn oil in a large skillet and sauté tofu until golden brown on both sides, about 4 minutes. Add reserved marinade and simmer, turning tofu once, for 10 minutes. Transfer tofu, with marinade, to a platter.

4 SERVINGS

Calories 245.6 • Protein 10.55 gm • Fat 19.45 gm • Percentage of calories from fat 70% • Cholesterol 0 mg • Dietary fiber 0.05 gm • Sodium 528 mg • Calcium 48.94 mg

Seitan Cutlets with Red Wine Sauce

I usually serve these cutlets with freshly cooked noodles, crusty French bread, and a lightly steamed vegetable.

1 pound seitan (see page 11), cut into ¼-inch cutlets
Salt and freshly ground black pepper
2 tablespoons corn oil
¾ cup dry red wine
1 shallot, finely minced
¼ teaspoon dried thyme, crumbled

1 cup Basic Vegetable Stock (see page 10)
1 tablespoon low-sodium tamari
1 tablespoon cornstarch dissolved in 1 tablespoon water
1 tablespoon minced fresh parsley
2 teaspoons snipped fresh chives
1 teaspoon minced fresh tarragon or ½ teaspoon dried

Preheat oven to 275 degrees. Sprinkle seitan with salt and pepper. Heat oil in a large skillet over medium-high heat. Add seitan and cook until brown, about 1 minute per side. Arrange in single layer on ovenproof platter, cover, and keep warm in oven. Reheat skillet, add wine, and bring to a boil, scraping up any browned bits. Add shallot and thyme. Boil until reduced to ¼ cup, stirring occasionally, about 2 minutes. Add stock and tamari. Boil for 5 minutes, whisking constantly. Reduce heat to low and whisk in cornstarch mixture, whisking until thickened. Stir in parsley, chives, and tarragon. Adjust seasonings. Spoon sauce over seitan.

4 SERVINGS

Calories 457.8 • Protein 17.5 gm • Fat 8.709 gm • Percentage of calories from fat 16% • Cholesterol 0 mg • Dietary fiber 12.63 gm • Sodium 544.7 mg • Calcium 55.83 mg

Sautéed Seitan with Basil Sauce

2 tablespoons corn oil
1 pound seitan (see page 11), cut into ¼-inch slices
1 cup chopped onion
½ cup chopped carrot
½ cup chopped celery
2 cups Basic Vegetable Stock (see page 10)
1 cup dry white wine
1 tablespoon minced fresh parsley
1 clove garlic, minced

1 bay leaf
¼ teaspoon minced fresh thyme or ⅛ teaspoon dried, crumbled
¼ teaspoon freshly ground black pepper
1 cup heavy cream
½ cup tightly packed fresh basil leaves
Salt
Basil leaves for garnish

Heat oil in a large skillet over medium-high heat. Add seitan and brown on both sides, about 5 minutes. Transfer to ovenproof platter and keep warm in a 275-degree oven. Reheat skillet over medium-low heat. Add onion, carrot, and celery. Cover and cook until very tender, stirring occasionally, about 20 minutes. Add stock, wine, parsley, garlic, bay leaf, thyme, and pepper and bring to a simmer for 5 minutes. Strain liquid, pour into a saucepan, and boil until reduced by half. Add cream and boil until reduced by half. Add basil and purée sauce in a food processor. Add salt to taste. Serve sauce over seitan slices, garnished with whole basil leaves.

4 SERVINGS

Calories 669.1 • Protein 19.34 gm • Fat 28.01 gm • Percentage of calories from fat 36% • Cholesterol 69 mg • Dietary fiber 14.24 gm • Sodium 469.6 mg • Calcium 126.8 mg

Sautéed Tofu with Spinach and Red Pepper Sauce

Instructions for roasting bell peppers are included elsewhere in the book (see below for page reference). It's not difficult and the flavor is well worth the effort.

½ cup dry white wine
6 tablespoons white wine vinegar
½ teaspoon fresh thyme or ¼ teaspoon dried, crumbled
3 red bell peppers, roasted, peeled, and seeded (see page 22)
Salt and freshly ground black pepper

1 pound fresh spinach, washed and trimmed
2 tablespoons corn oil
1 pound firm tofu, cut into ¼-inch slices

In a medium saucepan, boil wine, vinegar, and thyme until reduced to ¼ cup. Strain and return to saucepan. Purée roasted peppers in a food processor. Add pepper purée to wine reduction and bring to a boil. Season with salt and pepper and keep warm.

Steam spinach until tender, about 3 minutes. Heat 1 tablespoon of the oil in a medium skillet over low heat. Add spinach and stir until heated through. Season with salt and pepper. Reserve.

Sprinkle tofu with salt and pepper. Heat remaining 1 tablespoon oil in a large skillet over medium-high heat. Add tofu in batches and sauté about 1 minute each side. Spoon some of the sauce onto plates. Top with tofu. Arrange spinach on either side of tofu. Pass remaining sauce.

4 TO 6 SERVINGS

Calories 151.2 • Protein 10.32 gm • Fat 7.805 gm • Percentage of calories from fat 42% • Cholesterol 0 mg • Dietary fiber 3.121 gm • Sodium 131.7 mg • Calcium 131.9 mg

Lemon-Ginger Tofu

1 pound frozen firm tofu (see page 49), thawed
2 tablespoons low-sodium tamari
1 teaspoon toasted sesame oil
2 tablespoons fresh lemon juice
1 teaspoon corn oil
1 medium onion, thinly sliced
2 cloves garlic, minced
1 tablespoon grated fresh ginger

½ cup Basic Vegetable Stock (see page 10)
2 teaspoons cornstarch dissolved in 2 teaspoons cold water
Freshly cooked rice or other grain
1 tablespoon toasted sesame seeds (see page 176)

Squeeze thawed tofu gently to remove water. Cut into ½-inch thick slices. In a bowl, whisk together tamari, sesame oil, and lemon juice. Add tofu and marinate for 10 minutes, turning tofu once. Heat corn oil in a large skillet over medium heat. Add onion and sauté until translucent, about 5 minutes. Add garlic and ginger and sauté 1 minute. Remove tofu from marinade and reserve marinade. Add tofu to the skillet and sauté 1 minute. Add marinade and the stock and simmer 5 minutes. Add cornstarch mixture and stir constantly until liquid thickens. Serve immediately over cooked rice or other grain. Garnish with toasted sesame seeds.

4 SERVINGS

Calories 141.9 • Protein 11.2 gm • Fat 5.871 gm • Percentage of calories from fat 37% • Cholesterol 0 mg • Dietary fiber 1.43 gm • Sodium 410.2 mg • Calcium 83.57 mg

Seitan Cutlets with Tarragon-Mustard Sauce

1 pound seitan (see page 11), cut into ¼-inch cutlets
½ teaspoon salt
⅛ teaspoon freshly ground black pepper
2 tablespoons corn oil
¼ cup chopped onion
¼ cup chopped carrot
¼ cup chopped celery

1 tablespoon all-purpose flour
¾ cup Basic Vegetable Stock (see page 10)
¼ cup dry white wine
2 teaspoons minced fresh tarragon or ¾ teaspoon dried
¼ cup heavy cream
1½ tablespoons Dijon mustard
1 teaspoon minced fresh parsley

Season seitan with salt and pepper. Heat oil in a large skillet over medium-high heat. Add seitan slices and sauté until brown on both sides, about 2 minutes per side. Transfer seitan to an ovenproof platter and keep warm in a 275-degree oven. Reduce heat under skillet to medium, add onion, carrot, and celery, and cook, stirring occasionally, until softened, about 5 minutes. Reduce heat to low, add flour, and stir 3 minutes. Stir in stock, wine, and tarragon, scraping up browned bits. Return heat to medium-high and bring sauce to a boil, stirring occasionally. Simmer sauce for 10 minutes, then purée in a food processor. Return sauce to skillet and stir in cream. Raise heat to high and boil until thickened, about 3 to 5 minutes. Remove from heat and blend in mustard and parsley; adjust seasonings. Pour sauce over seitan and serve.

4 SERVINGS

Calories 490.8 • Protein 17.96 gm • Fat 13.89 gm • Percentage of calories from fat 24% • Cholesterol 17.25 mg • Dietary fiber 13.36 gm • Sodium 775.2 mg • Calcium 74.59 mg

Tempeh Normandy

Used in a recipe title, the word Normandy indicates that a dish is made with apples. A tart cooking apple such as Granny Smith works best in this recipe. Use Calvados, applejack, or apple cider to replace the brandy, if you prefer.

1 tablespoon corn oil
1 medium apple, peeled and sliced
1 teaspoon sugar or a natural sweetener
1 pound poached tempeh (see page 12), cut into ¼-inch slices

¼ cup apple juice
2 tablespoons brandy
⅓ cup heavy cream

Heat oil in a large skillet over medium heat. Add apple and sugar and cook until apple is tender, about 3 minutes. Remove slices with slotted spatula. Add tempeh to skillet and cook until golden, turning once, about 5 minutes. Add apple juice and brandy. Reduce heat to medium-low and cook about 5 minutes. Remove tempeh slices with slotted spatula. Add cream to skillet. Increase heat to medium-high and stir until slightly thickened, about 6 minutes. Return tempeh and apples to skillet and heat through, spooning sauce over all. Serve immediately.

4 SERVINGS

Calories 324.3 • Protein 18.53 gm • Fat 19.33 gm • Percentage of calories from fat 53% • Cholesterol 26.9 mg • Dietary fiber 3.789 gm • Sodium 15.83 mg • Calcium 93.6 mg

Seitan Pizzaiola

A meat-alternative version of Steak Pizzaiola that doesn't scrimp on flavor.

2 tablespoons olive oil
1 pound seitan (see page 11), cut
 into 3- × 1-inch strips
½ teaspoon salt
⅛ teaspoon freshly ground black
 pepper
½ pound mushrooms, sliced
1 medium onion, thinly sliced
2 cloves garlic, minced

5 ripe plum tomatoes or 1 cup
 canned Italian tomatoes,
 chopped
¼ cup minced fresh parsley
½ teaspoon dried oregano
1 teaspoon hot red pepper flakes
1 cup dry red wine
½ cup freshly grated Parmesan
 cheese

Heat olive oil in a large skillet over medium-high heat. Sprinkle seitan with salt and pepper, add to skillet, and brown quickly on both sides, about 5 minutes. Transfer seitan to a flameproof dish. Add mushrooms to skillet and sauté about 3 minutes. Remove with slotted spoon and place over seitan. Add onion and garlic to skillet and sauté about 5 minutes. Add tomatoes, parsley, oregano, red pepper flakes, and wine. Bring to a boil and reduce liquid by one half, about 10 minutes.

Top seitan and mushrooms with Parmesan cheese and place under broiler until cheese browns slightly. Spoon sauce onto dinner plates and top with seitan slices and mushrooms.

4 SERVINGS

Calories 547.1 • Protein 24.13 gm • Fat 12.66 gm • Percentage of calories from fat 20% • Cholesterol 9.875 mg • Dietary fiber 14.36 gm • Sodium 958.1 mg • Calcium 250.9 mg

Grilled Tempeh with Mexican-Style Tomato Sauce

3 tablespoons corn or safflower oil
1 medium onion, minced
2 cloves garlic, minced
¼ teaspoon ground cumin
2 pounds tomatoes, peeled (see page 375) and finely chopped
⅛ teaspoon cayenne

½ teaspoon salt
⅛ teaspoon freshly ground black pepper
2 teaspoons tomato paste
2 teaspoons minced fresh cilantro
1 pound poached tempeh (see page 12), cut into ¼-inch slices

Heat 1 tablespoon of the oil in a large saucepan over low heat. Add onion and cook until soft, stirring occasionally, about 10 minutes. Add garlic and stir 30 seconds. Add cumin and stir 30 seconds. Mix in tomatoes, cayenne, salt, and pepper. Bring to a boil. Reduce heat to low and cook until tomatoes are very soft, stirring occasionally, about 20 minutes; sauce will be chunky. Stir in tomato paste. Add cilantro, cover, and keep warm. Heat remaining 2 tablespoons oil in a large skillet over medium-high heat. Sprinkle tempeh with some salt and pepper and cook slices 2 minutes on each side, or until browned. Divide sauce among plates and top with tempeh. Serve immediately.

4 SERVINGS

Calories 340.9 • Protein 20.81 gm • Fat 19.64 gm • Percentage of calories from fat 50% • Cholesterol 0 mg • Dietary fiber 6.948 gm • Sodium 300.1 mg • Calcium 111.5 mg

Sautéed Tofu with Lemon-Caper Sauce

Use small capers for a more delicate flavor. Enjoy this light, refreshing dish on a hot summer day.

1 large lemon, peeled and white pith removed
1 tablespoon corn oil combined with 1 teaspoon water
1 pound firm tofu, cut into ¼-inch slices
Salt and freshly ground black pepper

¼ cup all-purpose flour
½ cup dry bread crumbs
5 tablespoons olive oil
¼ cup capers
2 tablespoons minced fresh parsley
Lemon wedges

Cut between lemon segments with small sharp knife to release the fruit. Discard membranes and seeds. Cut lemon segments into ¼-inch dice.

Preheat oven to 275 degrees. Place corn oil mixture in a shallow bowl. Sprinkle tofu with salt and pepper. Dust 1 slice with flour, shaking to remove excess. Dip in oil mixture, then bread crumbs, coating completely; pat and press lightly so crumbs adhere. Transfer to a large platter. Repeat with remaining slices, arranging them in a single layer.

Heat 2 tablespoons of the olive oil in a large skillet over medium-high heat. Sauté tofu in batches (do not crowd) and cook until golden brown, about 1 minute per side. Arrange tofu in a single layer on an ovenproof platter and keep warm in oven. Heat remaining 3 tablespoons olive oil in a medium saucepan over medium-low heat. Add capers, parsley, and lemon dice and simmer for 2 minutes. Pour sauce over tofu. Garnish with lemon wedges and serve.

4 SERVINGS

Calories 329.4 • Protein 11.78 gm • Fat 23.48 gm • Percentage of calories from fat 63% • Cholesterol 0 mg • Dietary fiber 0.843 gm • Sodium 480.8 mg • Calcium 72.03 mg

Sautéed Tempeh with Spicy Tomato Sauce

A quick and easy no-cook sauce, especially delicious made with ripe fresh tomatoes.

2 tablespoons plus ⅓ cup olive oil
1 pound poached tempeh (see page 12), cut into ¼-inch thick triangles
1 clove garlic, halved
½ teaspoon salt

2 large tomatoes, peeled and chopped, or 2 cups canned tomatoes, chopped
¼ teaspoon cayenne
1 tablespoon red wine vinegar

Heat the 2 tablespoons oil in a large skillet over medium-high heat. Add tempeh triangles and sauté until golden brown, about 2 minutes each side. Keep warm. In a food processor, combine garlic and salt. Add tomatoes and cayenne, mixing until smooth. With machine running, stream the remaining ⅓ cup olive oil slowly through feed tube and process until smooth and thick. Add vinegar and blend well. Spoon sauce over sautéed tempeh triangles.

4 SERVINGS

Calories 410.5 • Protein 18.66 gm • Fat 33.33 gm • Percentage of calories from fat 71% • Cholesterol 0 mg • Dietary fiber 4.111 gm • Sodium 280.2 mg • Calcium 85.19 mg

Seitan with Chutney Glaze

A few simple ingredients produce a zesty and delectable marinade that permeates the seitan with flavor.

½ cup chutney, homemade (see index) or commercial
1 cup low-sodium tamari
¾ cup brown sugar or a natural sweetener
1 teaspoon ground ginger

1 teaspoon grated lemon zest
2 tablespoons fresh lemon juice
¼ teaspoon Tabasco sauce
1 pound seitan (see page 11), cut into ¼-inch slices
2 tablespoons corn oil

In a food processor combine chutney, tamari, sugar, ginger, lemon zest, lemon juice, and Tabasco sauce until mixture is smooth. In a bowl, pour the chutney mixture over the seitan and let it marinate, covered and chilled, for at least 1 hour or overnight. Heat oil in a large skillet over medium-high heat, remove seitan from marinade and cook seitan until browned on both sides, about 5 minutes. Reduce heat to low, add marinade to skillet and simmer seitan 10 to 15 minutes, spooning marinade over the seitan slices.

4 SERVINGS

Calories 654.4 • Protein 23.58 gm • Fat 8.691 gm • Percentage of calories from fat 12% • Cholesterol 0 mg • Dietary fiber 12.41 gm • Sodium 2788 mg • Calcium 101.7 mg

Tempeh with Port and Ginger Sauce

The tempeh absorbs the pungent flavors of ginger and port for a sensational taste combination.

2 tablespoons corn oil
1 pound poached tempeh (see
   page 12), cut into ¼-inch slices
½ cup port
1½ cups Basic Vegetable Stock
  (see page 10)

1 teaspoon minced fresh ginger
1 teaspoon low-sodium tamari
Freshly ground black pepper

Preheat oven to 275 degrees. Heat oil in a large skillet over medium-high heat. Add tempeh (in batches if necessary; do not crowd) and sauté until golden brown, about 1 minute per side. Transfer to an ovenproof platter and keep warm in oven. Add port to skillet, scraping up any browned bits. Place over medium high heat and reduce to a syrup. Stir in stock and ginger and reduce by half. Add tamari. Strain sauce into saucepan, place over medium heat, and cook 1 minute. Season with pepper. Spoon a little sauce onto individual plates and arrange tempeh on top. Serve with remaining sauce.

4 SERVINGS

Calories 303.9 • Protein 18.87 gm • Fat 15.42 gm • Percentage of calories from fat 45% • Cholesterol 0 mg • Dietary fiber 3.939 gm • Sodium 155.3 mg • Calcium 91.04 mg

Lemon Tofu with Almond-Mint Pesto

The mint adds a surprising coolness to this intriguing pesto variation.

¼ cup packed fresh mint leaves
1 large clove garlic
1 pound firm tofu, cut into ½-inch slices
4 tablespoons fresh lemon juice
3 tablespoons olive oil

½ teaspoon salt
⅛ teaspoon freshly ground black pepper
⅓ cup whole blanched almonds
1 tablespoon minced fresh mint
Fresh mint sprigs

Mince together the ¼ cup mint leaves and the garlic. Arrange tofu slices in a shallow baking dish. Rub with mint mixture. Combine 3 tablespoons of the lemon juice, 1 tablespoon of the olive oil, salt, and pepper in a small bowl. Pour over tofu and turn to coat evenly. Cover tofu and refrigerate at least 2 hours or overnight. Remove tofu slices and scrape mint mixture off tofu back into marinade. Reserve marinade. Pat tofu dry and salt lightly.

Heat remaining 2 tablespoons olive oil in large skillet over medium heat. Add almonds and cook until golden, about 5 minutes, stirring frequently. Remove them with a slotted spoon and set aside. Add tofu to skillet and sauté until golden brown on both sides, about 2 minutes per side. Remove tofu from skillet and keep warm. Stir remaining 1 tablespoon lemon juice into skillet, scraping up browned bits. Add marinade. Reduce heat to low and cook 5 minutes. Add almonds and minced mint; cook another 2 minutes. Transfer tofu to a serving platter, pour sauce on top, and garnish with mint sprigs.

4 SERVINGS

Calories 230.2 • Protein 12.35 gm • Fat 18.31 gm • Percentage of calories from fat 68% • Cholesterol 0 mg • Dietary fiber 1.178 gm • Sodium 339.6 mg • Calcium 96.9 mg

Tofu with Lime-Wasabi Marinade

½ cup low-sodium tamari
1 tablespoon minced garlic
1 tablespoon finely grated fresh
  ginger
2 tablespoons minced scallion
1 tablespoon fresh lime juice

1 tablespoon wasabi (hot
  Japanese horseradish) powder
1 pound firm tofu, cut into ¼-inch
  slices
2 tablespoons olive oil

Combine tamari, garlic, ginger, scallion, lime juice, and wasabi powder in a
large bowl; stir until blended. Add tofu, spooning to coat. Marinate tofu in
refrigerator 1 hour. Heat oil in a large skillet over medium-high heat. Add
tofu pieces, reserving marinade. Sauté tofu about 2 minutes on each side.
Transfer to a serving platter and keep warm. Add marinade to skillet and
boil until liquid is slightly reduced. Serve tofu topped with marinade or use
marinade as dipping sauce.

4 SERVINGS

Calories 171.7 • Protein 13.07 gm • Fat 9.239 gm • Percentage of calories from
fat 49% • Cholesterol 0 mg • Dietary fiber 0.081 gm • Sodium 1287 mg • Calcium
57.42 mg

Seitan with Red and Green Peppers

1 pound seitan (see page 11), cut
  into 3 × 1 × ¼-inch slices
Salt and freshly ground black
  pepper
2 tablespoons corn or safflower oil
4 cups Basic Vegetable Stock (see
  page 10), reduced to 2 cups
2 fresh jalapeño chili peppers,
  seeded and cut into thin strips

1 red bell pepper, seeded and cut
  into thin strips
2 tablespoons minced fresh
  cilantro
2 tablespoons fresh lime juice
Freshly cooked brown rice

Season seitan with salt and pepper. Heat oil in a large skillet over medium-
high heat. Add seitan to skillet and brown 3 to 5 minutes on each side.

Transfer slices to a platter and keep warm. Combine stock and chilies in a medium skillet and boil until liquid is reduced to 1 cup. Reduce heat to low and add cilantro and lime juice. Pour mixture over seitan. Serve immediately over rice.

4 SERVINGS

Calories 468.3 • Protein 18.48 gm • Fat 8.933 gm • Percentage of calories from fat 16% • Cholesterol 0 mg • Dietary fiber 15.07 gm • Sodium 763.5 mg • Calcium 74.53 mg

Tofu Grenoble

The tofu absorbs the tangy flavors of the lemon and capers for a captivating yet simple preparation.

1 lemon, peeled and white pith removed
1 pound firm tofu, cut into ¼-inch slices
Salt and freshly ground black pepper
½ cup all-purpose flour
5 tablespoons olive oil
2 tablespoons capers
2 tablespoons minced fresh parsley

Chop lemon into small dice, discarding seeds and membrane. Set aside. Sprinkle tofu with salt and pepper; then dredge in flour and shake off excess. Heat 2 tablespoons of the oil in a large skillet over medium-high heat. Add tofu and cook, turning once, until crisp and golden, about 4 minutes. Transfer tofu to a warm plate. Reduce heat in skillet to low, add remaining 3 tablespoons olive oil, and heat about 1 minute. Remove pan from heat and stir in lemon pieces, capers, and parsley. Pour sauce over tofu and serve immediately.

4 SERVINGS

Calories 279 • Protein 10.96 gm • Fat 19.52 gm • Percentage of calories from fat 62% • Cholesterol 0 mg • Dietary fiber 0.629 gm • Sodium 231.5 mg • Calcium 65.35 mg

Sautéed Seitan with Shiitake Mushrooms

4 tablespoons corn oil
¼ pound shiitake mushrooms,
 stemmed and thinly sliced
1 large shallot, minced
Salt and freshly ground black
 pepper

¼ pound white mushrooms,
 stemmed and thinly sliced
⅓ cup Madeira wine
1 pound seitan (see page 11), cut
 into ¼-inch slices
1 tablespoon minced fresh parsley

Preheat oven to 275 degrees. Heat 1 tablespoon of the oil in a large skillet over medium heat. Stir in shiitake, shallot, salt, and pepper. Cook until shiitake are just tender, stirring frequently, about 4 minutes. Transfer to a plate using a slotted spoon. Heat 1 tablespoon of the oil in the skillet over medium-high heat. Add white mushrooms, salt, and pepper. Cook until light brown, stirring frequently, about 3 minutes. Return shiitake to the skillet and reheat until sizzling. Add Madeira, reduce heat to medium, and stir until all liquid is absorbed, about 3 minutes. Adjust seasonings. Remove mushroom mixture from heat.

Heat remaining 2 tablespoons oil in another large skillet over high heat. Sprinkle seitan with salt and pepper, and in batches cook seitan 1 minute on each side. Transfer slices to an ovenproof platter and keep warm in the oven while cooking remaining seitan. Reheat mushroom mixture, add parsley, and spoon over seitan.

4 SERVINGS

Calories 498.2 • Protein 17.54 gm • Fat 15.63 gm • Percentage of calories from fat 27% • Cholesterol 0 mg • Dietary fiber 13.16 gm • Sodium 314.5 mg • Calcium 43.94 mg

Herb-Rubbed Tempeh

½ teaspoon dried thyme, crumbled

½ teaspoon dried marjoram, crumbled

2 teaspoons corn oil

1 clove garlic, minced

½ teaspoon dried rosemary, crumbled

1 pound poached tempeh (see page 12), cut into ¼-inch slices

1 cup Basic Vegetable Stock (see page 10)

½ cup dry white wine

2 scallions, minced

1 teaspoon Dijon mustard combined with ½ teaspoon cornstarch

Fresh herb sprigs

Combine thyme, marjoram, oil, garlic, and rosemary and rub over tempeh. Refrigerate at least 30 minutes or overnight. Heat a large skillet over medium-high heat. Add tempeh, and cook about 3 minutes on each side. Keep warm. Meanwhile, simmer stock, wine, and scallions in a small saucepan until reduced to ½ cup. Strain and return liquid to pan. Bring to a boil; whisk in mustard mixture. Reduce heat and simmer until thickened, stirring constantly, about 1 minute. Arrange tempeh on a platter, pour sauce over tempeh, and garnish with fresh herb sprigs.

4 SERVINGS

Calories 237.7 • Protein 18.71 gm • Fat 10.99 gm • Percentage of calories from fat 41% • Cholesterol 0 mg • Dietary fiber 3.806 gm • Sodium 105.1 mg • Calcium 98.86 mg

Seitan with Peppers and Cilantro

2 green bell peppers
1 red bell pepper
3 tablespoons olive oil
1 pound tomatoes, peeled (see page 375), and chopped, or a 1-pound can whole tomatoes, drained and chopped
2 cloves garlic, minced
2 tablespoons minced fresh cilantro
2 tablespoons minced fresh parsley

1 teaspoon paprika
¼ teaspoon ground cumin
¼ teaspoon salt
⅛ teaspoon cayenne
1 pound seitan (see page 11), cut into ¼-inch slices
1 large onion, thinly sliced
Salt and freshly ground black pepper

Roast peppers directly over a gas flame or under the broiler until skin is charred, about 5 minutes. Place in paper bag or covered bowl and allow steam to build for 10 minutes. Rub off skin and discard seeds. Cut roasted peppers into 1-inch pieces. Heat 1 tablespoon of the olive oil in a large skillet over medium heat, add roasted peppers, chopped tomatoes, garlic, 1 tablespoon of the cilantro, the parsley, paprika, cumin, salt, and cayenne, and cook, stirring, for 15 to 20 minutes, or until the sauce is thick. Remove from heat and reserve.

In a large skillet, heat the remaining 2 tablespoons olive oil over moderately low heat and add seitan, with onion slices, remaining 1 tablespoon cilantro, salt, and pepper; cook, stirring, for 3 minutes. Add ½ cup water, bring liquid to a boil, and simmer for 15 minutes. Transfer seitan to a platter. Boil onion mixture, stirring, until thick and reduced to about ½ cup. Stir in the sauce, return seitan to pan, and simmer covered, over low heat, for 10 minutes.

4 SERVINGS

Calories 495.2 • Protein 18.79 gm • Fat 12.64 gm • Percentage of calories from fat 22% • Cholesterol 0 mg • Dietary fiber 15.54 gm • Sodium 448.2 mg • Calcium 71.28 mg

Sweet and Sour Tempeh

Tempeh replaces pork in this tangy interpretation of a Chinese restaurant classic. Serve over rice and enjoy.

3 tablespoons sugar or a natural sweetener
3 tablespoons white vine vinegar
3 tablespoons ketchup
3 tablespoons Basic Vegetable Stock (see page 10)
1 tablespoon low-sodium tamari
1½ teaspoons cornstarch

2 tablespoons corn oil
1 pound poached tempeh (see page 12), cut into ½- × 1-inch cubes
1 tablespoon minced scallion
1 large clove garlic, minced
2 teaspoons minced fresh ginger

Combine sugar, vinegar, ketchup, stock, tamari, and cornstarch in a small bowl; stir well. Heat oil in a skillet over medium-high heat. Add tempeh, scallion, garlic, and ginger; sauté about 2 minutes, or until tempeh is golden brown. Reduce heat to medium, add sweet–sour mixture. Sauté until ingredients are well combined and sauce has thickened, about 1 minute.

4 SERVINGS

Calories 295.5 • Protein 18.67 gm • Fat 15.37 gm • Percentage of calories from fat 46% • Cholesterol 0 mg • Dietary fiber 3.433 gm • Sodium 247.3 mg • Calcium 91.9 mg

Barbecued Seitan Strips

This meaty seitan drenched in a scrumptious finger-licking sauce is sure to become a family favorite.

3 tablespoons corn oil
1 medium onion, minced
1 clove garlic, minced
1 ½ teaspoons minced fresh ginger
1 8-ounce can plum tomatoes, mashed, with juice
½ cup chili sauce
2 tablespoons dark-brown sugar or a natural sweetener

2 tablespoons sugar or a natural sweetener
3 tablespoons low-sodium tamari
1 tablespoon mirin, white wine, or sherry
2 teaspoons chili powder
⅛ teaspoon cayenne
1 pound seitan (see page 11), cut into 1-inch strips

In a medium saucepan, heat 1 tablespoon of the oil over medium-low heat. Add onion, garlic, and ginger and cook 5 minutes, being careful not to brown. Stir in remaining ingredients except the seitan and remaining oil and bring to a boil, then reduce heat. Simmer, uncovered, stirring occasionally, about 20 minutes. Heat remaining 2 tablespoons oil in a large skillet, add seitan, and brown on both sides. Spread sauce on seitan after it browns, and continue cooking several minutes longer.

4 SERVINGS

Calories 546.6 • Protein 18.92 gm • Fat 12.32 gm • Percentage of calories from fat 20% • Cholesterol 0 mg • Dietary fiber 13.92 gm • Sodium 913.7 mg • Calcium 74.83 mg

Tempeh with Lime-Mustard Sauce

4 tablespoons corn oil
1 medium onion, minced
1 tablespoon arrowroot or cornstarch
1¾ cups Basic Vegetable Stock
  (see page 10)
¼ cup fresh lime juice
1 tablespoon apricot jam

1 tablespoon grated lime zest
1 teaspoon white wine vinegar
1 teaspoon tomato sauce
1 teaspoon Dijon mustard
¼ teaspoon Worcestershire sauce
1 pound poached tempeh (see
  page 12), cut into ¼-inch slices

Heat 2 tablespoons of the oil in a large saucepan over medium-low heat. Add onion and cook until translucent, stirring occasionally, about 5 minutes. Dissolve arrowroot in ¼ cup of the stock. Add dissolved arrowroot, remaining stock, and all ingredients except tempeh and remaining oil, to the saucepan and simmer 30 minutes or until thickened to saucelike consistency. Keep warm. Heat remaining 2 tablespoons oil in a large skillet over medium-high heat. Add tempeh to skillet and cook about 2 to 3 minutes on each side. Divide tempeh slices among plates. Spoon some of the sauce on top. Pass remaining sauce separately.

4 SERVINGS

Calories 365.4 • Protein 19.41 gm • Fat 22.39 gm • Percentage of calories from fat 54% • Cholesterol 0 mg • Dietary fiber 4.918 gm • Sodium 164 mg • Calcium 105.5 mg

Three-Mushroom Sauté with Seitan and Cognac Sauce

3 tablespoons olive oil

4 ounces shiitake mushrooms, stemmed and thinly sliced

4 ounces enoki mushrooms, bottom half of stems discarded

4 ounces Portobello mushrooms, thinly sliced

1 pound fresh spinach, stemmed, washed, and dried

1 pound seitan (see page 11), cut into 3 × ½ × ¼-inch strips

2 tablespoons Cognac

¼ cup Basic Brown Sauce (see page 13)

Salt and freshly ground black pepper

1 teaspoon fresh lemon juice

Heat 1 tablespoon of the olive oil in a large skillet over medium-high heat. Add mushrooms and sauté until liquid has evaporated, about 5 minutes. Transfer to a plate. Add spinach and sauté about 2 minutes longer. Transfer to the plate with mushrooms. Heat remaining 2 tablespoons olive oil in the skillet over medium-high heat. Add seitan and sauté until browned, about 4 minutes. Add Cognac and sauté another 30 seconds. Add Basic Brown Sauce, mushrooms, and spinach, and cook long enough to heat through, about 3 to 5 minutes. Season to taste with salt, pepper, and lemon juice. Serve immediately.

6 SERVINGS

Calories 339.4 • Protein 14.18 gm • Fat 8.416 gm • Percentage of calories from fat 21% • Cholesterol 0 mg • Dietary fiber 10.82 gm • Sodium 284.3 mg • Calcium 103.3 mg

Tofu with Shiitake Mushrooms and Garlic

The shiitake mushrooms impart a deep woodsy flavor to this flavorful dish.

1 tablespoon corn oil
1 tablespoon toasted sesame oil
1 pound firm tofu, cut into 2½ × 1 × ¼-inch slices
6 ounces shiitake mushrooms, stemmed and thinly sliced
2 ounces white mushrooms, thinly sliced
4 scallions, chopped
2 cloves garlic, minced

1 teaspoon minced fresh ginger
¼ teaspoon hot red pepper flakes
¼ cup low-sodium tamari
3 tablespoons mirin, white wine, or sherry
1 cup Basic Vegetable Stock (see page 10)
1 tablespoon cornstarch dissolved in 1 tablespoon water

Heat oils in a large skillet over medium-high heat. Add tofu and sauté until golden brown, about 2 minutes on each side. Add mushrooms, scallions, garlic, ginger, red pepper flakes, tamari, mirin, and stock. Simmer 2 minutes, adding cornstarch mixture to simmering skillet, stirring until sauce thickens, about 2 minutes.

4 TO 6 SERVINGS

Calories 161.9 • Protein 9.959 gm • Fat 7.569 gm • Percentage of calories from fat 41% • Cholesterol 0 mg • Dietary fiber 1.374 gm • Sodium 598.3 mg • Calcium 50.68 mg

Lemon-Tarragon Seitan

2 tablespoons corn oil
1 pound seitan (see page 11), cut
 into ¼-inch slices
Salt and freshly ground black
 pepper
½ cup Cognac
1 cup Basic Vegetable Stock (see
 page 10)

2 tablespoons Dijon mustard
2 tablespoons minced fresh
 tarragon or 1 teaspoon dried
2 tablespoons fresh lemon juice
1 tablespoon capers

Heat oil in a large skillet over medium heat. Sprinkle seitan slices with salt and pepper. Add seitan to the skillet and sauté, turning once, until lightly browned, about 5 minutes total. Meanwhile, warm Cognac in a small saucepan over medium heat. Pour it over the seitan, carefully ignite, and shake until the flames subside. Add stock, mustard, tarragon, and lemon juice, reduce heat to low, and simmer, turning once, until sauce reduces, about 10 minutes. Season to taste with salt and pepper. Arrange seitan on a warm platter. Spoon the sauce on top and sprinkle with capers.

4 TO 6 SERVINGS

Calories 394.7 • Protein 13.87 gm • Fat 7.339 gm • Percentage of calories from fat 16% • Cholesterol 0 mg • Dietary fiber 10.16 gm • Sodium 505 mg • Calcium 41 mg

Tofu with Pickled Pepper Sauce

Pickled red bell peppers can be found in most supermarkets. They impart a tangy flavor that is accented by the capers and lemon juice.

¼ cup plus 2 tablespoons olive oil
2 tablespoons minced fresh
  parsley
⅓ cup pickled red bell pepper
  strips, drained and diced
2 tablespoons minced scallions
3 tablespoons fresh lemon juice

1 teaspoon minced fresh oregano
  or ¼ teaspoon dried, crumbled
1 tablespoon capers
Salt and freshly ground black
  pepper
1 pound firm tofu, cut into ¼-inch
  slices

Combine ¼ cup of the olive oil, the parsley, bell pepper strips, scallions, 2 tablespoons of the lemon juice, the oregano, capers, salt, and pepper in a medium saucepan over low heat. Cook 5 minutes to blend flavors, stirring occasionally. Taste, adding more lemon juice and capers if desired. Keep sauce warm. Heat remaining 2 tablespoons olive oil in a large skillet over medium-high heat. Add tofu slices and sauté until golden brown on both sides, about 2 minutes per side. Transfer tofu to plates. Top with sauce and serve.

4 SERVINGS

Calories 234.6 • Protein 9.437 gm • Fat 20.32 gm • Percentage of calories from fat 75% • Cholesterol 0 mg • Dietary fiber 0.377 gm • Sodium 152.7 mg • Calcium 49.78 mg

Garlic-Infused Seitan with Brandy-Mustard Sauce

The seitan absorbs the flavor of the garlic and is further enhanced by the delectable sauce.

2 cloves garlic, finely minced
3 tablespoons olive oil
1 pound seitan (see page 11), cut into ¼-inch slices
2 shallots, minced
1 cup Basic Vegetable Stock (see page 10)
1 tablespoon brandy

1 tablespoon Dijon mustard
2 tablespoons minced fresh parsley
1 tablespoon cornstarch dissolved in 1 tablespoon water
Salt and freshly ground black pepper

Combine minced garlic with 1 tablespoon olive oil. Lay out seitan slices on a flat surface. Rub garlic-oil mixture into seitan slices. Heat remaining 2 tablespoons olive oil in a large skillet over medium heat. Add seitan and brown on both sides, being careful not to burn garlic. Remove seitan to ovenproof platter, and keep warm in a 275-degree oven. Reheat skillet, add shallots, and cook until softened, about 5 minutes. Stir in stock, scraping up browned bits. Boil until reduced by half. Add brandy and boil 1 minute.

Reduce heat to low. Whisk in mustard; stir in parsley. Whisk in cornstarch mixture, stirring until sauce thickens, about 3 minutes. Season with salt and pepper. Arrange seitan on individual plates and spoon sauce on top. Serve immediately.

4 SERVINGS

Calories 468.3 • Protein 17.26 gm • Fat 12.25 gm • Percentage of calories from fat 23% • Cholesterol 0 mg • Dietary fiber 12.7 gm • Sodium 459.7 mg • Calcium 52.63 mg

Seitan Cutlets with Porcini Mushrooms and Brandy-Port Sauce

If porcini mushrooms are unavailable, use any fresh mushrooms.

2 tablespoons corn oil
1 pound seitan (see page 11), cut into ½-inch slices
2 shallots, minced
4 ounces porcini mushrooms, trimmed and sliced
3 tablespoons low-sodium tamari

¼ cup brandy
½ cup Basic Vegetable Stock (see page 10)
1 tablespoon cornstarch dissolved in 1½ tablespoons water
¼ cup port

Heat oil in a large skillet over medium-high heat. Add seitan slices and sear quickly on both sides, about 2 minutes. Reduce heat to medium, add shallots, and cook about 3 minutes. Add mushrooms and cook another 2 minutes. Add tamari. Carefully pour brandy into pan and ignite. Add stock. Stir in cornstarch mixture, stirring until thick and clear, about 2 minutes. Stir in port. Reduce heat and simmer 2 minutes, stirring constantly. Arrange seitan slices on plates. Spoon sauce over them. Serve immediately.

4 SERVINGS

Calories 492.8 • Protein 18.62 gm • Fat 8.774 gm • Percentage of calories from fat 15% • Cholesterol 0 mg • Dietary fiber 12.79 gm • Sodium 789.3 mg • Calcium 50.58 mg

Seitan with Brown Sauce

3 tablespoons corn oil
1 tablespoon minced carrot
1 tablespoon minced celery
2 tablespoons minced shallot
⅓ cup dry red wine
1½ cups Basic Vegetable Stock
  (see page 10)
1 tablespoon tamari
⅛ teaspoon freshly ground black
  pepper

½ teaspoon tomato paste
1 tablespoon cornstarch dissolved
  in 2 tablespoons water
1 pound seitan (see page 11), cut
  into ¼-inch slices
Salt and freshly ground black
  pepper

Heat 1 tablespoon of the oil in a small saucepan over medium-high heat. Add minced carrot, celery, and shallot, and sauté, stirring until softened, about 2 minutes. Reduce heat to medium, add wine, and reduce until almost evaporated, about 3 minutes. Add vegetable stock, tamari, pepper, and tomato paste; cook, whisking constantly, for about 5 minutes to reduce sauce by one third. Whisk in cornstarch mixture and stir constantly to thicken, about 2 minutes. Keep warm.

Heat remaining 2 tablespoons oil in a large skillet over medium-high heat. Sprinkle seitan with salt and pepper, add to skillet, and brown both sides, about 2 minutes each side. Add half of the reserved sauce to seitan and simmer 1 to 2 minutes. Serve seitan slices topped with remaining sauce.

4 SERVINGS

Calories 477.8 • Protein 17.64 gm • Fat 12.12 gm • Percentage of calories from fat 22% • Cholesterol 0 mg • Dietary fiber 12.98 gm • Sodium 562.4 mg • Calcium 54.45 mg

Spiced Seitan

This pungent marinade also works well with tofu or tempeh.

1 pound seitan (see page 11), cut into 3- × 1- × ¼-inch slices
1 clove garlic, minced
1 teaspoon sugar or a natural sweetener
½ teaspoon sweet paprika
½ teaspoon ground ginger
½ teaspoon dry mustard

¼ teaspoon ground cinnamon
⅛ teaspoon ground turmeric
¼ teaspoon ground cumin
¼ teaspoon ground cloves
1 teaspoon fresh lemon juice
2 teaspoons low-sodium tamari
4 tablespoons olive oil

Place seitan in a large, shallow dish. In a small bowl whisk together garlic, sugar, paprika, ginger, mustard, cinnamon, turmeric, cumin, and cloves. Whisk in lemon juice, tamari, and 2 tablespoons of the olive oil, whisking until marinade is combined well. Pour marinade over the seitan, turning to coat, and marinate seitan for at least 1 hour or overnight.

Heat remaining 2 tablespoons olive oil in a large skillet over medium-high heat. Add seitan and brown on both sides, about 2 minutes for each side. Add reserved marinade for stronger flavor.

4 SERVINGS

Calories 470.9 • Protein 16.82 gm • Fat 15.45 gm • Percentage of calories from fat 28% • Cholesterol 0 mg • Dietary fiber 12.27 gm • Sodium 409.8 mg • Calcium 46.14 mg

Citrus-Glazed Tempeh

2 cups dry red wine
½ teaspoon freshly ground black
  pepper
1 medium lemon, thinly sliced
1 bay leaf
2 tablespoons corn oil
1 pound poached tempeh (see
  page 12), cut into 3- × 2- × ¼-inch
  slices

2 tablespoons frozen orange juice
  concentrate, thawed
¼ cup Grand Marnier
2 tablespoons low-sodium tamari
1 teaspoon cornstarch
Zest of 1 medium orange in
  julienne strips, blanched
2 tablespoons minced fresh
  parsley

Simmer wine, pepper, lemon, and bay leaf in a saucepan over medium-high heat until reduced by one half. Let wine mixture cool to room temperature, then strain and reserve. Heat oil in a large skillet over medium-high heat. Add tempeh and cook until golden brown on both sides, about 5 minutes. Set aside.

Combine orange juice concentrate, Grand Marnier, tamari, and cornstarch in a medium saucepan. Bring to a boil over low heat, stirring constantly. Add blanched orange strips. Blend in the reserved wine mixture. Reheat tempeh over medium-high heat. Stir in orange-wine mixture, simmering until sauce reduces and becomes syrupy, about 20 minutes. Arrange tempeh on a platter, sprinkle with parsley, and serve.

6 SERVINGS

Calories 275 • Protein 13.46 gm • Fat 10.34 gm • Percentage of calories from fat 33% • Cholesterol 0 mg • Dietary fiber 2.73 gm • Sodium 260.9 mg • Calcium 89.74 mg

Seitan Bordelaise

Seitan is a natural choice to complement this classic bordelaise sauce.

1 cup Basic Vegetable Stock (see page 10)
1 cup dry red wine
2 tablespoons corn oil
1 pound seitan (see page 11), cut into ¼-inch slices
½ teaspoon salt
½ teaspoon minced fresh thyme or ¼ teaspoon dried
⅛ teaspoon freshly ground black pepper
1 medium onion, thinly sliced
1 cup sliced mushrooms

Place stock and wine in a saucepan over high heat and boil until reduced by half. Remove from heat and set aside.

Heat oil in a large skillet over medium-high heat. Add seitan slices and season with salt, thyme, and pepper. Sauté 2 minutes, or until browned on each side. Remove seitan from skillet and keep warm. Add onions to skillet and cook for 3 to 5 minutes; then add mushrooms, reduce heat, add reserved wine reduction, and simmer until liquid is further reduced to a saucelike consistency. Adjust seasonings. Add seitan slices to sauce and heat through.

4 SERVINGS

Calories 475.1 • Protein 17.79 gm • Fat 8.8 gm • Percentage of calories from fat 16% • Cholesterol 0 mg • Dietary fiber 13.58 gm • Sodium 670.1 mg • Calcium 62.92 mg

Seitan Piccata

2 tablespoons corn oil
1 pound seitan (see page 11), cut
   into ¼-inch slices
¼ teaspoon salt
⅛ teaspoon freshly ground black
   pepper

1 scallion, minced
1 cup sliced mushrooms
2 tablespoons lemon juice
2 tablespoons dry white wine
2 tablespoons minced fresh
   parsley

Heat oil in a large skillet over medium-high heat. Add seitan and season
with salt and pepper. Sauté 2 to 3 minutes, until brown. Turn to brown other
side, add scallion and mushrooms, and sauté 2 more minutes. Add lemon
juice, wine, and parsley and simmer for 2 minutes, or until sauce reduces
and becomes slightly syrupy. Adjust seasonings.

4 SERVINGS

Calories 412.4 • Protein 16.84 gm • Fat 8.717 gm • Percentage of calories from
fat 18% • Cholesterol 0 mg • Dietary fiber 12.48 gm • Sodium 435 mg • Calcium
44.83 mg

Seitan Marsala

The slight sweetness of the Marsala permeates the seitan and mushrooms for a simple yet elegant dish. I've fed this to appreciative guest who thought they were eating veal.

2 tablespoons corn oil
1 pound seitan (see page 11), cut into ¼-inch slices
¼ teaspoon salt
⅛ teaspoon freshly ground black pepper
1 medium onion, thinly sliced

1 cup sliced mushrooms
½ teaspoon minced fresh thyme, or ¼ teaspoon dried
½ cup Marsala
1 cup Basic Brown Sauce (see page 13)

Heat oil in a large skillet on medium-high heat. Add seitan slices, season with salt and pepper, and sauté 2 minutes, or until browned. Turn, add onions, and brown seitan slices on the other side. Add mushrooms and thyme; cook for 2 to 4 minutes. Add Marsala and cook 2 minutes more, or until wine reduces and becomes syrupy. Reduce heat, add Basic Brown Sauce, and simmer 5 minutes. Adjust seasonings.

4 SERVINGS

Calories 461.3 • Protein 17.84 gm • Fat 8.823 gm • Percentage of calories from fat 16% • Cholesterol 0 mg • Dietary fiber 13.55 gm • Sodium 576.2 mg • Calcium 60.92 mg

Three-Grain Sauté

This is a great way to stretch leftover grains and also to experiment with various grain combinations. Kamut is an Egyptian wheat, known for its hearty texture and flavor. Add some chopped seitan or tempeh bacon if you have some on hand.

2 tablespoons corn oil
2 whole scallions, thinly sliced on the diagonal
1 tablespoon chopped red bell pepper
2 cups cooked brown rice
2 cups cooked kamut or other grain

1 cup fresh corn, off the cob
1 tablespoon minced fresh parsley
1 tablespoon low-sodium tamari
⅛ teaspoon freshly ground black pepper

Heat oil in a large skillet over medium-high heat. Add scallions and red pepper; cook for 1 minute. Add rice, kamut, corn, and parsley. Heat through, stirring. Add tamari and pepper. Adjust seasonings.

4 SERVINGS

Calories 348.7 • Protein 9.885 gm • Fat 9.05 gm • Percentage of calories from fat 21% • Cholesterol 0 mg • Dietary fiber 7.574 gm • Sodium 286.7 mg • Calcium 16.95 mg

Tofu with Snow Peas in Lemon Vinaigrette

3 tablespoons fresh lemon juice
1 teaspoon freshly grated lemon
  zest
2 shallots, finely minced
2 teaspoons Dijon mustard
¼ teaspoon salt
½ cup olive oil
1 pound firm tofu, cut into ½-inch
  slices

Salt and freshly ground black
  pepper
2 tablespoons corn oil
¼ pound snow peas, trimmed, cut
  diagonally into ½-inch pieces
12 small whole snow peas for
  garnish
1 tablespoon slivered lemon zest
  for garnish

In a small bowl whisk together lemon juice, grated lemon zest, shallots, mustard, and salt. Add olive oil in a stream, whisking, and whisk the vinaigrette until it is emulsified. Season tofu with salt and pepper. Heat corn oil in a large skillet over medium-high heat, add tofu slices, and sauté for 5 minutes, or until golden on both sides. While tofu is cooking, blanch the cut and whole snow peas for 5 seconds in boiling water, drain and refresh them under cold water. Transfer tofu carefully with a slotted spatula to 4 plates, sprinkle with cut snow peas and lemon zest slivers, and spoon vinaigrette over them. Garnish plates with whole snow peas.

4 SERVINGS

Calories 389.5 • Protein 10.28 gm • Fat 36.47 gm • Percentage of calories from fat 82% • Cholesterol 0 mg • Dietary fiber 1.092 gm • Sodium 270.3 mg • Calcium 60.78 mg

Seitan with Portobello Mushrooms and Red Wine Sauce

Some say the meaty Portobello mushrooms taste like filet mignon. I say they taste delicious, when teamed up with seitan and this flavorful sauce.

3 tablespoons olive oil
½ pound Portobello mushrooms, sliced
Salt and freshly ground black pepper

1 pound seitan (see page 11), cut into ¼-inch slices
2 shallots, minced
1 cup red wine
¼ cup minced fresh parsley

Heat 1 tablespoon of the oil in a large skillet and sauté mushrooms over medium-high heat, stirring, until mushroom liquid is almost evaporated, about 3 minutes. Season to taste with salt and pepper and set aside on a plate. Heat remaining 2 tablespoons olive oil in the skillet and sauté seitan over medium-high heat until seared on both sides, about 2 minutes total. Season with salt and pepper. Lower heat to medium and cook, turning once, about 2 more minutes. Put seitan on a warm serving platter and keep warm.

Sauté shallots in the same skillet until soft, about 3 minutes. Add wine and scrape up any browned bits. Bring to a boil and reduce to a thick, syrupy sauce, about 2 minutes. Stir in parsley and sautéed mushrooms. Season to taste with salt and pepper. Top seitan with the sauce and serve immediately.

4 SERVINGS

Calories 490.1 • Protein 17.97 gm • Fat 12.21 gm • Percentage of calories from fat 21% • Cholesterol 0 mg • Dietary fiber 12.93 gm • Sodium 342.5 mg • Calcium 52.11 mg

Tempeh with Orange Sauce and Golden Raisins

Grand Marnier is the best choice for this sauce, but feel free to substitute orange juice for the liqueur for a tasty non-alcoholic version.

2 tablespoons corn oil
1 pound poached tempeh (see page 12), cut into ¼-inch slices
¼ teaspoon salt
⅛ teaspoon freshly ground black pepper
½ cup fresh orange juice
¼ cup Grand Marnier or other orange liqueur

1 clove garlic, minced
¼ cup golden raisins
2 tablespoons tomato paste
2 tablespoons Dijon mustard
½ cup heavy cream
1 teaspoon fresh lemon juice
Freshly cooked pasta or rice
2 tablespoons minced fresh parsley

Heat oil in a large skillet over medium-high heat. Add tempeh and sauté until golden brown on both sides, about 5 minutes. Season with salt and pepper. Set aside to cool. In a shallow bowl, combine orange juice, 2 tablespoons of the liqueur, and the garlic. Add tempeh to marinade, and marinate for at least 2 hours. In the meantime, soak raisins in remaining orange liqueur. Drain marinade from tempeh and transfer marinade to a large skillet or saucepan. Add raisins with liqueur and bring to a boil. Add tomato paste, mustard, and cream; cook for 5 minutes and add lemon juice. Add tempeh to sauce and simmer until tempeh is heated through, about 5 minutes. Serve over pasta or rice and sprinkle with parsley.

4 SERVINGS

Calories 384.1 • Protein 20.4 gm • Fat 19.49 gm • Percentage of calories from fat 45% • Cholesterol 11.13 mg • Dietary fiber 4.374 gm • Sodium 351.7 mg • Calcium 128.4 mg

Piquant Seitan Cutlets

This recipe uses the bottled roasted peppers available in most supermarkets.
Keep them on hand, along with olives and capers, so you can make spectac-
ular dishes in a hurry. For a delicious variation, add a few tablespoons
crumbled feta to the sauce and sprinkle with chopped fresh parsley.

3 tablespoons olive oil
1 pound seitan (see page 11) cut
   into ¼-inch slices
¼ teaspoon salt
⅛ teaspoon freshly ground black
   pepper

½ cup dry white wine
1 cup sweet roasted red peppers,
   drained, cut in julienne
8 pitted green olives, thinly sliced
2 tablespoons capers

Heat 2 tablespoons of the olive oil in a large skillet over high heat. Add
seitan to the skillet in batches and sauté until golden, about 3 minutes per
side. Transfer to a heatproof platter, sprinkle with salt and pepper, and keep
warm in a 275-degree oven.

Heat remaining 1 tablespoon olive oil in the same skillet over high heat.
Add wine, scraping up browned bits. Reduce heat to medium. Add remaining ingredients and stir until heated through. Pour sauce over seitan and
serve immediately.

6 SERVINGS

Calories 317 • Protein 11.32 gm • Fat 8.721 gm • Percentage of calories from
fat 24% • Cholesterol 0 mg • Dietary fiber 8.906 gm • Sodium 445.9 mg • Calcium
36.8 mg

Grilled Seitan Cutlets

1 tablespoon Dijon mustard
½ teaspoon dry mustard
⅛ teaspoon cayenne
1 pound seitan (see page 11), cut
   into ¼-inch slices

1 tablespoon vegetable oil
4 tablespoons red wine
1 teaspoon Worcestershire sauce
¼ teaspoon salt

Combine both mustards with the cayenne and spread thinly over seitan slices on both sides. Set aside for at least 20 minutes. Heat oil in a large skillet over medium-high heat. Add seitan and fry rapidly for 2 to 3 minutes over high heat, turning once, to seal both sides. Lower heat to medium and cook 4 minutes longer, turning occasionally. Transfer seitan to a baking dish and keep warm in a 275-degree oven. Add wine and Worcestershire sauce to the pan juices and season with salt. Stir well, simmer for 1 minute, then pour over seitan and serve immediately.

4 SERVINGS

Calories 390.2 • Protein 16.84 gm • Fat 5.658 gm • Percentage of calories from fat 12% • Cholesterol 0 mg • Dietary fiber 12.24 gm • Sodium 550.1 mg • Calcium 44.41 mg

Parsleyed Tofu Cutlets

These cutlets are especially enjoyable served with a ratatouille or other assertive vegetable melange.

2 tablespoons all-purpose flour
Salt and freshly ground black
  pepper
1 pound firm tofu, cut into ½-inch
  slices
2 tablespoons olive oil

1 clove garlic, minced
¼ cup dry white wine
1 tablespoon white wine vinegar
3 tablespoons minced fresh
  parsley

Spread flour on a large plate and season with salt and pepper. Dredge tofu slices in the seasoned flour to coat on both sides.

Heat oil in a large skillet over medium-high heat and add tofu slices, in batches. Cook about 2 minutes on each side. Transfer fried tofu to a heated serving dish and keep warm in a 275-degree oven. Fry remaining tofu in the same way and transfer to the serving dish.

Add garlic to the skillet and cook over medium heat about 30 seconds, stirring often and adding more oil if necessary. Add wine and vinegar and stir for 30 seconds. Stir in parsley and pour sauce over tofu. Serve immediately.

4 SERVINGS

Calories 154.4 • Protein 9.682 gm • Fat 9.25 gm • Percentage of calories from fat 52% • Cholesterol 0 mg • Dietary fiber 0.137 gm • Sodium 74.87 mg • Calcium 52.93 mg

Tofu with Spicy Sauce

A long list of ingredients, but if you enlist your food processor to mince the vegetables, and assemble your spices ahead of time, this sauce can be prepared in minutes. The mild flavor of the tofu helps balance the fiery nature of the sauce.

3 tablespoons corn oil
1 red bell pepper, minced
1 green bell pepper, minced
1 small onion, minced
1 clove garlic, minced
2 dried red chili peppers
¼ teaspoon dry mustard
¼ teaspoon dried thyme
1 tablespoon chili powder
1 bay leaf, crumbled
2 tablespoons dry white wine

2 cups Basic Vegetable Stock (see page 10)
1 tablespoon cornstarch combined with 1 tablespoon water
Salt and freshly ground black pepper
¾ cup light cream or milk
½ teaspoon hot pepper sauce
1 pound tofu, cut into ½-inch slices
1 cup cornmeal for dredging

Heat 1 tablespoon of the oil in a large skillet over low heat. Add red and green bell peppers, onion, garlic, and chili peppers and cook gently, covered, for 5 minutes. Add mustard, thyme, chili powder, and bay leaf; continue to cook, covered, for 3 minutes. Deglaze skillet with wine and cook over medium-high heat until liquid is nearly evaporated, 1 to 2 minutes. Add stock and bring to a boil. Lower heat to medium and reduce by one half, about 15 minutes. Add cornstarch mixture to sauce, stirring, until sauce thickens. Simmer 10 minutes more; then strain sauce through a fine sieve. Season with salt and pepper. Stir in cream or milk and hot pepper sauce and keep warm.

Heat remaining 2 tablespoons oil in another large skillet over medium-high heat. Dredge tofu slices in cornmeal and fry until crisp and golden, about 2 minutes on each side. Serve fried tofu slices on pool of sauce, or spoon some sauce over tofu slices. Serve extra sauce separately.

4 SERVINGS

Calories 377.2 • Protein 15.68 gm • Fat 15.49 gm • Percentage of calories from fat 36% • Cholesterol 3.375 mg • Dietary fiber 8.901 gm • Sodium 257.5 mg • Calcium 142.5 mg

Seitan with Brandied Fruit Sauce

Boiling the brandy evaporates the alcohol, leaving only the delicious flavor. For a non-alcoholic version you can use apple juice, but the sauce won't be as flavorful.

½ cup pitted prunes
½ cup dried apricots
¾ cup brandy
2 cups Basic Vegetable Stock (see page 10)
1 pound seitan (see page 11), cut into ¼-inch slices

¼ teaspoon salt
⅛ teaspoon freshly ground black pepper
2 tablespoons corn oil
1 tablespoon red currant jelly

Combine prunes, apricots, and brandy in a bowl and let stand 30 minutes. Boil stock in a medium saucepan until reduced to 1 cup, about 10 minutes. Drain fruit, reserving brandy.

Season seitan with salt and pepper. Heat oil in a large skillet, add seitan slices, and sauté until browned on both sides, about 2 minutes for each side. Keep warm in a 275-degree oven. Add reserved brandy to skillet and bring to boil, scraping up any browned bits. Boil until reduced by half, about 3 minutes. Add reduced stock and jelly and boil until syrupy. Add fruit and heat through. Arrange slices of seitan on serving plates. Spoon sauce and fruit over and serve.

4 SERVINGS

Calories 614.8 • Protein 18.07 gm • Fat 8.905 gm • Percentage of calories from fat 12% • Cholesterol 0 mg • Dietary fiber 15.66 gm • Sodium 564.3 mg • Calcium 71.59 mg

Pan-Seared Seitan with Tahini Sauce and Vegetables

3 tablespoons tahini

3 tablespoons low-sodium tamari

3 tablespoons rice vinegar

1 tablespoon Dijon mustard

1 tablespoon sugar or a natural sweetener

1 clove garlic, sliced

1 teaspoon toasted sesame oil

½ teaspoon hot chili oil

1 carrot, cut into ¼-inch julienne strips

½ celery rib, cut into ¼-inch julienne strips

1 tablespoon corn oil

1 pound seitan (see page 11), cut into ¼-inch julienne strips

Salt and freshly ground black pepper

2 ounces enoki mushrooms, trimmed

2 scallions, minced

1 pound fresh spinach, washed and trimmed

4 cups freshly cooked brown rice

1 tablespoon toasted sesame seeds (see page 176)

Combine tahini, tamari, vinegar, mustard, sugar, garlic, sesame oil, and hot chili oil in a food processor. Reserve. In a steamer, lightly blanch carrot and celery. Heat corn oil in a large skillet over medium-high heat. Add seitan strips, season with salt and pepper. Sauté until browned, about 3 minutes. Add blanched carrot and celery, sauté 1 more minute. Transfer to a large bowl. Mix in mushrooms and scallions. Steam spinach lightly in steamer.

Divide rice among 4 serving plates. Arrange spinach on rice. Top with seitan-vegetable julienne. Drizzle with some of the tahini sauce and sprinkle sesame seeds on top. Pass extra sauce separately.

4 SERVINGS

Calories 712.2 • Protein 27.53 gm • Fat 12.4 gm • Percentage of calories from fat 15% • Cholesterol 0 mg • Dietary fiber 19.52 gm • Sodium 981.8 mg • Calcium 236.5 mg

Mixed Grill

For a special treat, fire up the outdoor grill and use vegetables fresh from the garden.

3 tablespoons olive oil
1 tablespoon Dijon mustard
¼ teaspoon dried thyme
4 ounces seitan (see page 11), cut into ¼-inch slices
2 baby eggplants, halved lengthwise

2 small zucchini, halved lengthwise
Salt and freshly ground black pepper
4 large white mushrooms, stemmed
2 plum tomatoes, halved crosswise
1 tablespoon minced fresh basil

In a small bowl, combine 2 teaspoons of the olive oil with mustard and thyme; blend well. Brush seitan with mustard mixture. Cover and refrigerate at least 1 hour.

Preheat oven to 350 degrees. Remove seitan from the refrigerator. Heat a large skillet over high heat. Brush the cut sides of eggplant with 1 tablespoon of the olive oil. Place eggplant halves, cut side down, in the skillet and cook over high heat, turning, until they are softened and well browned all over, about 10 minutes. Remove eggplant to a large oiled baking dish. Place in oven.

Brush the cut sides of the zucchini with 1 teaspoon of the olive oil. Place in the skillet and cook, turning, until browned on both sides, 3 to 4 minutes. Season with salt and pepper to taste and transfer to the baking dish. Brush the mushrooms with 1 teaspoon of the olive oil, place in hot skillet, and cook, turning, until brown, about 4 minutes. Season with salt and pepper and transfer to the baking dish. Brush the cut sides of the tomato halves with 1 teaspoon of the olive oil, place in the skillet with the basil and cook about 1 minute. Add to other vegetables in the baking dish. Add remaining teaspoon of olive oil to the skillet. Place seitan in the skillet and cook for 2 minutes on each side or until browned. Season with salt. Remove baking dish from the oven, add seitan, and arrange components aesthetically. Serve directly from the dish. If baking dish is too crowded, or you have grilled outdoors, divide components among individual plates to serve.

4 SERVINGS

Calories 206.9 • Protein 5.878 gm • Fat 11.1 gm • Percentage of calories from fat 46% • Cholesterol 0 mg • Dietary fiber 4.12 gm • Sodium 175.2 mg • Calcium 27.47 mg

Grilled Seitan with Yellow Pepper Purée

If you do not have a grill, simply sauté or broil the seitan.

4 yellow bell peppers, seeded and chopped
1 medium onion, chopped
1 garlic clove, minced
1 tablespoon plus ¼ cup olive oil
1 tablespoon red wine vinegar
1 tablespoon lemon juice
½ cup Basic Vegetable Stock (see page 10)

1 teaspoon minced fresh thyme or ¼ teaspoon dried
1 pound seitan (see page 11), cut into ¼-inch slices
Salt and freshly ground black pepper

Simmer peppers, onion, garlic, 1 tablespoon olive oil, vinegar, and lemon juice in a medium saucepan for 30 minutes on low heat, stirring mixture frequently and adding a little more olive oil if necessary to prevent scorching. Purée mixture in a food processor until smooth. Slowly add stock until desired consistency is reached. Strain through a medium sieve and keep warm. Combine the ¼ cup olive oil and thyme. Brush seitan with olive oil–thyme mixture. Grill slices about 2 minutes on each side until browned. Season to taste with salt and pepper. To serve, pour a layer of yellow pepper purée on each plate. Top purée with grilled seitan.

4 TO 6 SERVINGS

Calories 426.6 • Protein 14.19 gm • Fat 15.13 gm • Percentage of calories from fat 30% • Cholesterol 0 mg • Dietary fiber 11.53 gm • Sodium 267.8 mg • Calcium 49.09 mg

Grilled Seitan Sushi Style

1 teaspoon wasabi (hot Japanese horseradish) powder
1½ teaspoons water
1 pound seitan (see page 11), cut into ¼-inch slices
½ cup toasted sesame oil
½ cup low-sodium tamari
¼ cup rice vinegar
1 teaspoon arrowroot or cornstarch combined with 1 teaspoon water

2 tablespoons finely minced scallions
1 pound washed and trimmed spinach leaves, lightly steamed
2 cups cooked brown rice, kept warm
8 slices pickled ginger
Additional wasabi paste for garnish

Combine wasabi with 1½ teaspoons water to make a thick paste. Cover and set aside. Brush seitan with sesame oil. Heat a large skillet over medium-high heat and grill seitan slices for 1 minute on each side. Meanwhile, bring tamari and vinegar to a simmer in a small saucepan. Whisk in arrowroot mixture and stir until slightly thickened. Remove from heat. Add half the scallions. Cover plates with spinach and top with a mound of rice. Lay slices of seitan over rice. Spoon sauce over seitan. Garnish with remaining scallions, put a few slices of pickled ginger and a dab of wasabi to the side, and serve.

4 SERVINGS

Calories 745.3 • Protein 24.37 gm • Fat 30.14 gm • Percentage of calories from fat 35% • Cholesterol 0 mg • Dietary fiber 15.6 gm • Sodium 156.7 mg • Calcium 119.2 mg

9
Main-Dish Salads

Perfect for warm summer nights when you don't want to heat up the kitchen. Prepare the components for these salads early in the cool morning for assembly later in the day.

Using a varied complement of the freshest vegetables, grains and beans, and seitan, tofu, and tempeh, these hearty salads are well-balanced meals in themselves, needing little more than a loaf of crusty bread to satisfy even the most ravenous appetite.

Rotini Salad with Chick-peas and Seasonal Vegetables

Vary the vegetable choices according to what's fresh and in season.

⅓ cup toasted sesame oil
¼ cup corn oil
¼ cup rice vinegar
¼ teaspoon dry mustard
½ teaspoon salt
1 teaspoon low-sodium tamari
½ teaspoon sugar or a natural sweetener
½ teaspoon minced fresh ginger
1 pound rotini, cooked until just tender
1 cup cooked chick-peas

½ cup thinly sliced carrots, blanched
½ cup thinly sliced celery
½ cup sliced yellow squash, blanched
½ cup fresh snow peas or green beans, halved and blanched
½ cup sliced mushrooms
¼ cup minced fresh parsley
1 scallion, minced
4 cups torn mixed greens

Combine sesame oil, corn oil, vinegar, mustard, salt, tamari, sugar, and ginger in a small bowl and set aside. In a large bowl, combine cooked pasta with remaining ingredients except salad greens. Whisk reserved dressing and add some to the pasta salad, tossing to coat. Add more dressing if necessary and adjust seasonings. Serve on a bed of torn salad greens.

6 TO 8 SERVINGS

Calories 473.6 • Protein 11.58 gm • Fat 21.5 gm • Percentage of calories from fat 40% • Cholesterol 0 mg • Dietary fiber 4.461 gm • Sodium 287.3 mg • Calcium 60.33 mg

Brown Rice Salad

The flavors in this salad improve with time, making it an ideal choice to pre-pare ahead of time and refrigerate overnight.

½ cup olive oil
¼ cup fresh lemon juice
½ teaspoon salt
⅛ teaspoon cayenne
1 teaspoon chopped fresh basil
4 cups cooked brown rice
½ cup adzuki beans, cooked
1 rib celery, sliced thin on diagonal

1 carrot, peeled and grated
2 scallions, minced
½ red bell pepper, seeded and chopped
½ cup cooked green peas
2 tablespoons minced parsley
5 cups torn mixed greens

In a small bowl, whisk together olive oil, lemon juice, salt, cayenne, and basil and set aside. In a large bowl, combine rice, beans, and prepared veg-etables. Add dressing and toss to combine. Adjust seasonings. Serve in a shallow serving bowl lined with torn greens, or mound on individual plates lined with the greens.

4 TO 6 SERVINGS

Calories 429.7 • Protein 7.744 gm • Fat 23.31 gm • Percentage of calories from fat 48% • Cholesterol 0 mg • Dietary fiber 6.611 gm • Sodium 240.8 mg • Calcium 77.56 mg

Composed Chef Salad

Let your creativity be your guide in garnishing this salad.

½ cup olive oil
4 tablespoons cider vinegar
3 tablespoons low-sodium tamari
8 ounces seitan (see page 11), cut into ¼-inch strips
8 ounces firm tofu, cut into ¼-inch strips

6 cups torn mixed greens, such as romaine, Boston lettuce, red leaf
4 cups prepared Brown Rice Salad (see page 310)
Radish roses, cherry tomatoes, snow peas, etc., for garnish

Heat olive oil, vinegar, and tamari in a small saucepan. Pour liquid over seitan and tofu strips in a shallow bowl; allow to "cook" by marinating 30 minutes at room temperature. Line 4 large individual plates with torn mixed greens. Mound 1 cup of rice salad on one section of each plate. Place seitan strips in next third of plate, and tofu on third part of plate. Garnish with snow peas, radish roses, cherry tomatoes, and other colorful vegetables.

4 SERVINGS

Calories 588.4 • Protein 17.2 gm • Fat 35.07 gm • Percentage of calories from fat 52% • Cholesterol 0 mg • Dietary fiber 8.871 gm • Sodium 724.1 mg • Calcium 102.9 mg

White Bean and Tomato Salad

Let your food processor do the chopping and this salad will pull itself together in no time. You can substitute julienne strips of seitan for the beans, but I prefer to use the white beans as the meat alternative in this salad for their texture and creamy color.

For beans:

2 tablespoons plus ½ cup olive oil
1 medium onion, chopped
1 green bell pepper, chopped
1 cup chopped celery
½ teaspoon freshly ground black
  pepper
¼ teaspoon ground cinnamon
¼ teaspoon ground allspice

⅓ cup currants or raisins
¼ cup tomato paste
¼ cup cider vinegar
2 cups cooked Great Northern
  beans, rinsed and drained
½ cup packed fresh parsley leaves
1 medium clove garlic
1 teaspoon salt

For greens:

1½ tablespoons balsamic vinegar
¼ teaspoon salt
Pinch sugar or a natural sweetener
⅛ teaspoon freshly ground black
  pepper

5 tablespoons olive oil
6 cups torn mixed greens
  (romaine, Boston lettuce, etc.)
12 cherry tomatoes, halved

For beans:

Heat 2 tablespoons oil in a large skillet over medium-high heat. Add onion, bell pepper, and celery and cook, stirring frequently, about 10 minutes. Reduce heat to medium. Add pepper, cinnamon, and allspice and stir 1 minute. Add currants, tomato paste, and vinegar and cook 5 minutes, stirring frequently. Reduce heat to low. Add beans and cook 15 minutes to blend flavors, stirring occasionally. Transfer mixture to a large bowl and reserve. Place parsley, garlic, and salt in a food processor and mince finely. With machine running, gradually stream in the ½ cup oil. Stir parsley mixture into warm beans and let stand 30 minutes.

For greens:

Combine vinegar, salt, sugar, and pepper in a small bowl. Gradually whisk in oil in a thin, steady stream. Mix greens in a large bowl, then toss with dressing to taste. Divide greens onto individual plates, or place in a large shallow bowl. Mound beans in the center. Top with tomatoes and serve immediately.

6 SERVINGS

Calories 443 • Protein 7.656 gm • Fat 34.59 gm • Percentage of calories from fat 67% • Cholesterol 0 mg • Dietary fiber 6.827 gm • Sodium 586.3 mg • Calcium 115.6 mg

Curried Rice Salad with Tofu and Fruit

1½ tablespoons coarse-grained mustard
3 tablespoons cider vinegar
2 teaspoons curry powder
½ cup corn or safflower oil
½ cup Tofu Mayonnaise (see page 12)
2 teaspoons sugar or a natural sweetener
½ teaspoon salt

6 cups cooked brown rice
⅓ cup minced scallions
1 Red Delicious apple, unpeeled, cut into ½-inch dice
1 cup golden raisins
2 ribs celery, finely chopped
5 radishes, chopped
4 ounces firm tofu, cut into ¼-inch dice

In a small bowl whisk together mustard, vinegar, curry powder, oil, Tofu Mayonnaise, sugar, and salt until well blended. Place rice in a large bowl and add scallions, apple, raisins, celery, radishes, and tofu. Toss mixture with dressing until combined. Chill salad, covered, for at least 1 hour or overnight.

6 SERVINGS

Calories 596.9 • Protein 8.948 gm • Fat 32.68 gm • Percentage of calories from fat 48% • Cholesterol 0 mg • Dietary fiber 5.277 gm • Sodium 308.3 mg • Calcium 73.55 mg

Tofu and Mushroom Salad with Pesto Vinaigrette

Since this salad tastes better if allowed to marinate, it's an ideal choice to take along on a picnic. And there's no mayonnaise to worry about! If you can't find fresh porcini mushrooms, just increase the quantity of the other mushrooms.

1 pound firm tofu, halved lengthwise, cut into ½-inch crosswise slices
2 tablespoons plus ¼ cup olive oil
1 large onion, thinly sliced
2 cloves garlic, minced
½ teaspoon sugar or a natural sweetener
½ pound white mushrooms, thinly sliced
¼ pound porcini mushrooms, thinly sliced
¼ pound shiitake mushrooms, stems discarded, cut into ¼-inch slices
Salt and freshly ground black pepper
1 pound tomatoes, cut into ¼-inch slices
½ cup minced fresh parsley
Pesto Vinaigrette (recipe follows)

Preheat oven to 325 degrees. Arrange tofu slices on large baking sheets and bake about 10 minutes. Reserve. Heat 2 tablespoons of the olive oil in a large skillet over medium-high heat. Add onion and garlic; sprinkle with sugar and cook, stirring frequently, about 5 minutes. Transfer to a medium bowl.

Heat remaining ¼ cup olive oil in the same skillet over medium-high heat. Add white, porcini, and shiitake mushrooms and cook until tender, stirring frequently, about 3 minutes. Season with salt and pepper. Place one third of the onion mixture in a large, deep bowl. Layer with one third of the tofu, one third of the mushroom mixture, one third of the sliced tomatoes, one third of the parsley, some black pepper, and one third of the Pesto Vinaigrette. Repeat layering 2 times, ending with vinaigrette. Cover with plastic wrap and refrigerate at least 1 hour or overnight. Let stand 30 minutes at room temperature before serving.

6 SERVINGS

Calories 189.4 • Protein 7.806 gm • Fat 12.83 gm • Percentage of calories from fat 58% • Cholesterol 0 mg • Dietary fiber 2.1 gm • Sodium 60.59 mg • Calcium 50.53 mg

Pesto Vinaigrette

2 cups loosely packed fresh basil
 leaves
1 large clove garlic, halved
¼ cup pine nuts
¼ teaspoon salt

⅛ teaspoon freshly ground black
 pepper
½ cup olive oil
¼ cup white wine vinegar

In a food processor, combine basil, garlic, pine nuts, salt, and pepper. Process 10 seconds, or until basil is finely minced. With the machine running, stream in the olive oil and process about 10 seconds. Stop and scrape down the sides of the bowl. Add the vinegar and process 5 seconds longer.

MAKES 1 CUP

Calories 1185 • Protein 11.9 gm • Fat 128.8 gm • Percentage of calories from fat 92% • Cholesterol 0 mg • Dietary fiber 0.449 gm • Sodium 534.2 mg • Calcium 153.8 mg

Seitan and New Potato Salad

¼ cup olive oil
4 tablespoons cider vinegar
2 tablespoons low-sodium tamari
1 pound seitan (see page 11), cut
　into ½-inch strips
½ teaspoon sweet paprika
1 tablespoon safflower oil
6 new red potatoes, cut into 1-inch
　dice

1 clove garlic, minced
2 scallions, minced
1 teaspoon Dijon mustard
½ cup grated carrots
¼ cup minced fresh parsley
1 head romaine lettuce, cut
　crosswise into ¼-inch strips

Combine olive oil, 3 tablespoons of the vinegar, and the tamari in a medium bowl, add seitan slices, and marinate for 30 minutes, turning once to coat them. Remove seitan from the marinade; sprinkle with paprika. Reserve marinade. Heat safflower oil in a large skillet over medium-high heat and add seitan slices. Sear them quickly in the hot pan for 1 to 2 minutes on each side. Remove slices to a plate.

Cook potatoes in gently boiling salted water about 10 minutes, or until tender. Meanwhile, combine garlic, scallions, remaining 1 tablespoon cider vinegar, and mustard in a large bowl and mix well. Add reserved marinade. Drain cooked potatoes and gently toss them with the dressing while they are still hot. Refrigerate for 15 minutes, then add the seitan, carrots, and parsley. Toss salad carefully and serve on a bed of romaine lettuce.

6 SERVINGS

Calories 356.9 • Protein 13.18 gm • Fat 10.53 gm • Percentage of calories from fat 25% • Cholesterol 0 mg • Dietary fiber 9.565 gm • Sodium 474.5 mg • Calcium 49.75 mg

Curried Tempeh Salad

1 pound poached tempeh (see page 12), cut into ½-inch cubes
1½ teaspoon minced garlic
½ teaspoon salt
1 teaspoon cornstarch
½ cup soft tofu
¼ cup chutney, homemade (see index) or purchased
1 tablespoon plus ½ cup olive oil
2 tablespoons coarse-grained mustard

1½ teaspoons curry powder
⅛ teaspoon cayenne
2 oranges, peel and pith removed
¼ cup red wine vinegar
¼ cup fresh orange juice
1 teaspoon grated orange peel
Salt and freshly ground black pepper
8 cups torn mixed greens, such as Boston and red leaf lettuce
1 cup unsalted roasted peanuts

Place tempeh in a shallow dish. In a small bowl, combine 1 teaspoon garlic with salt and cornstarch. Mix in tofu, chutney, 1 tablespoon olive oil, 1 tablespoon of the mustard, the curry, and the cayenne. Pour mixture over tempeh, covering completely, and marinate for at least 1 hour.

Halve oranges lengthwise. Slice halves crosswise into ¼-inch half circles and transfer to a bowl and set aside. Mix vinegar, orange juice, remaining 1 tablespoon mustard, the grated orange peel, remaining ½ teaspoon garlic, salt, and pepper in a small bowl. Gradually whisk in the ½ cup olive oil.

Preheat broiler. Transfer tempeh to a broiling pan, reserving marinade. Brush tempeh with some of the marinade. Broil 4 inches from heat source, turning once and basting frequently, until slightly browned, about 10 minutes. Transfer to a plate and cool slightly.

Combine mixed greens and orange slices in a large bowl. Whisk dressing to blend, add some of it to the salad, and toss. Season with salt and pepper. Divide salad among 4 plates. Mound tempeh on top of salad, top with additional dressing, sprinkle with peanuts, and serve.

4 SERVINGS

Calories 807.3 • Protein 33.75 gm • Fat 59.52 gm • Percentage of calories from fat 64% • Cholesterol 0 mg • Dietary fiber 11.17 gm • Sodium 681.1 mg • Calcium 286.3 mg

Lentil and Rice Salad with Summer Vegetables

A showcase for all those great summer vegetables. Make this salad ahead of time so you can enjoy coming home after a day in the sun to a light supper that's ready to eat.

2 large cloves garlic
1 medium shallot
⅓ cup olive oil
2 tablespoons balsamic vinegar
3 tablespoons fresh orange juice
1 tablespoon coarsely chopped
  fresh parsley
½ teaspoon salt
3 large ripe tomatoes, seeded and
  cut into 6 wedges each

2 cups cooked lentils
1 medium red bell pepper, seeded
  and finely chopped
4 cups broccoli florets, steamed
1 cup minced fresh basil
½ cup cooked fresh corn off the
  cob
1 head romaine lettuce, cut
  crosswise into ½-inch strips
Fresh basil leaves

In a food processor, mince garlic and shallot. Add oil, vinegar, orange juice, 1 tablespoon water, parsley, and salt and process until smooth, about 2 minutes. Add fresh tomatoes to dressing in processor and chop coarsely with on/off pulses. Place lentils, red bell pepper, broccoli, basil, and corn, in a large bowl and toss with dressing. Arrange lettuce on plates. Divide lentil-vegetable mixture among the plates on top of the lettuce. Garnish with basil leaves.

6 SERVINGS

Calories 228.2 • Protein 9.51 gm • Fat 11.74 gm • Percentage of calories from fat 43% • Cholesterol 0 mg • Dietary fiber 7.03 gm • Sodium 248.2 mg • Calcium 71.91 mg

Tabbouleh with Chick-peas and Vegetables

1 cup bulgur
1 cup cooked brown rice
1 cup cooked chick-peas
1 large clove garlic
½ cup loosely packed fresh mint leaves
1 jalapeño chili pepper, seeded and coarsely chopped
¼ cup olive oil
2½ tablespoons red wine vinegar
½ teaspoon salt
1 small green bell pepper, chopped
1 medium red onion, chopped
1 cucumber, peeled and seeded, chopped
4 cups spinach leaves, washed and dried
3 large tomatoes
⅓ cup crumbled feta cheese

Add bulgur to 2 cups boiling water in a medium saucepan. Simmer, covered, until bulgur is tender, about 15 minutes. Drain well, transfer to a large bowl, and add rice and chick-peas. In a food processor, mince garlic, mint, and jalapeño pepper. Add oil, vinegar, and salt and process 5 seconds. Scrape dressing into grain mixture, add bell pepper, onion, and cucumber. Put 2 cups of the spinach in the processor and process until minced, about 5 seconds. Add to grain mixture. Cut 1 tomato into ¼-inch dice and add to grain mixture, tossing gently to combine. Cover and refrigerate tabbouleh for 2 hours.

To serve, toss tabbouleh, taste, and adjust seasonings, adding more vinegar if desired. Slice remaining tomatoes. Arrange remaining spinach leaves on each plate. Place tomato slices in a circle on top of the spinach, overlapping slightly. Mound some of the tabbouleh in the center and sprinkle feta cheese on top. Serve immediately.

6 SERVINGS

Calories 312.7 • Protein 9.574 gm • Fat 13.71 gm • Percentage of calories from fat 37% • Cholesterol 11.62 mg • Dietary fiber 10.16 gm • Sodium 563 mg • Calcium 154.8 mg

Creole Salad

A zesty and robust salad that's hearty enough to be a meal in itself. Filé powder is a crucial spice in gumbo.

1¼ cups olive oil
1 small onion, finely chopped
½ teaspoon hot red pepper flakes
½ teaspoon filé powder
½ teaspoon dried thyme
1 bay leaf
2 cups Basic Vegetable Stock (see page 10)
1 teaspoon salt
1 cup basmati rice
2 cups diced seitan (see page 11)
⅛ teaspoon cayenne
⅛ teaspoon ground allspice
⅛ teaspoon fennel seed, ground

⅓ cup cider vinegar
3 tablespoons coarse-grained mustard
1 teaspoon freshly ground black pepper
2 celery ribs, chopped
1 small green bell pepper, chopped
1 small red bell pepper, chopped
4 scallions, minced
6 cups torn iceberg or romaine lettuce
2 ripe tomatoes, cut into 6 wedges each, or 12 cherry tomatoes

In a medium saucepan, heat 2 tablespoons of the olive oil. Add onion and cook, stirring, over moderate heat until tender but not brown, about 5 minutes. Add red pepper flakes, filé powder, thyme, and bay leaf and cook, stirring, for 2 to 3 minutes, until fragrant. Stir in stock, ¾ teaspoon of the salt, and the rice. Increase the heat to moderately high and bring to a boil. Reduce the heat to low, cover the pan, and cook for 20 minutes, or until rice is tender and all the liquid is absorbed. Remove from the heat and let stand, covered, for 5 minutes. Remove bay leaf. Transfer rice to a large bowl and let stand, stirring occasionally, until cool.

Heat 2 tablespoons of the oil in a large skillet and add seitan, cayenne, allspice, and fennel seed. Cook until seitan is browned on all sides, about 5 minutes. Add to rice.

In a food processor, combine vinegar, mustard, remaining ¼ teaspoon salt, and the black pepper. Process for 1 minute. With the machine on, stream in remaining 1 cup olive oil. Pour dressing over rice mixture, add celery, bell peppers, and scallions. Toss well to mix and adjust seasonings. Serve on top of shredded lettuce and garnish with tomatoes.

6 SERVINGS

Calories 1273 • Protein 27 gm • Fat 75.55 gm • Percentage of calories from fat 52% • Cholesterol 0 mg • Dietary fiber 19.79 gm • Sodium 1143 mg • Calcium 120.4 mg

Lentil-Watercress Salad

The lentils are enhanced by the slightly peppery flavor of the watercress.

1 cup lentils	⅔ cup olive oil
¼ cup red wine vinegar	2 bunches watercress, stems
½ teaspoon salt	discarded (about 3 cups)
⅛ teaspoon freshly ground black	½ teaspoon minced garlic
pepper	¼ cup minced scallions

In a saucepan combine lentils with 5 cups water, bring water to a boil, and simmer the lentils, covered partially, for 30 minutes, or until just tender. Transfer lentils to a colander and drain for 5 minutes. In a small bowl combine vinegar, salt, and pepper. And olive oil in a stream, whisking, until it is emulsified. In a large serving bowl toss lentils, watercress, garlic, scallions, dressing, and salt and pepper to taste until the salad is combined.

4 SERVINGS

Calories 488.2 • Protein 13.98 gm • Fat 36.76 gm • Percentage of calories from fat 66% • Cholesterol 0 mg • Dietary fiber 0.134 gm • Sodium 276.2 mg • Calcium 55.41 mg

Lime-Marinated Tofu Salad

A refreshing summer salad brimming with a variety of texture and flavors.

1 large clove garlic

2 tablespoons grated lime zest

1 jalapeño pepper, seeded and cut in half lengthwise

4 tablespoons corn oil

1 pound firm tofu, cut into ½-inch cubes

1 large Granny Smith apple, peeled and chopped

3 tablespoons fresh lime juice

¼ cup minced fresh cilantro

3 scallions, minced

½ teaspoon salt

1 medium red bell pepper, seeded and chopped

1 large carrot, grated

2 cups green beans, trimmed and cut into ½-inch pieces, steamed

1 head romaine lettuce, coarsely chopped

Mince garlic, lime zest, and jalapeño pepper. Heat 1 tablespoon of the oil in a large skillet over medium heat. Add garlic mixture and cook about 2 minutes, stirring frequently. Add ¼ cup water and bring to a simmer. Add tofu and cook about 3 minutes. Transfer mixture to a large bowl; add apple and 1 tablespoon of the lime juice. Combine fresh cilantro and scallions with remaining 3 tablespoons oil, 2 tablespoons lime juice, and the salt. Add to tofu mixture. Then add bell pepper, carrot, and cooked green beans; toss gently. Line 4 plates with romaine. Spoon salad on top.

4 SERVINGS

Calories 267.9 • Protein 11.82 gm • Fat 16.6 gm • Percentage of calories from fat 53% • Cholesterol 0 mg • Dietary fiber 2.837 gm • Sodium 469.7 mg • Calcium 103.6 mg

Tempeh and Noodle Salad with Spicy Sesame Sauce

This salad tastes best if prepared in advance, making it a perfect do-ahead lunch entrée. If serving at a picnic or buffet, however, substitute rotini or other bite-sized pasta shape for the sometimes unwieldy linguine.

1 pound linguine
1 tablespoon plus 2 teaspoons toasted sesame oil
1 pound poached tempeh (see page 12)
2 tablespoons corn oil
½ cup tahini
¼ cup peanut butter
1 teaspoon minced garlic
⅓ cup low-sodium tamari
¼ cup sake

1 teaspoon hot chili oil
1 8-ounce can sliced water chestnuts, drained
2 scallions, minced
1 red bell pepper, cut into ¼-inch squares
1 cucumber, peeled, halved lengthwise, seeded, and thinly sliced
1 tablespoon sesame seeds

Cook pasta in a large pot of boiling salted water until tender, stirring occasionally, about 12 minutes. Drain. Toss with 1 tablespoon sesame oil in a bowl. Cover and chill 1 hour or more. Cut tempeh into ¼-inch strips. Heat corn oil in a large skillet, add tempeh, and cook until browned, about 5 minutes. Allow to cool. Blend tahini, peanut butter, and garlic in a small bowl. Gradually mix in remaining 2 teaspoons sesame oil, tamari, sake, 3 tablespoons water, and chili oil. Add to pasta. Mix in tempeh, water chestnuts, scallions, bell pepper, and cucumber. Transfer to a large, shallow serving bowl or divide among individual plates. Garnish with sesame seeds and serve.

4 TO 6 SERVINGS

Calories 800.8 • Protein 34.23 gm • Fat 33.52 gm • Percentage of calories from fat 37% • Cholesterol 0 mg • Dietary fiber 6.446 gm • Sodium 727.5 mg • Calcium 184.1 mg

White Bean Salad with Cashews and Chutney

For a truly quick fix, use canned beans and bottled chutney. Just be sure to rinse the beans well before using them in the recipe.

1 tablespoon corn oil
2 ounces tempeh bacon, chopped
2 cups cooked Great Northern beans
3 tablespoons olive oil
2 tablespoons white wine vinegar
2 tablespoons minced onion
¾ cup unsalted cashews
½ teaspoon salt
⅛ teaspoon freshly ground black pepper

3 tablespoons minced fresh parsley
2 tablespoons minced crystallized ginger
1 tablespoon minced fresh cilantro
3 tablespoons chutney, homemade (see index) or purchased
1 head romaine, cut into ¼-inch diagonal slices

Heat corn oil in a small skillet over medium-high heat. Add tempeh bacon and cook until browned, about 3 minutes. Remove from skillet and allow to cool. Place cooked beans and tempeh bacon in a large bowl. Add remaining ingredients except for the lettuce. Toss salad well and chill it, covered, for 1 hour. To serve, line plates with romaine and mound salad on top of lettuce.

4 SERVINGS

Calories 461.8 • Protein 13.75 gm • Fat 30.17 gm • Percentage of calories from fat 56% • Cholesterol 0 mg • Dietary fiber 7.297 gm • Sodium 506.6 mg • Calcium 115.2 mg

Piquant Two-Rice Salad

¾ cup wild rice, rinsed and drained
¾ cup brown rice, rinsed and drained
1 cup cooked adzuki beans
¼ cup apple cider vinegar
½ teaspoon salt
⅛ teaspoon freshly ground black pepper
½ cup olive oil
½ cup pimiento-stuffed green olives, sliced
1 tablespoon chopped capers
¼ cup minced scallions
¼ cup minced fresh parsley
6 cups torn mixed lettuces, such as Boston, romaine, red leaf

Bring a large pot of salted water to a boil. Add wild rice and cook, covered, over medium heat for 15 minutes. Add brown rice, stirring, and simmer, covered, for 45 minutes more. Drain rice in a large colander and rinse under running water. Transfer to a large bowl and add adzuki beans. In a small bowl whisk together vinegar, salt, and pepper. Add olive oil in a stream and whisk until it is emulsified. Pour dressing over rice and beans and toss to coat. Add olives, capers, scallions, parsley, and more salt and pepper to adjust seasonings. Toss gently to combine. Serve on a bed of mixed lettuces.

6 SERVINGS

Calories 390 • Protein 8.879 gm • Fat 20.37 gm • Percentage of calories from fat 46% • Cholesterol 0 mg • Dietary fiber 5.363 gm • Sodium 534.3 mg • Calcium 53.45 mg

Seitan, Green Bean, and Walnut Salad

¼ cup white wine vinegar
¼ cup walnut oil
½ cup plus 1 tablespoon corn oil
1 scallion, minced
1 teaspoon salt
⅛ teaspoon freshly ground black
  pepper

1 cup walnut halves
8 ounces seitan (see page 11), cut
  into ¼-inch strips
1 pound green beans, steamed
  until just tender
1 cup crumbled feta cheese

In a bowl, combine vinegar, walnut oil, ½ cup of the corn oil, scallion, salt, and pepper. Set vinaigrette aside.

Heat oven to 350 degrees. Toast walnuts on a baking sheet, stirring once, until lightly browned, about 5 minutes. Cool and then chop finely and set aside. Heat remaining 1 tablespoon corn oil in a large skillet over medium-high heat. Add seitan strips and sauté until brown, about 5 minutes. Remove from skillet and allow to cool. Arrange cooked beans on a serving platter in a circular fashion with the ends meeting in the center. Arrange seitan strips in a similar pattern on top of beans. Drizzle vinaigrette evenly over both. Sprinkle crumbled feta in the center of the plate. Sprinkle chopped walnuts in a circle around the cheese. Serve at room temperature.

4 SERVINGS

Calories 933.5 • Protein 23.67 gm • Fat 74.18 gm • Percentage of calories from fat 68% • Cholesterol 56.5 mg • Dietary fiber 9.319 gm • Sodium 1398 mg • Calcium 418.2 mg

Brown Rice–Ambrosia Salad

Fragrant with spices and studded with fruit, this is ambrosia worthy of the name.

3 cups cooked brown rice
½ orange, peeled, pith removed
¼ cup corn oil
1 tablespoon fresh lemon juice
½ cup fresh orange juice
¼ teaspoon ground cinnamon
¼ teaspoon ground allspice
½ teaspoon salt
⅛ teaspoon freshly ground black pepper
¼ cup chopped scallions
½ cup chopped unsalted cashews
¼ cup chutney, homemade (see index) or purchased
½ cup golden raisins
½ cup drained canned crushed pineapple
Boston lettuce leaves

Place cooked rice in a large bowl. Chop orange and add to rice along with the remaining ingredients except the lettuce and toss well. Refrigerate salad, covered, at least 1 hour or overnight. To serve, line lettuce leaves in a shallow serving dish, or on individual plates, and mound with the salad.

6 SERVINGS

Calories 320.7 • Protein 5.142 gm • Fat 15.34 gm • Percentage of calories from fat 41% • Cholesterol 0 mg • Dietary fiber 3.976 gm • Sodium 201.6 mg • Calcium 37.42 mg

White Bean Salad

½ cup olive oil
¼ cup fresh lemon juice
½ teaspoon minced garlic
1 teaspoon dry mustard
½ teaspoon salt
⅛ teaspoon freshly ground black
   pepper

4 cups cooked cannellini beans
1 cucumber, peeled, halved
   lengthwise, and seeded
¼ cup diced pimientos
6 cups torn mixed lettuces
¼ cup minced fresh parsley

Combine olive oil, lemon juice, garlic, mustard, salt, and pepper in a jar with a tight-fitting lid and shake until thoroughly mixed. Rinse beans under cold running water; drain well. Chop cucumber into a fine dice and combine with pimientos and beans. Pour dressing over bean salad in a large bowl; toss lightly with a fork. Let stand, covered, at room temperature at least 30 minutes. Drain off any excess dressing and adjust seasonings. To serve, mound salad on plates lined with mixed lettuces and sprinkle with parsley. Serve at room temperature.

6 SERVINGS

Calories 322 • Protein 11.37 gm • Fat 18.95 gm • Percentage of calories from fat 51% • Cholesterol 0 mg • Dietary fiber 7.557 gm • Sodium 187.8 mg • Calcium 125.2 mg

Couscous Salad with Currants and Pine Nuts

The currants and pine nuts add delightful texture and flavor to this delicious and colorful salad. Bring this to a pot luck or put on a buffet table and watch it disappear.

⅓ cup pine nuts
2 tablespoons corn oil
⅛ teaspoon ground turmeric
1½ cups Basic Vegetable Stock
  (see page 10)
1½ cups couscous
½ cup currants
1½ cups diced celery

¼ cup minced scallions
¼ cup minced fresh parsley
¼ cup fresh lemon juice
¼ teaspoon ground cinnamon
½ teaspoon salt
⅛ teaspoon freshly ground black
  pepper
½ cup olive oil

Toast pine nuts in a medium skillet over medium heat, shaking pan frequently until light brown, about 5 minutes. Reserve. In a large saucepan heat corn oil with turmeric over moderate heat, stirring; then add stock and bring to a boil. Stir in couscous and currants, cover the saucepan, and remove it from the heat. Let mixture stand for 5 minutes; then transfer it to a large bowl. Add celery, scallions, pine nuts, and parsley and toss to combine. In a small bowl whisk together lemon juice, cinnamon, salt, and pepper. Whisk in oil in a slow stream until emulsified. Add dressing to salad, toss, and season with additional salt and pepper, if desired.

6 SERVINGS

Calories 472.4 • Protein 9.187 gm • Fat 27.48 gm • Percentage of calories from fat 50% • Cholesterol 0 mg • Dietary fiber 8.299 gm • Sodium 274.8 mg • Calcium 50.95 mg

Southwestern Rice and Bean Salad

The zesty flavors of the Southwest permeate this hearty main dish salad.

⅓ cup fresh lime juice
2 tablespoons corn oil
1 teaspoon sugar or a natural
  sweetener
1 teaspoon Tabasco sauce
1 clove garlic, minced
1 jalapeño pepper, seeded and
  minced
½ teaspoon salt
⅛ teaspoon freshly ground black
  pepper

1½ cups cooked adzuki beans
¼ cup chopped scallions
1 7½-ounce jar roasted red
  peppers, drained, rinsed, and
  diced
2 tablespoons chopped fresh
  cilantro
4 cups cooked brown rice
4 cups torn mixed lettuces

In a large bowl, whisk together lime juice, corn oil, sugar, Tabasco sauce, garlic, jalapeño, salt, and pepper. Add beans, scallions, roasted red peppers, cilantro, and rice. Adjust seasonings with salt and pepper. Serve on a bed of mixed lettuces.

4 TO 6 SERVINGS

Calories 348.6 • Protein 10.67 gm • Fat 7.234 gm • Percentage of calories from fat 18% • Cholesterol 0 mg • Dietary fiber 9.031 gm • Sodium 315.2 mg • Calcium 80.55 mg

Cold Noodle Salad

This Asian-flavored pasta salad makes a complete and satisfying meal that can be prepared in advance.

¼ cup rice wine vinegar
¼ cup low-sodium tamari
2 tablespoons fresh lemon juice
2 teaspoons grated fresh ginger
2 cloves garlic, minced
¾ cup toasted sesame oil
8 ounces seitan (see page 11), cut into ¼-inch strips
2 tablespoons safflower oil
8 ounces shiitake mushrooms, stems discarded, sliced

4 scallions, minced
2 ounces fresh snow peas, strings removed
¼ teaspoon salt
⅛ teaspoon freshly ground black pepper
1 pound cooked udon noodles, tossed with 1 tablespoon toasted sesame oil

In a small bowl, blend vinegar, tamari, lemon juice, 1 teaspoon of the ginger, and half the garlic until smooth. Slowly add sesame oil. In a bowl, spoon some of the dressing over the seitan. Heat safflower oil in a large skillet over medium-high heat. Add remaining ginger and garlic. Add seitan slices and cook on both sides until brown, about 5 minutes. Add shiitake mushrooms, scallions, and snow peas and cook another 2 minutes. Season with salt and pepper and allow to cool. In a large bowl, combine cooked noodles with dressing and seitan mixture, and toss, combining well. Serve at room temperature.

6 SERVINGS

Calories 714 • Protein 18.63 gm • Fat 36.11 gm • Percentage of calories from fat 44% • Cholesterol 0 mg • Dietary fiber 8.083 gm • Sodium 1296 mg • Calcium 26.95 mg

Tempeh Waldorf Salad

A "meaty" version of the classic apple salad. Be prepared for comments like "This is the best chicken salad I've ever had!"

1 pound poached tempeh (see page 12)
⅓ cup lightly packed watercress leaves, stems removed
2 tablespoons cider vinegar
3 tablespoons corn oil
1 teaspoon Dijon mustard
2 tablespoons Tofu Mayonnaise (see page 12)
½ teaspoon sugar or a natural sweetener

¼ teaspoon salt
1 scallion, finely minced
2 cups finely chopped cabbage
2 Red Delicious apples, unpeeled, chopped
1 red bell pepper, seeded and finely chopped
⅓ cup raisins

Cut poached tempeh into ½-inch cubes. In a food processor, combine watercress, vinegar, oil, mustard, mayonnaise, sugar, and salt; pulse for about 6 seconds. Transfer to a large bowl, add scallion, cabbage, and apples to dressing. Mix in tempeh, bell pepper, and raisins. Adjust seasonings and serve.

4 TO 6 SERVINGS

Calories 299.2 • Protein 15.85 gm • Fat 16.22 gm • Percentage of calories from fat 47% • Cholesterol 0 mg • Dietary fiber 5.114 gm • Sodium 159.6 mg • Calcium 98.19 mg

10
One-Dish Meals

Especially handy when cooking for a crowd, these one-dish meals take the fuss out of entertaining. Many of these dishes freeze well, so if you're cooking for only one or two, make the whole recipe and store the surplus in small portions.

All-time favorites such as Jambalaya and Lasagne are given a lift with new ingredients. Tricolored Beans with Summer Vegetables and the Moroccan Couscous with Tempeh are sure to please.

Couscous with Seitan and Walnuts

4 tablespoons olive oil
1 cup ground seitan (see page 8)
½ cup walnut halves
1 teaspoon salt
1 small red bell pepper, seeded
  and cut into ¼-inch strips

1 cup couscous
1 teaspoon fresh lemon juice
3 tablespoons minced fresh
  parsley
2 tablespoons chopped fresh basil
Salt and pepper

In a medium skillet heat 2 tablespoons of the oil over moderate heat, add seitan, walnuts, and salt, and cook them, stirring, for 3 minutes or until golden brown. Set aside.

Heat remaining 2 tablespoons olive oil in a large skillet over medium heat, add bell pepper strips, stirring, until softened, then add couscous and stir to coat it with the oil. Remove the skillet from the heat, shaking it to spread the couscous in an even layer; then pour 1 cup boiling water over couscous and cover skillet immediately. Let mixture stand for 5 minutes, then fluff it with a fork and add reserved seitan-walnut mixture and lemon juice. Toss lightly. Add parsley, basil, and salt and pepper to taste. Toss again. Transfer couscous to a serving dish and serve immediately.

4 SERVINGS

Calories 736 • Protein 24.67 gm • Fat 25.07 gm • Percentage of calories from fat 30% • Cholesterol 0 mg • Dietary fiber 20.18 gm • Sodium 840.5 mg • Calcium 74.51 mg

Jambalaya

Jambalaya is a Creole dish that usually contains whatever meats are on hand. Following that pattern, this recipe uses a variety of meat alternatives. Serve over freshly cooked rice.

4 tablespoons corn oil
4 ounces firm tofu, cut into ½-inch cubes
8 ounces meatless sausage links, cut into 1-inch pieces
4 ounces poached tempeh (see page 12), cut into ½-inch cubes
1 onion, chopped
1 cup chopped celery
1 clove garlic, minced
1 green bell pepper, chopped

1 cup peeled and chopped tomatoes (see page 375 for peeling)
2 tablespoons tomato paste
1 teaspoon filé powder
1 teaspoon salt
1 tablespoon chopped fresh parsley
½ teaspoon dried thyme
1 teaspoon Tabasco sauce

Heat 2 tablespoons of the oil in a large skillet over medium-high heat. Add tofu, meatless sausage, and tempeh and brown lightly; set aside.

In a large pot, heat remaining 2 tablespoons oil over medium heat and add onion, celery, garlic, and bell pepper. Sauté until onion is translucent; then add tomatoes, tomato paste, filé powder, salt, parsley, thyme, and Tabasco. Stir to combine, and add browned tofu, tempeh, and meatless sausage. Simmer 20 minutes. Adjust seasonings, adding more Tabasco if desired.

6 TO 8 SERVINGS

Calories 213.1 • Protein 10.88 gm • Fat 15.48 gm • Percentage of calories from fat 62% • Cholesterol 0 mg • Dietary fiber 1.917 gm • Sodium 625.7 mg • Calcium 58.68 mg

Couscous with White Beans and Carrots

The fragrant addition of vanilla adds a delightful scent to this light and lovely dish. Prepare the beans and vegetables the night before, and dinner can be ready in minutes.

2 tablespoons olive oil
1 pound carrots, cut into ¼-inch diagonal slices
⅔ cup minced onions
¼ teaspoon sugar or a natural sweetener
¼ teaspoon salt
¼ teaspoon freshly ground black pepper

⅛ teaspoon vanilla extract
1 cup cooked Great Northern beans
3 to 6 tablespoons plus 2 cups Basic Vegetable Stock (see page 10)
1 cup couscous
½ cup shredded Jarlsberg cheese

Heat olive oil in a large skillet over medium heat. Add carrots and cook until beginning to soften, stirring frequently, about 10 minutes. Add onions, increase heat to medium high, and stir until onions begin to brown, about 5 minutes. Sprinkle with sugar, salt, and pepper and stir 30 seconds. Add vanilla and remove from heat. Add beans to skillet, mix in 3 tablespoons of the stock, and season to taste with additional salt. Set aside in a bowl to cool, then refrigerate several hours or overnight.

Preheat oven to 350 degrees. Reheat beans and vegetables in a covered saucepan over low heat, stirring occasionally (adding 2 to 3 tablespoons more stock to moisten), about 10 minutes. While beans are reheating prepare couscous: Bring 2 cups stock to a boil, add couscous, cover, and remove from heat. Allow to sit for 5 minutes. Spread couscous in a baking dish, layer with bean-carrot mixture, then top with shredded cheese. Bake until cheese is melted.

4 SERVINGS

Calories 349.5 • Protein 13.38 gm • Fat 11.33 gm • Percentage of calories from fat 29% • Cholesterol 12.98 mg • Dietary fiber 11.59 gm • Sodium 343.7 mg • Calcium 223.4 mg

Herbed Tofu and Vegetables with White Wine Sauce

Prepare this dish when your herb garden is at its peak, since this is a glorious celebration of fresh herbs.

1 tablespoon corn oil

1 carrot, cut into ¼-inch julienne strips

1 leek, white part only, cut into ¼-inch julienne strips

2 ribs celery, cut into ¼-inch julienne strips

1 pound firm tofu, cut into ¼-inch slices

½ teaspoon salt

⅛ teaspoon freshly ground black pepper

1 cup dry white wine

1 teaspoon minced fresh basil

1 teaspoon minced fresh thyme

¼ teaspoon grated lemon zest

½ teaspoon minced fresh mint

½ teaspoon minced fresh tarragon

1 cup milk

1 tablespoon cornstarch dissolved in 1 tablespoon water

Heat oil in a large skillet over medium heat. Add carrot, leek, and celery julienne and stir until beginning to soften, about 3 minutes. Remove from heat and transfer julienne to a plate using a slotted spoon. Season tofu with salt and pepper. Arrange in a single layer in the same skillet, add wine, then julienne. Simmer about 5 minutes. Transfer tofu and vegetables to a heated platter using a slotted spoon. Keep warm. Add basil, thyme, lemon zest, mint, and tarragon to liquid in skillet. Boil until reduced by half, about 5 minutes. Add milk and any liquid accumulated on platter and bring to a boil. Add cornstarch and stir to thicken, about 3 minutes. Adjust seasonings, pour sauce over tofu and vegetables, and serve immediately.

4 SERVINGS

Calories 223.1 • Protein 12.44 gm • Fat 7.266 gm • Percentage of calories from fat 28% • Cholesterol 4.5 mg • Dietary fiber 2.244 gm • Sodium 414.9 mg • Calcium 172 mg

Polenta with Braised Seitan and Mushrooms

3 quarts Basic Vegetable Stock
(see page 10)
1 teaspoon salt
2⅓ cups yellow cornmeal
½ cup minced scallions
6 tablespoons corn oil
¼ cup minced fresh parsley
⅛ teaspoon freshly ground black
pepper

¾ pound seitan (see page 11), cut
into ½-inch strips
4 ounces shiitake mushrooms,
stemmed and sliced
Salt and freshly ground black
pepper
¼ cup red wine

In a large saucepan, bring 2 quarts of the stock and the salt to a boil over high heat. Stir in cornmeal in a thin stream, reducing heat to medium. Stir polenta constantly with a wooden spoon, about 30 minutes, adding more stock as necessary to maintain creamy consistency. Stir in scallions, 4 tablespoons of the oil, the parsley, and the pepper. Adjust seasonings. Keep warm.

Heat remaining 2 tablespoons oil in a large skillet. Add seitan and mushrooms. Cook over medium-high heat for 2 minutes, turning to brown. Sprinkle with salt and pepper. Add red wine, scraping pan to remove browned bits. Reduce liquid by boiling until it becomes syrupy. To serve, spoon sauce and seitan over polenta.

4 TO 6 SERVINGS

Calories 688.1 • Protein 18.67 gm • Fat 19.99 gm • Percentage of calories from fat 25% • Cholesterol 0 mg • Dietary fiber 20.65 gm • Sodium 1248 mg • Calcium 98.82 mg

Tofu Provençal

Redolent with herbs and spices, the aroma of this sauce will beckon your guests to the dinner table.

1 pound firm tofu, cut into ½-inch slices
2 tablespoons olive oil
1 tablespoon fresh lemon juice
1 teaspoon salt
¼ teaspoon freshly ground black pepper
1 green bell pepper, seeded and cut into ½-inch dice
1 small onion, cut into ¼-inch dice
½ teaspoon sugar or a natural sweetener
1 clove garlic, finely minced

1 16-ounce can Italian plum tomatoes, drained and chopped (reserve juice)
¼ cup anise liqueur
1 tablespoon chopped fresh basil
½ teaspoon fennel seed, crushed
1 teaspoon finely minced fresh thyme
Salt and freshly ground black pepper
1 tablespoon minced fresh parsley
Freshly cooked brown rice

Place tofu in a small baking dish. In a small bowl combine 1 tablespoon of the olive oil, the lemon juice, ½ teaspoon of the salt, and ⅛ teaspoon of the pepper. Pour over tofu and set aside at room temperature 1 hour.

Heat 2 teaspoons of the olive oil in a large skillet over medium heat. Add bell pepper and onion, sprinkle with sugar, cover, and cook until vegetables begin to soften, about 5 minutes. Add garlic and tomatoes, increase heat to medium-high, and cook until juices are thickened, about 2 minutes, stirring occasionally. Stir in reserved tomato juice, then the liqueur, basil, fennel seed, thyme, salt, and pepper; cook 5 minutes, stirring occasionally. Reduce heat to low, uncover, and simmer until sauce thickens and vegetables are soft, about 15 minutes. Adjust seasonings.

In a separate pan, heat remaining 1 teaspoon olive oil over medium-high heat, add tofu, and sauté on both sides until lightly browned. Transfer to individual plates. Spoon sauce around tofu slices. Garnish with parsley. Serve immediately with brown rice.

4 SERVINGS

Calories 236.3 • Protein 11.05 gm • Fat 9.349 gm • Percentage of calories from fat 35% • Cholesterol 0 mg • Dietary fiber 2.194 gm • Sodium 850.7 mg • Calcium 92.7 mg

Cajun Tofu

Not for the timid, this simple recipe is hot stuff. Be sure to serve over cooked rice or with a loaf of warm crusty bread to help put out the fire.

¼ cup olive oil
2 cloves garlic, minced
4 scallions, minced
4 dried red chili peppers

¼ teaspoon hot pepper sauce
1 pound firm tofu, cut into ½-inch cubes
¼ cup low-sodium tamari

Heat oil in a large skillet over medium-high heat. Add garlic and sauté 1 minute. Stir in scallions, chilies, and hot pepper sauce and simmer 2 minutes. Add tofu and tamari and stir just until tofu is heated through, about 2 to 4 minutes. Remove chilies before serving.

4 SERVINGS

Calories 211.7 • Protein 11.08 gm • Fat 15.95 gm • Percentage of calories from fat 68% • Cholesterol 0 mg • Dietary fiber 0.833 gm • Sodium 699.8 mg • Calcium 58.66 mg

Baked Tofu Vinaigrette with Roasted Vegetables

1 pound firm tofu, cut into ½-inch slices
2 large cloves garlic, minced
½ cup olive oil
¼ cup balsamic vinegar
8 fresh sage leaves
¼ teaspoon salt

⅛ teaspoon freshly ground black pepper
8 small red potatoes
4 small zucchini, halved lengthwise
4 small yellow squash, halved lengthwise
Salt and freshly ground pepper

Arrange tofu in a large shallow dish, sprinkle with half the garlic, drizzle with half the oil, half the vinegar, and half the sage. Season with salt and pepper. Turn tofu over and repeat with remaining garlic, oil, vinegar, and sage. Sprinkle with salt and pepper. Marinate 2 hours or overnight in the refrigerator, turning occasionally. Meanwhile preheat oven to 400 degrees.

Steam potatoes until almost tender, about 15 minutes, then cut in half. Steam zucchini and yellow squash until starting to soften, about 5 minutes. Place potatoes, zucchini, and yellow squash in a large baking dish. Sprinkle with salt and pepper. Reserving marinade, arrange tofu alongside vegetables in pan. Bake for 15 minutes, turning tofu and vegetables and brushing all with reserved marinade. Serve directly from baking dish.

4 SERVINGS

Calories 418.4 • Protein 13.57 gm • Fat 29.99 gm • Percentage of calories from fat 62% • Cholesterol 0 mg • Dietary fiber 3.941 gm • Sodium 212.3 mg • Calcium 92.15 mg

Tricolored Beans with Summer Vegetables

In addition to being a nourishing and flavorful meat alternative, the beans add color and texture to this recipe. Make it when fresh corn and tomatoes are at their peak for a real taste treat.

½ pound green beans, trimmed and cut into 2-inch pieces
4 ears fresh corn
¾ cup Basic Vegetable Stock (see page 10)
2 tablespoons corn oil
2 scallions, minced
1 cup cooked navy beans

1 cup cooked pinto beans
1 small clove garlic, minced
Salt and freshly ground black pepper
2 medium tomatoes, peeled (see page 375) and chopped
1 tablespoon chopped fresh basil
Freshly cooked rice

Steam green beans until tender, about 5 minutes. Rinse with cold water and drain. Cut kernels from corn. Bring stock to a boil in a large skillet. Reduce heat to low, add corn, and simmer 5 minutes, or until tender. Remove corn, using slotted spoon. Boil liquid until reduced to about 3 tablespoons. Pour over corn.

Heat oil in the same skillet over medium heat. Add scallions, navy and pinto beans, garlic, salt, and pepper. Stir over low heat about 2 minutes. Add corn, green beans, tomatoes, and basil. Cook 3 minutes longer. Adjust seasonings, and transfer to a serving dish. Allow to come to room temperature. Serve on a bed of freshly cooked rice.

6 SERVINGS

Calories 275.9 • Protein 11.91 gm • Fat 5.946 gm • Percentage of calories from fat 18% • Cholesterol 0 mg • Dietary fiber 4.793 gm • Sodium 43.41 mg • Calcium 75.42 mg

Seitan Pot Roast

What could be more comforting on a cold winter night than a blazing fire and the aroma of this pot roast wafting through the house?

2 cups dry red wine
3 tablespoons olive oil
1 medium onion, chopped
2 cloves garlic, crushed
2 bay leaves
½ teaspoon dried thyme
¼ teaspoon freshly ground black pepper
1½ pounds seitan (see page 11)
2 tablespoons corn oil
1 large onion, minced
1 large carrot, minced
1 cup minced celery

3 cups Basic Vegetable Stock (see page 10)
2 tablespoons tomato paste
Salt and freshly ground black pepper
4 small yellow onions, quartered
1 pound small new potatoes, cut in half
1 pound carrots, cut into ½-inch slices
1 pound green beans, trimmed, cut in half

Combine first 7 ingredients in a large, shallow bowl. Add seitan, turning to coat all sides. Cover and refrigerate at least 1 hour or overnight. Drain seitan and set aside. Strain marinade through fine sieve, pressing on vegetables with the back of a spoon to extract liquid. Reserve marinade and discard solids.

Heat oil in a large saucepan or Dutch oven over medium-high heat. Add seitan and brown on all sides; set aside. Return pot to medium-high heat. Add minced onion, carrot, and celery and cook 5 minutes. Add stock, tomato paste, salt, pepper, and reserved marinade and bring to a simmer. Return seitan to pot. Add onions, potatoes, and carrots. Reduce heat to low, cover tightly, and simmer gently for 45 minutes. Add green beans and continue cooking 15 minutes. Slice the seitan roast and arrange slices on serving platter. Remove vegetables from sauce using slotted spoon and arrange around seitan. Taste sauce and reduce to desired flavor and consistency. Spoon some sauce over seitan and serve. Serve remaining sauce separately.

6 TO 8 SERVINGS

Calories 608.8 • Protein 20.39 gm • Fat 11.99 gm • Percentage of calories from fat 17% • Cholesterol 0 mg • Dietary fiber 18.31 gm • Sodium 474.2 mg • Calcium 153 mg

Seitan Bourguignonne

No one will ask "where's the beef?" when they taste this delicious meat alternative version of Beef Bourguignonne.

2 tablespoons corn oil
½ pound sliced mushrooms
2 slices tempeh bacon, diced
1 pound seitan (see page 11), cut into 1-inch cubes
2 tablespoons all-purpose flour
½ teaspoon salt
⅛ teaspoon freshly ground black pepper

¾ teaspoon minced fresh thyme or ¼ teaspoon dried
1 bay leaf
½ cup Basic Vegetable Stock (see page 10)
1 cup dry red wine
½ pound pearl onions
4 cups freshly cooked rice

Heat oil in a large pot and sauté mushrooms until softened and lightly browned. Remove mushrooms and liquid and set aside. Fry tempeh bacon until browned; then remove and set aside. Add seitan to the oil and brown it well. Blend in flour, stirring, and add salt, pepper, thyme, and bay leaf. Add stock, wine, and onions that have been peeled first, by blanching them in boiling water and then removing skins. Cover and simmer for 45 minutes, stirring occasionally. Add mushrooms and tempeh bacon. Simmer 10 minutes longer. Add more wine if liquid has evaporated. Remove bay leaf. Serve over rice.

4 SERVINGS

Calories 796.4 • Protein 25.34 gm • Fat 14.7 gm • Percentage of calories from fat 16% • Cholesterol 0 mg • Dietary fiber 14.24 gm • Sodium 904.8 mg • Calcium 74.98 mg

Vegetable Bean Bake

½ pound tempeh bacon, diced
2 shallots, chopped
¼ cup olive oil
4 small red potatoes, thinly sliced
1 zucchini, thinly sliced
1 yellow squash, thinly sliced

½ pound fresh or frozen green
 peas
1 large tomato, thinly sliced
1 cup cooked pinto beans
½ pound Monterey Jack cheese,
 grated

Preheat oven to 350 degrees. Fry tempeh bacon and shallots in 1 table-spoon of the oil in a small skillet until browned. Set aside. Oil the bottom and sides of a large baking dish. Place a layer of sliced potatoes, zucchini, yellow squash, peas, and tomato on the bottom of the dish and sprinkle with half the tempeh bacon, pinto beans, oil and the cheese. Layer the remaining vegetables, then sprinkle with remaining tempeh bacon, beans, oil, and all but ⅓ cup of the cheese. Bake covered for 45 minutes. Remove from oven. Top with remaining cheese. Bake uncovered for 10 minutes, or until cheese melts.

4 SERVINGS

Calories 789.7 • Protein 34.7 gm • Fat 48.38 gm • Percentage of calories from fat 54% • Cholesterol 50.31 mg • Dietary fiber 6.701 gm • Sodium 1144 mg • Calcium 521.6 mg

Wheat Meat Hash

This is comfort food at its finest, and a great way to use leftover seitan pot roast (see page 344).

2 tablespoons corn oil
1 large Spanish onion, chopped
1 medium red bell pepper, seeded and chopped
1 pound boiling potatoes, cooked and cooled

3 cups cooked seitan (see page 11), shredded or ground, or leftover seitan roast
½ teaspoon salt
⅛ teaspoon freshly ground black pepper

Heat oil in a large skillet over medium-high heat. Add onion and bell pepper and sauté until soft, about 5 minutes. Chop potatoes into ¼-inch dice. Add potatoes and seitan to the skillet and cook until browned, stirring frequently. Add salt and pepper. Serve with Tomato Chutney (see page 233) or ketchup.

6 SERVINGS

Calories 794 • Protein 35.11 gm • Fat 8.351 gm • Percentage of calories from fat 9% • Cholesterol 0 mg • Dietary fiber 26.66 gm • Sodium 780.7 mg • Calcium 95.34 mg

Baked Tempeh with Brown Rice Syrup

Brown rice syrup, a natural sweetener available at natural foods stores, imparts a mellow and subtly sweet flavor to the tempeh.

2 tablespoons corn oil
1 pound poached tempeh (see page 12), cut into ½-inch slices
1 medium onion, chopped
4 large mushrooms, thinly sliced
⅛ teaspoon salt

⅛ teaspoon freshly ground black pepper
1 tablespoon mirin, white wine, or sherry
¼ cup brown rice syrup
Freshly cooked rice

Preheat oven to 350 degrees. Heat oil in a large skillet over medium-high heat. Add tempeh and onion and sauté until tempeh is brown on both sides and onion is tender, about 5 minutes. Transfer tempeh to a baking dish. Reheat skillet and add mushrooms, salt, and pepper; sauté for 2 minutes or until mushrooms are softened. Remove mushrooms with a slotted spoon and spoon over tempeh. Add mirin and rice syrup to pan and blend with pan juices. Pour pan sauce evenly over tempeh and mushrooms. Bake until heated through, about 20 minutes. Serve immediately over rice.

4 SERVINGS

Calories 282.8 • Protein 18.7 gm • Fat 15.56 gm • Percentage of calories from fat 49% • Cholesterol 0 mg • Dietary fiber 4.085 gm • Sodium 83.74 mg • Calcium 89.77 mg

Seitan with Rice and Olives

Beer is the secret ingredient in this dish, but for a non-alcoholic version, substitute more stock.

3 tablespoons olive oil
2 cloves garlic, minced
1 pound seitan (see page 11), cut into 1-inch cubes
½ pound tempeh bacon, chopped
1 large onion, chopped
½ green bell pepper, chopped
1½ cups brown rice
2 cups Basic Vegetable Stock (see page 10)

1 16-ounce can whole tomatoes, drained and chopped
1 cup beer
½ cup pitted green olives, chopped
¼ cup chopped pimientos
¾ teaspoon salt
¼ teaspoon freshly ground black pepper

Preheat oven to 375 degrees. In a large skillet, heat oil with garlic. Add seitan and cook over moderate heat until browned, about 5 minutes. Transfer to a baking dish. Add tempeh bacon, onion, and bell pepper to the skillet. Cook over moderate heat until softened, about 5 minutes; then scoop into casserole. Add rice to the skillet and cook 2 to 3 minutes, stirring constantly. Add stock to rice and cover. Simmer over low heat for 15 minutes. Add rice and stock, along with remaining ingredients, to the casserole, stirring to combine. Cover and bake until rice is tender, about 30 minutes.

4 SERVINGS

Calories 979.6 • Protein 31.04 gm • Fat 33.03 gm • Percentage of calories from fat 28% • Cholesterol 0 mg • Dietary fiber 17.31 gm • Sodium 2004 mg • Calcium 157 mg

Polenta with Portobello Mushrooms and Tomato-Basil Sauce

The meaty texture of Portobello mushrooms is a pleasant surprise. I like them so much I often grill a few extra brushed with garlic, olive oil, and a dash of Worcestershire, and serve them along side the polenta.

½ cup pine nuts
3 tablespoons olive oil
2 cloves garlic, minced
4 cups Basic Vegetable Stock (see page 10)
4 sun-dried tomatoes, chopped
4 tablespoons Pesto Sauce (see page 126)
Salt and freshly ground black pepper

¼ pound Portobello mushrooms, thinly sliced
1 medium onion, finely chopped
½ teaspoon salt
1 cup yellow cornmeal
2 tablespoons grated Pecorino Romano cheese
Fresh basil leaves as garnish

Toast pine nuts in a medium skillet over low heat, shaking pan frequently, about 5 minutes. Remove from heat and reserve. Heat 1 tablespoon of the oil in a medium saucepan over medium heat. Add garlic and stir until light brown. Add 1 cup of the stock and the tomatoes. Increase heat and boil until reduced by half, about 10 minutes. Stir in pesto, salt, and pepper. Keep warm. Heat remaining 2 tablespoons olive oil in medium skillet over medium-high heat. Add mushrooms and onion and sauté until soft, about 5 minutes. Set aside.

Preheat oven to 350 degrees. Bring remaining 3 cups stock and the salt to a boil in a large saucepan. Stir in cornmeal in a thin stream. Boil until polenta is thick, stirring constantly, about 20 minutes. Blend in mushroom mixture. Turn polenta into an oiled baking dish. Smooth out top and sprinkle with cheese. Bake for 15 minutes. To serve, spoon onto plates or cut into squares or wedges and top with reserved sauce. Sprinkle with pine nuts and garnish with fresh basil leaves.

6 SERVINGS

Calories 337.5 • Protein 8.807 gm • Fat 22.18 gm • Percentage of calories from fat 56% • Cholesterol 2.469 mg • Dietary fiber 3.076 gm • Sodium 616.6 mg • Calcium 72.1 mg

Tempeh Marengo

1 pound poached tempeh (see page 12), cut into 1-inch cubes
2 tablespoons corn oil
1 cup chopped onions
1 teaspoon minced garlic
1 red bell pepper, seeded and diced
1 cup diced carrots
1 bay leaf
½ teaspoon dried thyme
¼ cup tomato paste
1 cup plus 2 tablespoons white wine
2 cups Basic Vegetable Stock (see page 10)
½ pound mushrooms
1 tablespoon cornstarch
1 tablespoon grated lemon zest

In a large saucepan, brown tempeh in oil, about 5 minutes. Add onions, garlic, bell pepper, carrots, bay leaf, and thyme. Cook for 5 minutes; then add tomato paste, 1 cup white wine, and the stock. Cover and simmer over medium heat for 45 minutes. Add mushrooms and cook 10 minutes longer. Transfer tempeh and vegetables to a serving casserole; strain the sauce, pour it back into the saucepan, and bring to a boil. Lower heat till it is at a simmer. Blend cornstarch with 2 tablespoons white wine and stir into sauce until it begins to thicken. To serve, pour sauce over tempeh and vegetables in casserole and sprinkle with lemon zest.

4 SERVINGS

Calories 378.7 • Protein 21.71 gm • Fat 16.01 gm • Percentage of calories from fat 37% • Cholesterol 0 mg • Dietary fiber 7.493 gm • Sodium 163.3 mg • Calcium 130.2 mg

Red Beans and Rice

2 tablespoons corn oil
1 green bell pepper, chopped
1 red bell pepper, chopped
1 cup finely minced onion
½ cup chopped scallions
½ cup chopped celery
1 cup ground seitan (see page 8)
2 large cloves garlic, minced
1 teaspoon sweet paprika
¾ teaspoon dried thyme, crumbled

½ teaspoon dried basil, crumbled
¼ teaspoon cayenne
½ teaspoon salt
½ teaspoon freshly ground black pepper
2 cups cooked adzuki beans or red kidney beans
4 cups freshly cooked brown rice
2 tablespoons minced fresh parsley

Heat oil in a large, heavy skillet or Dutch oven over medium heat. Add all but the last 3 ingredients and cook, stirring occasionally, until vegetables are softened and lightly browned, about 20 minutes. Add cooked beans. Cook another 5 minutes, or until heated through. Adjust seasonings. Serve the beans on top of the rice and garnish with parsley.

4 SERVINGS

Calories 545.7 • Protein 18.56 gm • Fat 9.292 gm • Percentage of calories from fat 15% • Cholesterol 0 mg • Dietary fiber 15.28 gm • Sodium 369.4 mg • Calcium 99.37 mg

Tofu Stroganoff

Served over freshly cooked noodles, this stroganoff, with its rich creamy sauce, is sure to satisfy the hungriest appetite—and don't expect any leftovers.

1 pound firm tofu, cut into 1-inch cubes
½ teaspoon salt
¼ teaspoon freshly ground black pepper
½ teaspoon sweet paprika
2 tablespoons corn oil
1 tablespoon minced shallot
1 tablespoon chopped fresh parsley
2 tablespoons brandy
2 cups sliced mushrooms
1 tablespoon tomato paste
¼ cup dry sherry
1 cup Basic Brown Sauce (see page 13)
1 tablespoon soft tofu
1 teaspoon fresh lemon juice
1 tablespoon milk
Freshly cooked wide egg noodles

Season tofu cubes with salt, pepper, and paprika. Heat 1 tablespoon of the oil in a large skillet over high heat, add tofu, and brown quickly on all sides, about 2 minutes. Add shallot and parsley and sauté about 30 seconds. Remove skillet from heat. Add brandy carefully, and ignite. Shake pan until flames subside. Transfer tofu to a warm dish and reserve.

Heat remaining 1 tablespoon oil in the same skillet over high heat. Add mushrooms; sauté quickly for 2 minutes, stirring frequently. Blend tomato paste with sherry and add to skillet. Heat over medium-high heat to boiling, and boil 1 minute. Add Basic Brown Sauce and reduce heat to medium. Let sauce reduce until slightly thickened, about 2 minutes. Return tofu to skillet; stir briefly over heat to combine with sauce and heat through. Remove skillet from heat. Blend soft tofu with lemon juice and milk until smooth. Add to skillet, stir to combine flavors, and adjust seasonings. Serve immediately over freshly cooked noodles.

4 SERVINGS

Calories 190.8 • Protein 10.92 gm • Fat 9.766 gm • Percentage of calories from fat 44% • Cholesterol 0.281 mg • Dietary fiber 0.894 gm • Sodium 501.1 mg • Calcium 63.97 mg

Tofu Curry with Plum Chutney

A bottled chutney will certainly suffice, but when you see how easy chutney is to prepare, you may crave the satisfaction of making your own.

2 tablespoons corn oil
1 medium onion, chopped
1 cup diced fresh or canned jalapeño peppers
2 cloves garlic, minced
1 teaspoon minced fresh ginger
1 teaspoon ground turmeric
2 teaspoons curry powder
1 teaspoon ground coriander
1 cup Basic Vegetable Stock (see page 10)

1 pound firm tofu, cut into ½-inch cubes
1½ cups milk or coconut milk
1 cup raisins
1 teaspoon sugar or a natural sweetener
⅛ teaspoon cayenne
Salt and freshly ground black pepper
Plum Chutney (recipe follows)

Heat oil in a large saucepan over medium-low heat. Add onion, jalapeños, garlic, and ginger and cook until softened, stirring occasionally, about 10 minutes. Add turmeric, curry powder, and coriander; cook, stirring, 5 minutes. Add stock and simmer 20 minutes. Add tofu, milk, raisins, sugar, cayenne, salt, and pepper and simmer about 15 minutes. Serve with Plum Chutney.

4 SERVINGS

Calories 352.1 • Protein 14.51 gm • Fat 11.5 gm • Percentage of calories from fat 29% • Cholesterol 6.75 mg • Dietary fiber 4.998 gm • Sodium 988.8 mg • Calcium 196.2 mg

Plum Chutney

This is a good basic chutney recipe that lends itself to other fruits, so if plums are unavailable, experiment with fruits that are in season.

1½ pounds unpeeled plums, pitted and chopped
½ cup sugar or a natural sweetener
⅓ cup apple cider vinegar
½ cup golden raisins

2 cloves garlic, minced
1 dried red chili pepper
1 tablespoon minced fresh ginger
½ teaspoon salt
¼ teaspoon cayenne

Combine all ingredients in a large saucepan and bring to a boil. Reduce heat and simmer until thickened, stirring occasionally, about 1 hour. Remove chili pepper, serve at room temperature. Chutney may be stored in a jar or other container with a tight-fitting lid and refrigerated for several weeks.

MAKES 4 CUPS (½-CUP SERVING)

Calories 110.5 • Protein 0.991 gm • Fat 0.098 gm • Percentage of calories from fat 1% • Cholesterol 0 mg • Dietary fiber 1.126 gm • Sodium 141.7 mg • Calcium 22.37 mg

Tempeh with Fennel and New Potatoes

2 tablespoons vegetable oil
1 pound poached tempeh (see page 12), cut into 1-inch cubes
1 medium onion, chopped
2 shallots, chopped
2 large cloves garlic, minced
1 small fennel bulb, trimmed and cut into ¼-inch slices
½ cup plus 2 tablespoons dry white wine

½ cup Basic Vegetable Stock (see page 10)
1 teaspoon dried thyme, crumbled
½ teaspoon salt
⅛ freshly ground black pepper
1 tablespoon cornstarch
1 pound small new red potatoes, quartered
2 tablespoons snipped fresh chives

Preheat oven to 350 degrees. Heat oil in a large saucepan over medium-high heat. Brown tempeh on all sides in batches, transferring to a plate with a slotted spoon when done. Reheat saucepan over medium-high heat. Stir in onion, shallots, garlic, and fennel and cook for 5 minutes. Blend in ½ cup wine, stock, thyme, salt, and pepper and bring to a boil. Transfer to a baking dish and bake, covered, for 20 minutes.

Mix cornstarch and remaining 2 tablespoons wine in a small bowl until smooth. Stir into vegetables. Meanwhile, cook potatoes in large saucepan of boiling salted water until just tender, about 8 to 10 minutes. Drain. Carefully add potatoes and tempeh to casserole. Cover and bake another 15 minutes. Adjust seasonings. Garnish with chives and serve immediately.

6 SERVINGS

Calories 263.8 • Protein 14.37 gm • Fat 10.41 gm • Percentage of calories from fat 35% • Cholesterol 0 mg • Dietary fiber 3.998 gm • Sodium 215.6 mg • Calcium 81.8 mg

Spring Vegetable Platter

Accompany this display of vegetables with some sautéed tofu, if you wish. I usually let the vegetables be the stars of the show. Oyster mushrooms are available in Asian markets.

4 carrots, cut diagonally in ½-inch slices
½ pound green beans, trimmed
½ pound Brussels sprouts, trimmed
2 heads Belgian endive, halved lengthwise
3 cups broccoli florets
2 yellow squash, halved lengthwise and cut into ½-inch half-moons

1 cup sliced fresh oyster mushrooms (about ¼ pound)
2 scallions, chopped
2 teaspoons fresh lemon juice
1 teaspoon minced fresh mint
¼ teaspoon salt
⅛ teaspoon freshly ground black pepper
Minted Tofu-Pea Sauce (recipe follows)

Preheat oven to 350 degrees. In an oiled baking dish, arrange carrots, green beans, Brussels sprouts, endive, broccoli, and squash in rows or circles, depending on shape of baking dish. Scatter mushrooms and scallions over all. Combine lemon juice with ¼ cup water and pour over the vegetables, then sprinkle with mint, salt, and pepper. Cover tightly and bake until tender, about 40 minutes. Serve with Minted Tofu-Pea Sauce.

4 SERVINGS

Calories 120.8 • Protein 7.188 gm • Fat 1.283 gm • Percentage of calories from fat 8% • Cholesterol 0 mg • Dietary fiber 5.886 gm • Sodium 196.6 mg • Calcium 126.9 mg

Minted Tofu-Pea Sauce

2 cups cooked fresh or frozen
 green peas
1 teaspoon salt
⅛ teaspoon freshly ground black
 pepper

2 teaspoons chopped fresh mint
1 cup soft tofu
1 tablespoon fresh lemon juice
¼ cup olive oil

In a food processor, pureé peas, salt, pepper, and mint. Add tofu and lemon juice and process until smooth. Add oil in a thin stream with machine running. Then stream in ¼ cup warm water with the machine running. Adjust seasonings, transfer to bowl, and serve with Spring Vegetable Platter.

MAKES 3½ CUPS (¼-CUP SERVING)

Calories 58.57 • Protein 2.328 gm • Fat 4.16 gm • Percentage of calories from fat 62% • Cholesterol 0 mg • Dietary fiber 1.345 gm • Sodium 135.1 mg • Calcium 23.01 mg

Tempeh-Mushroom Polenta Casserole with Tomato-Feta Sauce

2 tablespoons olive oil
4 ounces mushrooms, chopped
4 ounces poached tempeh (see
 page 12), chopped
1½ tablespoons fresh lemon juice
4¼ cups Basic Vegetable Stock
 (see page 10)
¼ cup cream or milk
1¼ teaspoon salt
⅛ teaspoon freshly ground black
 pepper
2 tablespoons grated Pecorino
 Romano cheese
1⅓ cups yellow cornmeal
1 cup minced shallots

¼ cup tightly packed fresh basil
 leaves, chopped
2 large cloves garlic, minced
⅛ teaspoon dried thyme
1 bay leaf
2 cups canned Italian tomatoes,
 drained and chopped
½ cup dry white wine
2 cups Basic Vegetable Stock (see
 page 00), boiled until reduced to
 ⅔ cup
⅛ teaspoon cayenne
4 ounces feta cheese, crumbled
Salt and freshly ground black
 pepper

Preheat oven to 275 degrees. Heat 1 tablespoon of the olive oil in a large skillet over medium-high heat. Add mushrooms and tempeh and sauté for

2 to 4 minutes, or until tempeh is golden brown. Sprinkle with lemon juice. Add ¼ cup of the stock and the cream and boil 30 seconds. Using slotted spoon, transfer tempeh and mushroom mixture to a bowl. Boil liquid until thick, then pour over mixture in bowl. Season with ¼ teaspoon salt and the pepper. Stir in cheese and set aside.

Lightly oil a large baking dish. Bring remaining 4 cups stock and 1 teaspoon salt to boil in a large saucepan. Gradually whisk in cornmeal in a thin stream. Continue whisking until mixture comes to boil. Reduce heat to medium and stir slowly with a wooden spoon until very thick, about 30 minutes (if too thick to stir, add ¼ cup more stock). Stir in tempeh-mushroom mixture; then spread polenta evenly in prepared dish and keep warm in oven.

Heat remaining 1 tablespoon olive oil in a medium saucepan over medium-low heat. Add shallots, basil, garlic, thyme, and bay leaf. Cover and cook until shallots are soft, stirring occasionally, about 5 minutes. Uncover, increase heat to high, add tomatoes, and stir until all liquid evaporates, about 2 minutes. Add wine and cook until almost evaporated, about 10 minutes. Stir in reduced stock and cayenne and simmer uncovered until liquid reduces by half. Add feta and season with salt and pepper. To serve, cut hot polenta into squares or wedges and top with sauce.

6 SERVINGS

Calories 350 • Protein 12.95 gm • Fat 11.58 gm • Percentage of calories from fat 30% • Cholesterol 19.03 mg • Dietary fiber 4.842 gm • Sodium 1118 mg • Calcium 210.8 mg

Five-Jewel Rice

3 tablespoons corn oil
½ pound seitan (see page 11), cut into ½-inch strips
3 tablespoons mirin, white wine, or sherry
1 teaspoon salt
½ teaspoon sugar or a natural sweetener
1 teaspoon minced garlic
1 small head napa cabbage, trimmed, cut into ½-inch slices (about 4 cups)

2½ cups basmati rice
6 shiitake mushrooms, sliced
2 medium carrots, cut into diagonal ½-inch slices
1 cup Basic Vegetable Stock (see page 10)
3 tablespoons low-sodium tamari
1 tablespoon minced scallion
½ teaspoon hot red pepper flakes
1½ teaspoons toasted sesame oil
2 ounces snow peas, trimmed

Heat 1 tablespoon of the oil in a large skillet over medium-high heat. Add seitan and sauté until browned on both sides, about 5 minutes. Remove slices and set aside on a plate. Stir 2 tablespoons of the mirin, ½ teaspoon of the salt, and the sugar in a small bowl. Set aside. Heat remaining 2 table-spoons oil in the skillet over medium-high heat, add garlic, and sauté about 5 seconds. Add cabbage and cook, stirring, until coated with oil. Add mirin mixture and continue cooking until cabbage is slightly limp, about 2 min-utes. Transfer cabbage to a bowl, first draining off liquid.

Heat rice, 2½ cups water, and remaining ½ teaspoon salt in a large sauce-pan or Dutch oven over medium heat to boiling; reduce heat to low. Layer mushrooms, seitan, cabbage, and carrots over rice. Cook, covered, 20 min-utes. Meanwhile, stir together remaining 1 tablespoon mirin, the stock, tamari, scallion, red pepper flakes, and sesame oil in small bowl. Uncover pot after 20 minutes; pour stock mixture over rice and vegetables and add snow peas. Cover and cook until rice is tender and water is absorbed, about 15 minutes. If rice is not tender, add ¼ cup water; cook, covered, until water is absorbed and rice is tender.

4 SERVINGS

Calories 832.8 • Protein 21.21 gm • Fat 13.95 gm • Percentage of calories from fat 15% • Cholesterol 0 mg • Dietary fiber 11.26 gm • Sodium 1250 mg • Calcium 131.7 mg

Italian-Style Cabbage and Beans

If tempeh bacon is unavailable, use crumbled tempeh, and garnish with soy bacon bits to impart a smoky flavor.

3 tablespoons olive oil
3 ounces tempeh bacon, cut into
 ¼-inch julienne strips
2 large cloves garlic, minced
1 small onion, chopped
½ teaspoon hot red pepper flakes

1½ pounds cabbage, shredded
2 tablespoons tomato paste
2 cups cooked cannellini beans,
 rinsed and drained
¼ cup minced fresh parsley
½ teaspoon salt

Heat oil in a large skillet, add tempeh bacon, garlic, and onion, and cook over moderately high heat until onion is softened, about 5 minutes. Add red pepper flakes and stir for 30 seconds. Add cabbage and toss well till coated. In a small bowl, blend tomato paste with 1 cup water; pour over the cabbage. Stir, then cover pan, reduce heat to medium, and cook, stirring occasionally, until cabbage is tender, about 10 minutes. Add beans and parsley and cook, covered, until beans are heated through, about 5 minutes. Season with salt. Boil over medium-high heat to evaporate any excess liquid.

6 SERVINGS

Calories 218.1 • Protein 8.447 gm • Fat 11.5 gm • Percentage of calories from fat 45% • Cholesterol 0 mg • Dietary fiber 5.947 gm • Sodium 414.9 mg • Calcium 111.5 mg

Moroccan Couscous with Tempeh

The complexity of flavor and texture in this recipe belies its ease of preparation.

1 cup couscous
⅔ cup golden raisins
¾ cup boiling Basic Vegetable Stock (see page 10)
¼ cup olive oil
12 ounces poached tempeh (see page 12), chopped
1 large clove garlic, minced
½ teaspoon salt
3 medium carrots, cut into ¼-inch dice

1 unpeeled Granny Smith apple, chopped
1 red bell pepper, seeded and chopped
½ cup minced scallions
½ cup pine nuts
2 teaspoons fresh lemon juice
1 teaspoon ground cinnamon
¼ teaspoon cayenne

Place couscous and raisins in a bowl. Pour boiling stock over and stir with a fork. Cover bowl and set aside. Heat oil in a large skillet over medium-high heat. Add tempeh, garlic, and salt and stir 15 seconds. Reduce heat to medium, stir in carrots, cover, and cook, stirring occasionally, about 4 minutes. Add couscous, mixture, apple, bell pepper, scallions, pine nuts, lemon juice, cinnamon, and cayenne, tossing gently to blend. Cover and cook to heat through and blend flavors, stirring occasionally, about 5 minutes. Adjust seasonings and serve immediately.

6 SERVINGS

Calories 443.3 • Protein 17.57 gm • Fat 20.53 gm • Percentage of calories from fat 40% • Cholesterol 0 mg • Dietary fiber 9.161 gm • Sodium 231.9 mg • Calcium 85.03 mg

Seitan au Vin

Serve over freshly cooked noodles with a crisp green salad or marinated green beans and hot crusty bread.

3 tablespoons corn oil
1 pound seitan (see page 11), cut into ½-inch slices
½ teaspoon salt
⅛ teaspoon freshly ground black pepper
½ pound small pearl onions
1 tablespoon all-purpose flour
2 cups dry red wine

1 cup Basic Vegetable Stock (see page 10)
1 tablespoon tomato paste
½ teaspoon minced fresh basil or ¼ teaspoon dried
1 bay leaf
1 pound large mushrooms, trimmed and quartered

Heat 2 tablespoons of the oil in a large skillet over medium heat, add seitan, salt, and pepper, and cook slices until browned on both sides, about 5 minutes. While seitan is browning, peel onions by plunging them into boiling water and then removing their skins. To keep onions intact while cooking, cut a small cross in root end of each. Remove seitan slices with a slotted spoon and set aside. Reheat skillet over medium heat, add pearl onions, and cook, stirring occasionally, until onions are golden brown, about 5 minutes. Remove them and set aside.

Stir flour into remaining 1 tablespoon oil in skillet. Cook over medium heat, stirring constantly, 2 minutes. Whisk in wine and stock; then add tomato paste, basil, and bay leaf. Heat to boiling; reduce heat. Return seitan and onions to skillet and simmer, covered, until onions are tender, about 20 minutes. Add mushrooms and cook, covered, about 3 minutes. Uncover and continue to cook, stirring gently, to blend flavors, about 5 minutes. Remove bay leaf before serving.

4 SERVINGS

Calories 587.2 • Protein 20.56 gm • Fat 12.72 gm • Percentage of calories from fat 19% • Cholesterol 0 mg • Dietary fiber 15.31 gm • Sodium 714.8 mg • Calcium 78.45 mg

Tangy Twice-Cooked Seitan and Potatoes

A quick-fix way to transform leftovers. Use a good-quality bottled barbecue sauce for best results.

2 tablespoons corn oil
1 medium onion, chopped
1 pound leftover Seitan Pot Roast (see page 344) roast or sautéed seitan slices, cut into ½-inch dice
2 pounds boiling potatoes, cooked and cut into ½-inch dice

¾ cup barbecue sauce
½ cup Basic Vegetable Stock (see page 10)
Salt and freshly ground black pepper

Heat oil in a large skillet over medium-high heat. Add onion and cook, stirring occasionally, until they begin to brown, about 10 minutes. Add diced seitan, potatoes, barbecue sauce, and stock. Simmer for 10 minutes, stirring frequently. Season with salt and pepper to taste.

6 SERVINGS

Calories 441.3 • Protein 15.02 gm • Fat 7.026 gm • Percentage of calories from fat 14% • Cholesterol 0 mg • Dietary fiber 11.48 gm • Sodium 506.5 mg • Calcium 47.96 mg

Baked Rice with Peas, Celery, and Almonds

2 tablespoons plus 1 teaspoon corn oil
1 small onion, minced
1 cup sliced celery
1 cup basmati rice
2 cups hot Basic Vegetable Stock (see page 10)

⅓ cup sliced almonds
1 cup cooked fresh peas or thawed frozen peas
Salt and freshly ground black pepper

Preheat oven to 375 degrees. Heat 2 tablespoons of the oil in a large saucepan over medium heat and cook onion and celery, stirring, for 8 to 10 minutes. Add rice and cook, stirring, until coated with oil. Stir in hot stock and bring to a boil. Transfer mixture to a large casserole and bake, covered, for 20 minutes.

While rice is baking, sauté almonds in remaining 1 teaspoon oil over moderately high heat, stirring, until they are golden, 4 to 5 minutes. After 25 minutes, stir almonds, peas, and salt and pepper to taste into the rice and bake the mixture 5 minutes more, or until rice is tender and all the liquid is absorbed. Allow rice to stand, covered, for 5 minutes. Fluff with a fork just before serving.

6 SERVINGS

Calories 256.3 • Protein 6.035 gm • Fat 9.028 gm • Percentage of calories from fat 32% • Cholesterol 0 mg • Dietary fiber 3.732 gm • Sodium 105.2 mg • Calcium 46.55 mg

Fava Beans with Tomatoes and Chilies

Keep canned favas, tomatoes, and chilies on hand for those times when you need a quick dinner on the run.

2 tablespoons oil
1 onion, finely chopped
1 clove garlic, minced
2 cups cooked fava beans
½ pound ripe tomatoes, peeled (see page 375) and chopped, or 1-pound can whole tomatoes, drained and chopped

2 canned jalapeño chili peppers, rinsed, seeded, and chopped
½ teaspoon salt
⅛ teaspoon freshly ground black pepper
6 cups freshly cooked rice
¼ cup minced fresh parsley

Heat oil in a large skillet over medium-low heat, add onion, and cook, stirring, until onion softens, about 8 to 10 minutes. Add garlic and cook, stirring, for 1 minute. Stir in fava beans, tomatoes, jalapeños, salt, and pepper and cook, stirring occasionally, for 10 minutes, to blend flavors. Divide the rice onto 4 plates and top with bean–tomato mixture. Sprinkle with parsley.

4 SERVINGS

Calories 564.9 • Protein 15.1 gm • Fat 8.022 gm • Percentage of calories from fat 13% • Cholesterol 0 mg • Dietary fiber 7.84 gm • Sodium 486.5 mg • Calcium 49.51 mg

Seitan with Orzo and Feta

Orzo is a tiny rice-shaped pasta. If unavailable, substitute any small-shaped pasta such as radiatore or shells.

¼ cup olive oil
1 pound seitan (see page 11), cut into 1-inch cubes
1 cup chopped onions
1 32-ounce can tomatoes, chopped, juice reserved
½ teaspoon minced fresh oregano or ¼ teaspoon dried

½ teaspoons salt
⅛ teaspoon freshly ground black pepper
1 cup orzo (or other very small pasta)
1 cup crumbled feta cheese
¼ cup minced fresh parsley

Heat oil in a large saucepan over medium-high heat and brown seitan. Transfer to a plate. In the same saucepan, cook onions over medium-low heat, stirring, for 8 to 10 minutes. Add the tomatoes and juice, oregano, salt, and pepper and bring to a boil. Simmer mixture, covered, for 30 minutes. Add reserved seitan. In a saucepan of boiling salted water, cook orzo for 8 minutes; then drain and refresh under cold water. Add orzo, feta, and parsley to seitan mixture and simmer for 5 minutes.

6 SERVINGS

Calories 563.9 • Protein 22.34 gm • Fat 20.11 gm • Percentage of calories from fat 31% • Cholesterol 37.67 mg • Dietary fiber 10.82 gm • Sodium 1100 mg • Calcium 289.9 mg

Tofu Lasagne

The tofu provides ample protein, but if you're used to having ground meat in your lasagne, add the TVP or some crumbled tempeh or seitan to your tomato sauce instead.

2 pounds firm tofu, crumbled
¼ cup minced fresh parsley
1 tablespoon minced fresh basil
¼ cup grated Pecorino Romano cheese
½ teaspoon salt
½ teaspoon freshly ground black pepper

½ cup TVP combined with ½ cup water (optional)
4 cups tomato sauce
1 pound lasagne noodles, cooked and drained
8 ounces mozzarella, shredded

Preheat oven to 350 degrees. Combine tofu, parsley, basil, Pecorino Romano cheese, salt, and pepper in a large bowl. Mix filling well and adjust seasonings. Add TVP to tomato sauce, if using. Spread a thin layer of tomato sauce in a large baking dish. Line dish with a layer of noodles. Top noodles with a layer of filling, another layer of noodles, more sauce, and a sprinkle of shredded mozzarella. Repeat process until all ingredients are used, ending with top layer of sauce and shredded cheese. Bake for 45 to 50 minutes. Let lasagne set for 5 minutes before cutting. Pass extra sauce separately.

6 TO 8 SERVINGS

Calories 454.7 • Protein 28.18 gm • Fat 9.625 gm • Percentage of calories from fat 19% • Cholesterol 3.515 mg • Dietary fiber 2.914 gm • Sodium 377.8 mg • Calcium 235 mg

Seitan Stroganoff

This stroganoff is so rich and flavorful that it's hard to believe it's also good for you.

3 tablespoons corn oil
12 ounces seitan (see page 11), cut into 2 × ½-inch strips
2 tablespoons dry sherry
1 large onion, chopped
8 ounces mushrooms, sliced
3 tablespoons low-sodium tamari
1 teaspoon prepared mustard
½ teaspoon minced fresh basil or ¼ teaspoon dried
½ teaspoon minced fresh thyme or ¼ teaspoon dried

½ teaspoon salt
⅛ teaspoon freshly ground black pepper
1 bay leaf
2 tablespoons cornstarch dissolved in 2 tablespoons water
1 cup milk
Freshly cooked wide egg noodles
Tofu Sour Cream (recipe follows)
2 tablespoons chopped fresh parsley

Heat 2 tablespoons of the oil in a large skillet over medium-high heat. Brown seitan strips on both sides; sprinkle with sherry. Transfer seitan to a platter and keep warm. Reheat skillet, scraping up browned bits, and pour over seitan. Add remaining 1 tablespoon oil and onion to skillet and cook over medium-high heat for 5 minutes. Add mushrooms; sauté 2 minutes longer. Reduce heat; add tamari, mustard, basil, thyme, salt, pepper, and bay leaf. Stir in co rnstarch mixture. Slowly add milk, stirring over low heat until sauce thickens. Add reserved seitan. Cook 10 minutes on low heat and adjust seasonings. Remove bay leaf. Serve over cooked noodles. Top with Tofu Sour Cream or a dairy sour cream, if you prefer. Sprinkle with parsley.

4 SERVINGS

Calories 450.5 • Protein 17.6 gm • Fat 13.12 gm • Percentage of calories from fat 25% • Cholesterol 4.5 mg • Dietary fiber 10.99 gm • Sodium 1042 mg • Calcium 135.4 mg

Tofu Sour Cream

Miso, a nutritious soybean paste used to make soups and sauces, is available at natural foods stores in a variety of flavors. Choose a mellow white miso for this recipe.

1 cup soft tofu
¼ cup lemon juice
2 tablespoons corn oil

1 tablespoon light miso
¼ teaspoon prepared mustard
1 tablespoon low-sodium tamari

Combine all the ingredients in a food processor until well blended. Use as sour cream.

MAKES ABOUT 1½ CUPS (¼-CUP SERVING)

Calories 62.1 • Protein 3.01 gm • Fat 5.02 gm • Percentage of calories from fat 74% • Cholesterol 0 mg • Dietary fiber 0.102 gm • Sodium 158.6 mg • Calcium 35.8 mg

Tempeh with Red Wine Sauce

2 tablespoons corn oil
1 pound poached tempeh (see page 12), cut into 1-inch slices
½ teaspoon salt
⅛ teaspoon freshly ground black pepper
1 cup sliced mushrooms

¼ teaspoon minced fresh thyme or ⅛ teaspoon dried
1 cup dry red wine
1 cup pearl onions, cooked
1 cup Basic Brown Sauce (see page 13)
Freshly cooked noodles

Heat oil in a large skillet over medium-high heat. Add tempeh, season with salt and pepper, and sauté 2 minutes, or until browned and crisp. Turn and brown the other side. Add mushrooms and thyme and cook for 1 minute. Add red wine and onions. Cook for 5 minutes. Reduce heat, add Basic Brown Sauce, and simmer 5 minutes. Adjust seasonings. Serve over noodles.

6 SERVINGS

Calories 215.5 • Protein 13.16 gm • Fat 10.36 gm • Percentage of calories from fat 43% • Cholesterol 0 mg • Dietary fiber 3.113 gm • Sodium 302.9 mg • Calcium 68.52 mg

Quick Cabbage Rolls

You could use rice instead of barley in this recipe, but the barley imparts a chewy Old World flavor that's hard to surpass.

1 large head cabbage
2 tablespoons corn oil
1 medium onion, minced
1 cup ground seitan (see page 11)
2 cups cooked barley or brown rice

½ teaspoon salt
⅛ teaspoon freshly ground black
  pepper
Tomato Chutney (see page 233) or
  tomato sauce of choice

Wash and core cabbage. Blanch 16 large leaves in boiling salted water until tender, about 5 minutes. Reserve remaining cabbage for another use. Set leaves aside to cool. Heat oil in a large skillet, add onion, and sauté 5 minutes or until translucent. Add seitan and cook 5 minutes longer. Scoop into a bowl and add barley, salt, and pepper. Place a cabbage leaf stem side down and put a small amount of mixture in the center of the leaf. Roll up, stem end first, tucking in sides. Repeat with additional cabbage leaves until all mixture is used. Place cabbage rolls in a steamer and steam for 10 minutes to heat through. Serve with Tomato Chutney or a tomato sauce.

4 SERVINGS

Calories 569.7 • Protein 23.05 gm • Fat 9.544 gm • Percentage of calories from fat 14% • Cholesterol 0 mg • Dietary fiber 23.65 gm • Sodium 621.9 mg • Calcium 188.2 mg

Hoppin' John with Collard Greens

I came up with this recipe during my years as a chef in Charleston, South Carolina. It's based on a traditional Southern New Year's Day dish said to bring good luck in the coming year. If collard greens are unavailable, substitute kale or other dark leafy green.

3 tablespoons olive oil
1 medium onion, chopped
4 ounces tempeh bacon, finely chopped
2 cups cooked black-eyed peas
3 cups cooked brown rice

2 cups boiled collard greens, chopped
½ teaspoon salt
⅛ teaspoon freshly ground black pepper

Heat oil in a large skillet over medium-high heat. Add onion and sauté 5 minutes or until beginning to soften. Add tempeh bacon and cook until browned. Add peas, rice, and collards. Cook 5 minutes, stirring often, or until heated through. Season with salt and pepper.

4 SERVINGS

Calories 464.1 • Protein 14.45 gm • Fat 20.53 gm • Percentage of calories from fat 39% • Cholesterol 0 mg • Dietary fiber 12.17 gm • Sodium 698.8 mg • Calcium 70.92 mg

Tofu Risi e Bisi

2 tablespoons olive oil
1 pound firm tofu, cut into ½-inch
  cubes
2 ounces tempeh bacon, cooked
  and minced
3 cups cooked brown rice
½ teaspoon salt

⅛ teaspoon freshly ground black
  pepper
2 cups cooked fresh or frozen peas
1 tablespoon lemon juice
1 tablespoon chopped fresh
  parsley

Heat olive oil in a large skillet over medium-high heat. Sauté tofu until golden. Add tempeh bacon, rice, salt, and pepper. Add peas and lemon juice. Cook for 5 minutes or until heated through. Adjust seasonings. Sprinkle with chopped parsley and serve.

4 SERVINGS

Calories 402.4 • Protein 18.77 gm • Fat 14.87 gm • Percentage of calories from fat 33% • Cholesterol 0 mg • Dietary fiber 7.868 gm • Sodium 556.3 mg • Calcium 85.3 mg

Tofu Yung

3 tablespoons light sesame oil
½ cup chopped scallions
1 cup chopped mushrooms
2 cups bean sprouts
1 pound soft tofu, mashed

¼ teaspoon ground turmeric
2 tablespoons low-sodium tamari
Freshly cooked brown rice
1 cup Basic Brown Sauce (see
  page 13)

Heat oil in a large skillet over medium-high heat. Add scallions, mushrooms, and bean sprouts and stir-fry until vegetables are tender, about 2 minutes. Set aside. In a bowl, blend mashed tofu with turmeric and tamari. Add cooked vegetables and combine. Reheat skillet, spoon ½ cup of the mixture into it, flatten slightly, and cook until lightly browned, about 5 minutes. Carefully turn patty over to cook other side about 5 minutes. Repeat until all mixture is used. Keep cooked patties warm in a 275-degree oven. Serve over brown rice and top with Basic Brown Sauce.

4 SERVINGS

Calories 228.4 • Protein 12.78 gm • Fat 15.89 gm • Percentage of calories from fat 59% • Cholesterol 0 mg • Dietary fiber 1.68 gm • Sodium 456 mg • Calcium 144.3 mg

Simmered Seitan with Winter Vegetables

A variation on pot roast, with the seitan prepared on top of the stove while the vegetables bake in the oven.

2 large carrots, cut into 1-inch diagonal slices
2 parsnips, cut into 1-inch diagonal slices
2 cups winter squash in 1-inch cubes
4 new red potatoes, halved
1 medium onion, quartered
1 tablespoon minced fresh basil or 1 teaspoon dried

1 teaspoon minced fresh marjoram or ½ teaspoon dried
½ teaspoon salt
⅛ teaspoon freshly ground black pepper
2 tablespoons corn or safflower oil
12 ounces seitan (see page 11), cut into ¼-inch slices
1 cup Basic Brown Sauce (see page 13)

Preheat oven to 350 degrees. Lightly oil a baking dish and place prepared vegetables in it. Add ½ cup water, the basil, marjoram, salt, and pepper. Cover and bake 1 hour, or until vegetables are tender. Remove cover during last 10 minutes to brown vegetables. As they brown, heat oil in a large skillet over medium-high heat. Add seitan in batches, browning each side. Season with salt and pepper to taste. Add Brown Sauce and bring to a simmer. When vegetables are cooked, pour seitan and sauce over them and serve directly from baking dish.

4 SERVINGS

Calories 540.4 • Protein 18.23 gm • Fat 8.827 gm • Percentage of calories from fat 14% • Cholesterol 0 mg • Dietary fiber 17.29 gm • Sodium 657.7 mg • Calcium 137.8 mg

Curried Tempeh with Pear Chutney

3 tablespoons safflower oil
1 medium onion, chopped
2 scallions, chopped
1 pound poached tempeh (see page 12), cut into ½-inch cubes
1 tablespoon curry powder
2 tablespoons low-sodium tamari
1 teaspoon sugar or a natural sweetener
1 carrot, sliced diagonally, steamed

¼ cup raisins
¼ cup or more Basic Vegetable Stock (see page 10)
1 cup chopped peanuts
2 tablespoons chopped fresh parsley
Freshly cooked brown rice
Fresh Pear Chutney (recipe follows)

Heat oil in a large skillet over medium-high heat and cook onion for 5 minutes. Add scallions and sauté 2 minutes. Add tempeh and curry powder; sauté 2 minutes longer. Add tamari and sugar. Stir in carrot, raisins, and stock. Simmer 5 minutes. If liquid evaporates, add more stock. Adjust seasonings. Add peanuts and parsley. Serve over brown rice with Pear Chutney.

4 TO 6 SERVINGS

Calories 444.4 • Protein 23.14 gm • Fat 29.78 gm • Percentage of calories from fat 58% • Cholesterol 0 mg • Dietary fiber 6.388 gm • Sodium 508 mg • Calcium 106.7 mg

Pear Chutney

¼ cup minced onion
1 clove garlic, minced
¼ cup brandy
¼ cup apple juice
3 tablespoons fresh lemon juice

¼ cup sugar or a natural sweetener
1 teaspoon ground cinnamon
¼ teaspoon salt
2 ripe pears, peeled and chopped

In a medium saucepan, combine onion, garlic, brandy, apple juice, lemon juice, sugar, cinnamon, and salt. Bring to a boil over medium heat. Reduce heat and simmer for 5 minutes. Add pears and 2 tablespoons water. Simmer, stirring frequently, until chutney is thick, about 20 minutes. Serve warm, or let cool to room temperature.

MAKES ABOUT 2 CUPS (¼-CUP SERVING)

Calories 74.2 • Protein .281 gm • Fat .193 gm • Percentage of calories from fat 2% • Cholesterol 0 mg • Dietary fiber 1.28 gm • Sodium 67.3 mg • Calcium 11.2 mg

Tofu Creole

2 ripe tomatoes
3 tablespoons corn oil
1 pound firm tofu, cut into 1-inch cubes
1 medium onion, chopped
1 clove garlic, minced
1 cup chopped celery
1 green bell pepper, chopped
¼ cup tomato paste blended with ¼ cup water
½ teaspoon minced fresh thyme or ⅛ teaspoon dried

1 bay leaf
2 tablespoons chopped fresh parsley
½ teaspoon filé powder
1 teaspoon Tabasco sauce
¾ teaspoon salt
⅛ teaspoon freshly ground black pepper
Freshly cooked brown rice

First peel the tomatoes. Plunge them in boiling water for 1 minute, remove from water, and let cool a few seconds; the skin peels away easily. Chop tomatoes and set aside.

Heat 1 tablespoon of the oil in a large skillet over medium-high heat; add tofu cubes, sauté until golden, and set aside. Heat remaining 2 tablespoons oil in skillet, add onion, garlic, celery, and green pepper. Sauté 4 to 5 minutes. Add tomatoes and remaining ingredients except tofu and rice. Simmer 15 minutes. Add reserved tofu, adjust seasonings, and simmer 5 minutes longer. Serve over brown rice.

4 SERVINGS

Calories 213.3 • Protein 11.27 gm • Fat 13.19 gm • Percentage of calories from fat 53% • Cholesterol 0 mg • Dietary fiber 3.038 gm • Sodium 517.5 mg • Calcium 81.33 mg

Tofu Rancheros

Tofu makes eggs a thing of the past in this spicy south-of-the-border recipe. Serve as a Sunday brunch or light supper, with hot rolls and home-fried potatoes.

2 tablespoons corn oil
1 medium onion, chopped
1 green bell pepper, chopped
1 medium tomato, peeled (see page 375) and chopped
2 tablespoons low-sodium tamari
⅛ teaspoon freshly ground black pepper

¼ teaspoon chili powder
2 minced scallions
1 pound firm tofu, crumbled
¼ teaspoon ground turmeric
½ teaspoon salt

Heat 1 tablespoon of the oil in a large skillet over medium-high heat. Add onion and bell pepper and sauté till tender, about 5 to 8 minutes. Add tomato, tamari, pepper, and chili powder. Keep warm.

Heat remaining 1 tablespoon oil in a another large skillet over medium-high heat. Add scallions and sauté 1 minute; add tofu, turmeric, and salt, and sauté for 5 minutes. Serve tofu topped with warm vegetable mixture.

4 SERVINGS

Calories 165.1 • Protein 10.98 gm • Fat 9.486 gm • Percentage of calories from fat 50% • Cholesterol 0 mg • Dietary fiber 1.487 gm • Sodium 646.8 mg • Calcium 59.99 mg

Tofu Almondine

3 tablespoons low-sodium tamari
3 tablespoons almond butter
1 pound firm tofu, cut into ½-inch cubes
2 tablespoons corn oil
1 medium onion, chopped
1 green bell pepper, seeded and chopped
1 carrot, sliced diagonally, steamed

1 cup Basic Vegetable Stock (see page 10)
2 tablespoons cornstarch dissolved in 2 tablespoons water
½ cup toasted slivered almonds (see page 142)
Freshly cooked brown rice or noodles

Combine tamari and almond butter in a bowl, stirring until smooth. Toss with tofu cubes to coat. Set aside. Heat 1 tablespoon of the oil in a large skillet over medium-high heat. Add onion and bell pepper and cook until onion is translucent, about 5 minutes. Add carrot slices. Transfer vegetables to a bowl and keep warm. Heat skillet with remaining 1 tablespoon oil and add tofu. Cook until lightly browned. Transfer to a platter and keep warm. Return cooked vegetables to the skillet and heat over medium-high heat. Add stock. When stock comes to a simmer, add cornstarch mixture and simmer, stirring, until thick. Add reserved tofu and almonds. Adjust seasonings. Serve over brown rice or noodles.

4 SERVINGS

Calories 364.9 • Protein 17.84 gm • Fat 24.64 gm • Percentage of calories from fat 58% • Cholesterol 0 mg • Dietary fiber 4.812 gm • Sodium 601.2 mg • Calcium 162.1 mg

Tofu Tetrazzini

2 tablespoons corn oil

1 pound firm tofu, cut into ½-inch cubes

1 cup sliced mushrooms

¼ teaspoon salt

⅛ teaspoon freshly ground black pepper

2 tablespoons dry sherry

1 cup Basic Vegetable Stock (see page 10)

2 tablespoons cornstarch dissolved in 2 tablespoons water

1 cup milk

8 ounces linguine, cooked

½ cup slivered almonds

1 cup grated Monterey Jack cheese

Preheat oven to 375 degrees. Heat oil in a large skillet over medium-high heat. Add tofu, mushrooms, salt, and pepper. Sauté 2 minutes. Add sherry and set aside. In a medium saucepan, heat stock to a boil, whisk in cornstarch mixture, stirring to thicken, then lower heat. Slowly stir in milk. Combine cooked linguine, tofu mixture, almonds, and sauce. Transfer mixture to a large oiled baking dish. Top with grated cheese and bake for 30 minutes.

6 SERVINGS

Calories 397.4 • Protein 20.3 gm • Fat 18.74 gm • Percentage of calories from fat 42% • Cholesterol 19.77 mg • Dietary fiber 2.4 gm • Sodium 332.7 mg • Calcium 272.9 mg

Sweet and Sour Seitan

1½ cups apple juice
¼ cup lemon juice
⅓ cup sugar or a natural
    sweetener
2 tablespoons cornstarch
2 tablespoons corn oil
1 pound seitan (see page 11), cut
    into ½-inch cubes
1 teaspoon grated fresh ginger
2 scallions, minced

2 medium carrots, cut into
    matchstick julienne strips
2 medium yellow squash, cut into
    half rounds
¼ pound snow peas, trimmed
½ cup Basic Vegetable Stock (see
    page 10)
3 tablespoons low-sodium tamari
Freshly cooked rice

Combine apple juice, lemon juice, and sugar with cornstarch and set aside. In a large skillet, heat oil and sauté seitan until golden brown on all sides, about 5 minutes. Remove cubes with a slotted spoon and set aside. Sauté ginger, scallions, and carrots in the skillet 3 to 5 minutes. Add squash and snow peas; sauté 2 minutes more. Add stock and tamari, cover, and cook until vegetables are slightly tender, about 3 to 5 minutes. Add seitan and juice-cornstarch mixture. Stir gently until sauce thickens. Adjust seasonings and serve over rice.

6 SERVINGS

Calories 388.1 • Protein 13.08 gm • Fat 6.019 gm • Percentage of calories from fat 13% • Cholesterol 0 mg • Dietary fiber 10.14 gm • Sodium 536.3 mg • Calcium 59.47 mg

Tempeh in Curried Mustard Sauce

¾ cup Dijon mustard
½ cup honey or a natural
 sweetener
⅛ cup lime juice
¼ teaspoon curry powder

2 tablespoons corn oil
1 pound poached tempeh (see
 page 12), cut into ¼-inch slices
Freshly cooked brown rice

In a small bowl, combine mustard, honey, lime juice, and curry powder. Set aside. Heat oil in a large skillet over medium-high heat. Add tempeh, brown on both sides (about 5 minutes), lower heat, and add about ½ cup of the sauce. Coat tempeh and let sauce heat through. Serve over rice. Reserve remaining sauce for another use, or heat and pass separately.

4 SERVINGS

Calories 427.2 • Protein 21.14 gm • Fat 18.27 gm • Percentage of calories from fat 38% • Cholesterol 0 mg • Dietary fiber 3.806 gm • Sodium 1169 mg • Calcium 91.16 mg

Tempeh with Sauerkraut

1 pound poached tempeh (see
 page 12), cut into 3 × ½ × ¼-inch
 slices
2 tablespoons corn oil
2 cups drained sauerkraut
½ cup sliced carrots, steamed

1 cup apple sauce
1 tablespoon sugar or a natural
 sweetener
½ teaspoon dry mustard
⅛ teaspoon freshly ground black
 pepper

Preheat oven to 350 degrees. In a large skillet, sauté tempeh in oil over medium-high heat until lightly browned on both sides. Set aside. Combine remaining ingredients in a large baking dish. Add tempeh. Cover and bake 30 minutes.

4 SERVINGS

Calories 306.6 • Protein 19.4 gm • Fat 15.58 gm • Percentage of calories from fat 44% • Cholesterol 0 mg • Dietary fiber 7.696 gm • Sodium 794 mg • Calcium 119.8 mg

Tempeh Alsacienne

2 Granny Smith apples, peeled and
  sliced
1 tablespoon fresh lemon juice
3 cups shredded cabbage
2 tablespoons corn oil
1 pound poached tempeh (see
  page 12), cut into 1-inch cubes
1 medium onion, finely chopped

1 cup white wine
1 teaspoon caraway seeds
¼ teaspoon salt
⅛ teaspoon freshly ground black
  pepper
2 tablespoons chopped fresh
  parsley

Place apples in a bowl with lemon juice and enough water to cover apples. Steam cabbage for 5 minutes and set aside. Heat oil in a large skillet over medium-high heat, add tempeh, and sauté for 5 minutes, or until golden brown. Remove tempeh with a slotted spoon and reserve.

Reheat skillet, add onion, and sauté for 5 minutes. Add reserved cabbage, drained apples, wine, caraway seeds, salt, and pepper. Bring to the boil, stirring constantly; then lower heat to medium-low and simmer, covered, for 20 minutes. Remove cover, add reserved tempeh, and cook 15 minutes longer. Sprinkle with parsley and serve immediately.

4 SERVINGS

Calories 371.6 • Protein 20.71 gm • Fat 15.98 gm • Percentage of calories from fat 37% • Cholesterol 0 mg • Dietary fiber 7.534 gm • Sodium 173.8 mg • Calcium 173.1 mg

Tempeh Teriyaki

½ cup low-sodium tamari
2 tablespoons toasted sesame oil
2 tablespoons sugar or a natural
 sweetener
1 tablespoon grated fresh ginger
1 clove garlic, minced

1 tablespoon fresh lemon juice
1 pound poached tempeh (see
 page 12), cut into 3 × 1 × ¼-inch
 slices
2 tablespoons corn oil
Freshly cooked brown rice

Combine tamari, sesame oil, sugar, ginger, garlic, and lemon juice in a shallow bowl. Add tempeh to bowl, turning to coat with sauce, and marinate for 2 hours, turning at least once. Drain and reserve marinade. Heat the corn oil in a large skillet over medium-high heat. Brown tempeh on both sides, about 5 minutes. Add marinade and cook at a simmer for about 5 minutes to reduce sauce. Serve over brown rice.

4 SERVINGS

Calories 358.4 • Protein 21.68 gm • Fat 22.16 gm • Percentage of calories from fat 56% • Cholesterol 0 mg • Dietary fiber 3.331 gm • Sodium 1222 mg • Calcium 92.58 mg

Barbecued Tempeh

2 tablespoons corn oil
1 pound poached tempeh (see
 page 12), cut into ¼-inch slices
1 medium onion, minced
1 cup tomato sauce
3 tablespoons sugar or a natural
 sweetener

2 tablespoons cider vinegar
1 teaspoon Dijon mustard
1 teaspoon low-sodium tamari
1 teaspoon Worcestershire sauce
⅛ teaspoon freshly ground black
 pepper

Preheat oven to 350 degrees. Heat 1 tablespoon of the oil in a large skillet over medium-high heat, add tempeh, and brown on both sides, about 5 minutes. Set aside. Heat remaining 1 tablespoon oil in a medium saucepan over low heat, add onion, cover, and cook 5 minutes or until translucent. Add remaining ingredients except reserved tempeh. Bring to a boil, stirring;

then reduce heat. Simmer for 20 minutes. Adjust seasonings. Add about 1 cup sauce to reserved tempeh. Transfer tempeh to an oiled baking dish, bake for 15 minutes, turn, bake 15 more minutes on the other side. As tempeh absorbs sauce in the baking, add additional sauce.

4 SERVINGS

Calories 319.5 • Protein 19.68 gm • Fat 15.67 gm • Percentage of calories from fat 44% • Cholesterol 0 mg • Dietary fiber 4.936 gm • Sodium 540.1 mg • Calcium 103.2 mg

Seitan Bobotie

Ground beef or "minced meat" is used in the original version of this popular South African dish. Substitute 2 tablespoons almond butter for the eggs, if desired.

2 tablespoons corn oil
1 medium onion, chopped
1 pound ground seitan (see page 8)
1 tablespoon curry powder
½ teaspoon salt
⅛ teaspoon freshly ground black pepper

1 slice white bread
1 cup milk
3 tablespoons fresh lemon juice
¼ cup chopped almonds
8 dried apricots, chopped
¼ cup apricot jam
6 bay leaves
2 eggs, beaten

Preheat oven to 350 degrees. Heat oil in a large skillet, add onion, and sauté 5 minutes. Add seitan, curry powder, salt, and pepper and cook 5 minutes. Soak bread in milk a few seconds, remove, and squeeze dry. Add bread to seitan mixture, reserving milk. Stir into skillet the lemon juice, almonds, apricots, jam, and half the milk. Place mixture in an oiled baking dish, place bay leaves on top, and bake for 20 minutes. Meanwhile, combine remaining milk with eggs in a small bowl, blending well. Remove bay leaves and pour milk mixture over top of casserole. Bake 25 minutes longer.

4 TO 6 SERVINGS

Calories 512.4 • Protein 20.64 gm • Fat 13.6 gm • Percentage of calories from fat 23% • Cholesterol 88.8 mg • Dietary fiber 12.68 gm • Sodium 529.9 mg • Calcium 157.6 mg

Seitan with Walnut and Pomegranate Sauce

Pomegranate juice, sold as grenadine, is used as a flavoring in mixed drinks, and is usually available in liquor stores and some specialty stores.

4 tablespoons corn oil
1 large onion, chopped
½ teaspoon ground turmeric
1 cup ground walnuts
2 cups Basic Vegetable Stock (see page 10)
½ teaspoon salt
⅛ teaspoon freshly ground black pepper

1 pound seitan (see page 11), cut into 1- × ¼-inch slices
½ cup fresh or concentrated pomegranate juice
⅓ cup fresh lemon juice
2 tablespoons tomato paste
¼ cup sugar or a natural sweetener
Freshly cooked basmati rice

Heat 2 tablespoons of the oil in a large saucepan over medium heat. Add onion and turmeric and sauté 5 minutes. Add walnuts, stock, salt, and pepper and bring to a boil. Lower heat and simmer for 15 minutes.

Heat remaining 2 tablespoons oil in a large skillet over medium-high heat, add seitan, and sauté slices over moderate heat for 5 minutes, turning once, until browned. Then transfer seitan to walnut mixture in saucepan, stir to coat with sauce, and simmer, covered, over a low heat for 10 minutes, stirring occasionally. Combine pomegranate juice with lemon juice, tomato paste, and sugar and add to the saucepan, stirring gently to mix. Simmer for 15 minutes. Serve seitan over rice, topped with some of the sauce. Pass remaining sauce separately.

4 TO 6 SERVINGS

Calories 616.9 • Protein 17.85 gm • Fat 27.4 gm • Percentage of calories from fat 38% • Cholesterol 0 mg • Dietary fiber 12.23 gm • Sodium 563.9 mg • Calcium 75.35 mg

Spinach and Seitan Curry

Serve this hearty curry with basmati rice, chutney, and paratha.

2 tablespoons safflower oil
1 large onion, minced
1 garlic clove, minced
½ teaspoon salt
1 teaspoon minced fresh ginger
1 teaspoon ground turmeric
½ teaspoon chili powder
1 tablespoon ground coriander
1 teaspoon ground mustard

1 pound seitan (see page 11), cut into ½-inch dice
1 10-ounce package frozen whole-leaf spinach, thawed and squeezed dry
8 ounces yogurt (or 8 ounces soft tofu mixed with 2 tablespoons lemon juice)

Heat oil in a large skillet or Dutch oven over medium heat. Add onion, garlic, salt, ginger, turmeric, chili powder, coriander, and mustard and sauté for 5 minutes. Add seitan and cook, stirring, until brown on all sides, about 5 minutes. Add spinach, then gradually stir in half the yogurt or tofu mixture. Cover the pan and cook for 30 minutes. If the curry becomes too dry during the cooking time, add a little water. Stir in the remaining yogurt or tofu mixture just before serving.

4 SERVINGS

Calories 384 • Protein 18.32 gm • Fat 7.557 gm • Percentage of calories from fat 17% • Cholesterol 0 mg • Dietary fiber 11.75 gm • Sodium 537.9 mg • Calcium 226.2 mg

Index